Boarding Schools and Colleges 1999

Twelfth Edition

Editor: Derek Bingham

 John Catt Educational Ltd

Published in 1999 by John Catt Educational Ltd,
Great Glemham, Saxmundham, Suffolk IP17 2DH.
Tel: 01728 663666   Fax: 01728 663415
E–mail: enq@johncatt.co.uk   Internet: http://www.johncatt.co.uk

First published 1987
Twelfth edition 1999

The Sex Discrimination Act 1975.
The publishers have taken all reasonable steps to avoid a contravention of Section 38 of the Sex Discrimination Act 1975. However, it should be noted that (save where there is an express provision to the contrary) where words have been used which denote the masculine gender only, they shall, pursuant and subject to the said Act, for the purpose of this publication, be deemed to include the feminine gender and vice versa.

British Library Cataloguing in Publication Data.

Boarding Schools and Colleges. Vol 12. (1999)
        1. Boarding Schools - Europe - Directories
373.2'22'0254 L914.5
ISBN: 0 901577 26 X
ISSN: 0951 872X

Designed and typeset by John Catt Educational Limited, Great Glemham, Saxmundham, Suffolk IP17 2DH.

Printed and bound in Great Britain by The Lavenham Press Ltd, Sudbury, Suffolk.

Contents

EDITORIAL

Foreword 5

How to use the Guide 6

A home rather than a house 8

In praise of Mixed Boarding, *Philip Watson, BSC, MA* 11

Boarding – the complete education, *Cathryn Rogerson* 12

Your questions answered 14

Who's Who at Boarding School 20

Finding the Fees, *Chris Heyes* and *David Belchamber* 22

Section One: Pre-Preparatory and Preparatory Schools 25

Section Two: Senior Independent Schools .49

Directory of Pre-Preparatory, Preparatory
and Senior Independent Schools D133

Section Three: State Boarding Schools 199

Directory of State Boarding Schools D211

Section Four: Boarding at the age of 16 and above 219

Directory of Boarding at the age of 16 and above D225

Section Five: International Schools in the UK and Overseas 229

Directory of International Schools in the UK and Overseas D239

Continued overleaf

ADDITIONAL INFORMATION

Glossary of abbreviations 243

Map of Great Britain 244

General Index 247

Order Form for the 2000 Guide

Advisory service

Reader enquiry Cards

Foreword

We are extremely grateful to the many people who have helped to compile this the twelfth edition of **Boarding Schools and Colleges**. It will be seen in this country and abroad as an indication that boarding schools continue to provide a quality of education and experience second to none.

In particular we thank Mrs B A Evans, BSc, HNC, Headmistress of The Royal Wolverhampton School; Mr Mark Johnson, BEd, Headmaster of Cheam Hawtreys ; Mr P H Moody, MA, Headmaster of Hillstone, Malvern College; Mrs Cathryn Rogerson of Cottesmore School; Mr Patrick Tobin, MA, FRSA, Principal of Stewart's Melville College and The Mary Erskine School and Mr Philip Watson BSc, MA, Headmaster of Burleigh Community College.

We also extend our warm gratitude to the many schools and colleges for providing us promptly and efficiently with the accurate information this guide contains.

How to use the Guide

by the Editor

Parents will consult this Guide with a great variety of needs and levels of awareness. Some will already have a good knowledge of Boarding schools and colleges and will use the Guide simply to locate known institutions and update the information they have previously acquired. Others will search the lists of schools and colleges to find a caring environment, long-lasting friendships, security and the kind of facilities and courses of study which offer their children the qualifications they need for their future career. Some will be looking for schools in a particular geographical area. Others will be approaching the idea of boarding for the first time and will browse through the schools listed in the following pages. Whatever the need or interest, the answer is here, within the sections, educational categories and institutional entries that make up the content of this Guide.

How to proceed

First, whatever your degree of knowledge of Boarding schools and colleges, do explore the various articles introducing the Guide. They cover many, if not all of the most important aspects of boarding and will undoubtedly save those readers unfamiliar with the subject a great deal of time and possible confusion. Do read them. They are written by experts in their own field and aimed at helping you to make the 'right' choice.

From here on, your method of using the Guide will depend on your level of awareness of the different educational sectors and the institutions contained within them.

The Guide is divided into five sections, each consisting of paid listings and a directory.

> Section One covers Pre-Preparatory and Preparatory Schools in the age range 4 to 14.

> Section Two covers Senior Independent Schools in the age range 10 to 18.

> Section Three covers State Boarding Schools.

> Section Four covers Boarding at the age of 16 and above.

> Section Five covers International Schools in the UK and Overseas.

The geographical Directory provides basic information about boarding schools in each county; listings are intended to amplify this basic information. Schools in the Directory are presented by county, town and alphabetically.

If you are looking for a specific school or college, and know the name, simply turn to the index at the back, locate the school and turn to the relevant page.

If you are looking for a school or schools within a particular geographical area, again consult the Directory relevant to the section. Schools which also have a listing are marked with a *.

Appendices at the back provide information on single-sex and co-educational schools.

If you are trying to decide which is the 'Right School' for your son or daughter, you may well soon discover that 'Right" is relative. Each child's needs are different. Some may feel most at home in a small school, others will thrive in a larger school, some may prefer weekly to full-time boarding. Only you can be the the final judge of what is right for your child or children, but the Guide can assist you in making this extremely important decision by providing you with a way of comparing schools.

Abbreviations

A large number of abbreviations occur within the school and college listings, most of them being the traditional contractions of academic qualifications, examinations and professional organisations. The Glossary of Abbreviations will explain any unfamiliar abbreviations.

School fees and VAT

VAT is not normally chargeable by schools since most are charitable trusts. There is however a small number that are not trusts and these do charge VAT. If you are in any doubt enquire at the school(s) in which you are interested.

School Search

All the listings in this Guide also appear on John Catt Educational's website http://www.schoolsearch.co.uk which attracts large numbers of visitors from around the world every week.

Free Reader Enquiry Service

If you wish to receive a prospectus or further information on any school or college in this Guide, you will find Reader Enquiry Service cards at the back. Simply write the names of the institution(s) that interest(s) you on the card and post it. The card is pre-paid and needs no stamp, regardless of where in the world you post it.

We will contact the institution(s) or advertiser(s) on your behalf and ask them to send further details to you. This service is completely free and you will receive information from a number of schools or colleges of your choice. It is designed to help you make the right choice.

A home rather than a house

Some Heads share their views on the best things about a boarding education

" The best thing about boarding is the other people. They can be the worst aspect too! I have been involved with boarding schools or with day schools which have boarding houses since 1971. The old austerities were disappearing then, but I am struck by the extent to which the good boarding school offers to its boys and girls 'a home rather than a house' – the title which we give to our own boarding prospectus. Today's boarders experience a sensitivity, an openness and a comfort which are light years removed from the world of *If*.

The relatively small number of boarders at The Mary Erskine School and Stewart's Melville College live next door to each other in an Edinburgh street adjoining a busy day school. It is a far cry physically from the rural acres of the typical boarding school but the essential realities are the same. One of these today is that the physical barriers between the boarding experience and the outside world have vanished. Telephone, television, e-mail and internet ensure this. This creates problems; no boarding school can be 'sanitised' against unwholesome influences, however zealously the guard is mounted. For that reason, most of us focus more intently on personal, social and health education which will address the needs of boarders both in term time and in their holidays and university careers, while continuing to attach priority to the inculcation of lifelong values.

In an age of personal upheaval, instant impression and shallow consumerism, a great strength of boarding education is that it affirms community and stability. I think of two particularly good Sixth Year groups in our boys' and girls' boarding houses, all of whom have contributed a great deal to their respective schools. They have gained hugely from the example and influence of one-another, from learning to look for the best in other people, from the security which they have found in the rules of their extended family and from the values which will have been implicit and explicit throughout their boarding experience. "

Patrick Tobin, MA, FRSA,
Principal, Stewart's Melville College and The Mary Erskine School

" From a personal point-of-view, boarders tend to become more confident and self-reliant as a result of living away from their parents, which stands them in good stead in later life. At recent reunions at the School, I have also noticed that borders develop very deep and lasting friendships, as they are continually in each other's company 24 hours a day, as opposed to a few hours each day for day pupils. At our School in particular, I think that one of the big advantages of boarding is the opportunity to mix with and become friends with children from so many different backgrounds.

As pupils get older, particularly in the Sixth Form, day pupils often find that they spend too much time travelling to and from school each day, when they could be studying. In this respect, boarding is both convenient and time-saving.

The School has a small number of weekly boarders, whose parents do not generally live far from the School but who, due to work or personal commitments, are unable to look after their children during the week. Again, children are provided with security and stability, but are able to spend time with their families at the weekend. **"**

Mrs B A Evans, BSc, HNC, Headmistress, The Royal Wolverhampton School

" The burning issue amongst prospective parents considering a boarding education for their children remains a time-honoured one. Whilst they want to give their children the opportunity to enjoy and benefit from the boarding experience, they are increasingly reluctant to commit themselves to it at too early a stage in the child's prep school career. When a more flexible option is available, then a whole new world can open up. With children becoming more and more involved in the selection process, it is quite natural for their views on boarding to be taken into account by their parents. Institutions that leave the timing of this critical decision to families themselves can look forward to the future of boarding in their schools with a great deal of optimism. At Cheam we have experienced a reversal in the downward boarding trend by offering such a range in our boarding provision – full, weekly and 'flexi' are available to all the children (boys and girls 7-13) and there are relatively few who have not yet sampled boarding in one guise or another. No longer should there be any stigma attached to boarding if both the home and the school are very much involved in the initial decision making process. **"**

Mark Johnson, BEd, Headmaster, Cheam Hawtreys

" I have just returned from an evening visit to the boys' boarding house. Some were chatting about the day's events – matches against another school – over bowls of cereal, there is talk of last weekend's overnight trip to the hills, the charismatic French teacher, recently returned from a school trip across the Channel is playing animated board games in a 'dorm'. There is a lovely atmosphere, they are at ease, at home. And in the girls' house too there are happy faces and plenty of laughter. Real education never stops, goes beyond the 'normal' day.

So much of what we offer is intangible but precious. In our schools standards are high; there is invariably a stimulating range of activity beyond the classroom. Ordinary miracles happen in many classrooms and an enduring love is kindled of art, literature, drama, music or sporting activity. Skills are taught which are invaluable in the world of today – in technology, languages, innovative science, spoken English, personal and social education. But less tangibly qualities are fostered – of initiative, adaptability, a sensitivity to the needs of others; the ability to communicate and get on with people, the determination to persevere and see a difficult task through to fruition. Our pupils, through the rich educational experience we provide come to believe in themselves, to feel a real sense of pride in their achievements, to reach for the stars and to become good citizens.

Recently views have been gathered from former pupils as they reflect on their prep school days:

'I particularly remember the warm, friendly, tight-knit community that enabled you to grow at your own pace.'

'There is always someone who cares, who has time to talk and to discuss your day, your work, your hopes, your fears.'

'Being given a position of responsibility gave me much more confidence in myself and helped me come out of my proverbial shell.'

These reflections speak eloquently of the real difference our schools make in children's lives.
"

Mr P H Moody, MA, Headmaster, Hillstone, Malvern College

In praise of mixed boarding

Philip Watson, Principal of Burleigh Community College, *argues the merits of having to learn to get on with each other from an early stage*

Whilst many of our boarding schools are single-sex, there are a good many reasons why some have chosen to offer instead a totally different experience – that of mixed boarding. The reasons may be financial. With reductions in the Armed Forces abroad causing some schools to consider the prospect of closure, a move from two small single-sex houses to a single mixed provision has obvious attractions. Spare accommodation can be sold or used for other more profitable ventures, staff can be utilised more cost-effectively, significant budgetary savings can be made in energy, catering, laundry, transport and so on. A simplified management structure is another bonus.

However the welfare and happiness of the pupils has always to be the prime consideration and in this respect mixed boarding offers many pluses. The atmosphere in girls' houses differs markedly from that in boys' houses. Boys tend to be more noisy and boisterous, girls can be over-protective and cautious. In a mixed situation girls tend to modify the boys' behaviour and boys seem to bring life to the overly staid existence of girls. Certainly the relationships which form are of the very healthiest kind and traditional stereotypes often fall by the wayside. The two sexes learn very quickly to respect their differences which are far more exposed in the tightly knit community of a boarding house than they are in day time school. All become more caring, thoughtful and considerate, prepared to share their emotions without fear of shame or embarrassment. Equally those in a position of influence – senior boarders – exert their power more sensitively, more constructively.

Clearly there are strict requirements to which mixed boarding houses have to conform. These may include, for example, separated rooms and bathrooms, separate staircases and clear rules regarding freedom of movement, bed times *etc*. Outside of these restrictions boys and girls mix quite naturally during dinner, in social areas, at prep times and walking to and from school. The boundaries are clear and pupils soon learn to operate happily within them – of course they test them from time to time but then young people would, wouldn't they!

The overall sense in a mixed boarding house is one of a large family sharing the same values, caring for one another, responsible for one another. Given that boarding can never truly mirror life with loving parents, then arguably mixed boarding is as close as it is possible to get.

Boarding – the complete education

Cathryn Rogerson, A Headmaster's wife, argues that boarding provides children with time and space, as well as facilities and activities to help them to develop

The Headmaster's study at Cottesmore is oak panelled, cosy and warm. It is divided into two parts. On one side there are some comfortable armchairs, an often used coal fire, books and photographs. On the other side are two desks: one for the Headmaster and one for me, his wife. Staff, parents, boys and girls have been popping in and out of the study for many, many years.

From my desk as wife of the Headmaster, I have a privileged view, and have been able to observe the workings of this School and many others - independent and maintained, boarding and day, from a unique perspective.

There is a completeness to life in a boarding school. Each member of staff has a pastoral rôle besides teaching, and takes on myriad duties as part of school life. The high expectations of the classroom spill out into all areas of the School, and every child academically gifted or not, will be given the opportunity to discover and develop his or her full potential.

All children have their own special talents. Sometimes it takes time and patience to discover them, but one must be there to recognise and capture the spark. There is no greater joy to anyone who loves children than to see it kindled. A child never leaves this School without setting the world on fire in some small way. I feel sure that this can be said of all good boarding schools.

Children need to be loved, listened to and respected. They must have time and space to make their own mistakes and to learn from them. Most boarding schools are set in beautiful surroundings. They can provide children with the freedom so lacking in large parts of England today. A weekend means time to play, make friends, climb trees, be silly, get muddy, make believe, take risks, run, jump, hide, compete, relax. A team of experienced adults will always be nearby keeping a watchful eye from a discreet distance, conscious that there are times when children need to be separate from the world of adults, but aware of their responsibility for the children's safety.

One of the major developments I have seen over the years is the introduction of girls into some of the most traditional boarding schools. It has been a huge success. Boys and girls together mean fun. The combination is as natural as a family, which is after all what a good boarding Prep school should be. When girls first came to Cottesmore in 1974, after 75 years of boys only, the School became warmer in atmosphere and more challenging. Boys began to tolerate and take a greater interest in the arts whilst with an appreciative audience, match results got better and better! The girls integrated well, quick to learn and to take advantage of the huge range of games, hobbies and activities on offer – there were more than 25 to choose from at the last count. In the classroom, the natural competition between male and female, and their unique approach to each subject, enhanced academic performance hugely.

News of those early co-ed generations makes interesting reading. Most have been through university and are now earning their livings in various ways. Some work in the City, some have joined the medical profession. Some are dentists, aid workers, journalists, professional musicians, computer experts or lawyers. Some are married and have their own families. The common thread running through the lives of these young men and women seems to be their ease with each other. Firm friendships were forged at an early age, and a remarkable sense of tolerance and understanding has been carried through to the work place and beyond.

The advantages of a boarding school for those living abroad are plain to see. The high academic standards, continuity and stability that this style of schooling offers must be a major factor when parents are making that important decision. But many local parents will also allow their children the privilege of boarding. The completeness of the education, the fun and friendships of the safe environment makes it an attractive option. Daily travel to and from school is eliminated. So too are those evening runs to the children's myriad after school classes all of which will be on hand and time-tabled in a boarding school.

Although separation from one's children, even for short periods of time, is not easy, especially in the early stages, all schools are more open to parents than ever before and boarding schools are no exception. Frequent exeats, fax machines, e-mail and the telephone ensure that families keep in very close touch with each other, school and home working in harmony towards a common goal.

Siblings can often benefit from being distanced from one another for a short while. Younger children at home have a chance to grow and develop with their parents' full attention, whilst an older brother or sister at school can make a mark before a young sibling arrives. Many younger ones clamour to be allowed to follow a big brother or sister to school after a term. I can honestly say that in more than 25 years, I have never known a parent/child relationship to deteriorate because a child has been allowed to come to boarding school. Quite the contrary, relationships have been enhanced through mutual appreciation, as both parents, particularly those who work, put aside special time for their children when they come home, and children begin to discover their own talents and independence in school.

Many myths surround boarding schools. Some are true some are not. One thing is sure, a visit is essential. All schools will be glad to see you and be proud to show you what they can offer.

You will know what is right for your child when you see a school full of bright, shiny confident children who look you in the eye and say "Welcome"!

Mark and Cathryn Rogerson have been running Cottesmore for more than 25 years.
They have four children of their own, all of whom came to the School, and went on to
Independent boarding schools.

Your questions answered

Why consider a boarding school?

Boarding schools still form a major part of the independent sector: in 1998 just under 80,000 boarding pupils attended independent schools throughout the UK. Parents are sometimes surprised to learn that there are also state boarding schools, where tuition is free and a fee is charged for boarding only.

The need for boarding provision remains undiminished. For some groups it is the only real option: children whose parents are resident outside the UK or regularly posted abroad may find boarding the only means of maintaining stability and continuity. Similarly, some youngsters require special education which cannot be provided within the limits of a day school. Despite escalating fee levels, many parents choose boarding in preference to a day school education and are prepared to make sacrifices to meet the cost. Certainly parents willing to consider the boarding option in their initial selection will find their choice widened enormously.

Unlike state schools, independent schools are not subject to Local Authority control although they are required to meet regulations set by the Department for Education and Employment. At present, independent schools are not required to teach the National Curriculum, although many choose to do so, and nearly all prepare pupils for the GCSE and A level examinations, although some do offer the International Baccalaureate.

The freedom given to schools in this way encourages enormous choice and variety within the independent sector. There are single-sex and co-educational schools, specialist music and choir schools, schools with a particular religious foundation, such as the Quaker group which place great emphasis on the individual, and schools with

specific ideals such as those in the Round Square Conference, which follow the style of education developed by Kurt Hahn. Many of the country's oldest and best-known schools are boarding schools which have maintained their own traditions and philosophies. Some schools are privately owned, but most are now run as charitable trusts under the control of a board of Governors.

What are the main features?

Modern boarding schools take great pains to provide a caring environment and community life which encourage children to give as well as to receive. The carefully-structured day and the immediate availability of staff and resources in the evenings and at weekends lay the foundations for good work habits and organisation of time. Periods set aside daily specifically for supervised homework or private study avoid the arguments over television programmes and other distractions which may arise at home.

In recent years boarding schools have invested enormously in improvements to their teaching, boarding, arts and sports facilities, which may outclass anything students find in colleges and universities later on. These are available to pupils seven days a week, for academic or extra-curricular purposes, offering the best possible opportunities either to study or develop a hobby or personal interest.

The time outside normal lessons is used to the full. Most schools offer a wealth of different activities – sporting, cultural, creative – which encourages involvement and allows opportunities for pupils to discover and develop their talents in areas outside the timetabled curriculum. Personal and social development are further important aspects; living away from home in a large community helps to build self-confidence and self-reliance and to foster tolerance and understanding. Friendships made at boarding school often last a lifetime.

What are the usual entry requirements?

Some children begin boarding at eight or nine, when schools normally require a simple test in English and Mathematics and an interview.

Most pupils begin boarding when they enter senior school, at age 11 for girls and 13 for boys. A few schools set their own entrance examinations but most require applicants to sit the Common Entrance examination. At 11, this includes papers in English, Mathematics, Science, a Verbal Reasoning Test and, from the age of 12, elementary French. At 13, papers are set in English, Mathematics, Science, French, History, Geography and Religious Studies. Latin is an optional subject but a few schools require it.

The papers are set centrally by the Common Entrance Examinations Board but marked by the individual schools who set their own entry standards. There is no agreed national standard as such; a child gains entrance to a particular school by Common Entrance according to the performance standards accepted by that school.

For entry at 16, schools require a report from the student's present school and specify the grades needed at GCSE.

Are boarding schools accredited in any way?

Until 1978 independent schools were inspected by Her Majesty's Inspectorate and, on the basis of a satisfactory report, granted the status 'recognised as efficient', which indicated standards well above the minimum required for registration. This scheme was abandoned by the Department of Education and Science in 1978 and was not replaced.

Independent schools are much concerned with self-regulation. Many schools belong to the official associations such as HMC, GSA, SHIS, IAPS and ISA, all of which set standards to which their member schools must conform. A list of abbreviations appears at the end of this guide.

Currently eight such associations form the Independent Schools Council. Apart from the criteria set by its own associations, the ISC has also developed, in response to the demise of the DES inspection procedure, an accreditation scheme which schools may apply for voluntarily.

All boarding schools, both state and independent, are now subject to inspection by local authorities and social services under the regulations set out in the Children Act 1989.

How do I find the right school?

Finding the school which best suits your child among the hundreds available need not be as daunting as it seems! The first step, before all else, is to establish your child's academic needs. Even within the busy environment of a boarding school your child will spend most of the time at study, so this must come first. Be realistic about your child; boarding schools offer a wealth of choice for all abilities. Fast-moving academic schools are for fast-moving academic children and it can be very demoralising for a child to find himself always struggling at the bottom of the class. Think ahead, particularly at secondary level, to likely options after GCSEs or A levels and consider any special needs or interests which merit particular attention.

Then consider the type of school you are looking for and the geographical areas within reach. Once you have established the basics you can begin to gather information from the many sources available. The Head of your child's present school, other parents and friends may be helpful. Schools should be happy to send you a prospectus on request; it is a good idea to obtain a selection for comparative purposes. These will tell you something about the curriculum, the range of subjects, extra-curricular activities and pastoral care.

However the only way to gain a proper feel for a school is to visit it, ideally during term-time when classes are in progress. Make sure you visit at least two, so that you have some form of comparison, and note down those areas not covered in the prospectus on which you would like more information.

Are there any guidelines on making the most of my visit?

Normally when you arrive you will spend some time with the Head to discuss your child. The Head will then show you the school or ask another member of staff or a pupil to take you round.

Above all, don't be afraid to ask questions, however minor they may seem. Heads are used to answering all sorts of awkward questions, and you are about to make a major investment to which you may be committed for several years. The following may be a useful reminder of areas to be discussed during your visit:

Arrival and first impressions Is the school tidy and well-kept? Some schools are housed in magnificent buildings and beautiful grounds, but others take equal pride in somewhat less elaborate surroundings and take great pains to make the school look attractive. Are the pupils neat and well-behaved? Did any of them offer to direct you? How easy was it to find the Head's office? Were the staff welcoming and interested?

Academic matters What is the main thrust of the curriculum and where do leavers go? What are the school's special curricular strengths? At preparatory level, is the school preparing pupils chiefly for Common Entrance and boarding at 11 or 13 or is there more movement to day schools or the maintained sector? At secondary level, what is offered at GCSE and A level? How strong is the Sixth-Form? Is there a leaning towards sciences or the arts? What proportion of leavers go on to universities, professional courses or vocational studies? If your child has a more practical mind, does the school offer any vocational courses at Sixth-Form level?

What is the average class size? How large are the teaching groups for GCSE and A level? How are the pupils organised? Schools may cater for a broad range of ability and pupils are often taught in 'sets' taking account of their ability in individual subjects. Ask the Head about the school's policy.

What provision is there for special individual needs or learning difficulties and, at senior level, careers advice?

Since 1993 independent schools have been required to publish exam results, although many did so already. Schools should be happy to let you have their results on request, but make sure you know what you are being given – schools may list results in different ways.

Staff It is important that you should meet the staff who will be responsible for your child, not only the Head but also form and subject teachers and, as important, the House staff who will provide pastoral support and act *in loco parentis*, dealing with day-to-day personal matters and providing a source of guidance or comfort when problems arise.

Discipline This will vary from one school to another, but all schools will have a system of rules which are essential within a large community. Ask the Head about the school's approach. What constitutes punishable conduct? Are there clear guidelines for staff and for pupils? Is corporal punishment ever used? What sort of offence could lead to suspension or expulsion? Are parents informed about any misconduct on the part of their child?

The general level of supervision and control is also important, although you should be able to get a 'feel' of this simply by using your eyes. To what extent are pupils supervised during prep periods and leisure time? What rules are there with regard to bedtimes, television viewing and use of free time? Are pupils allowed out of school unaccompanied? On what terms?

Pastoral care Make sure that you are shown the boarding accommodation, warts and all. Is it warm, welcoming and comfortable? What sort of leisure facilities are there? Are the areas set aside for study outside normal lessons adequate, particularly for older students? Are they spacious, quiet and organised? Many schools have a House system, where pupils are accommodated in smaller groups in the care of a resident Housemaster or Housemistress, assistant staff and matron. Most boarding schools today offer comfortable, high quality and homely accommodation for their pupils, who are generally encouraged to personalise their own space.

Younger pupils may sleep in bedrooms housing small groups. Older pupils, particularly at V and VI Form level, often have shared or single study bedrooms, comfortably furnished and often with excellent bathroom and kitchenette facilities.

Extra-curricular activities A look at the noticeboards will tell you something about the various activities going on in school. What is the main thrust of activities –sports, art, music, outdoor pursuits? Is participation compulsory or voluntary? Is there sufficient provision for all types of interest? Are there areas in which the school truly excels? To what extent are pupils encouraged to develop their interests to the full potential?

Contact with parents How often do parents receive reports? Does the school organise regular parents' evenings where progress can be discussed? To what extent will the school help with forward planning and choice of subjects? How often are pupils allowed out for exeat weekends?

Overall impressions Much can be learned simply by observation. Is there a sense of purpose and organisation? Are pupils alert and interested? Is their work displayed on classroom walls? Are the standards of work what you would expect? How do pupils behave towards the Head and staff? Is there a rapport and a sense of respect? How do the pupils behave towards you as a visitor?

Coming from overseas?

Overseas parents seeking a boarding school have special requirements. Information on schools should be available locally, from British Council offices, British diplomatic representation abroad or possibly British companies with local bases who may hold the information for the benefit of their staff.

For children whose first language is not English it will be important to establish the level of English language acceptable to schools and the extent to which they can offer extra tuition where necessary.

All boarding schools will insist that children from overseas have a guardian in the UK who can offer a happy and secure home for weekends and half-terms, attend events at school and act as a point of contact for day-to-day matters.

What arrangements are made for travel? Does the school provide escorts to and from airports? Is it conveniently located for access to rail and air links?

How much will it cost? Why do fees vary so much?

School fees normally rise at a rate higher than inflation. In 1998 approximate annual fees for boarding preparatory schools were £6500 to £10,500, for secondary boarding up to £15,500. Fees for weekly boarding are normally the same as, or a little less than, the full boarding fee. Fees are normally paid termly in advance, but there are often extras to allow for in the form of music lessons, sports kit, trips abroad, pocket money and so on, although schools rarely charge for text books.

Beware of making the assumption that higher fees mean a better school. The best school for your child will be the one which best suits his or her individual needs. However, if the fees are very much lower than expected, find out why. Some schools receive special endowments which enable them to keep fees at a relatively low level.

In addition, many schools offer scholarships, given on the basis of academic excellence or a particular talent in a specific area, or bursaries, which may be granted in cases of hardship. Special mention should be made of Choir Schools for younger boys. Fees for choristers are very much reduced and there is sometimes help available for fees at senior schools, although many choristers obtain music scholarships at this level. In addition, some schools have scholarships restricted to children of clergy, the Services, the medical and teaching professions.

Who's Who at Boarding School

The Governors

Governors of independent schools, unlike many maintained schools, are the source of all authority within the school and are responsible for overall policy. They control finance and administration, responsibility for which is normally delegated to the Head or the Bursar, and – probably their single most important task – appoint the Head. Governors give their time and expertise in various fields voluntarily

and a good rapport between Governors and Head is essential for a well-run school.

The Head

The Head is responsible to the Governors for all aspects of school life including, for example, the safety and welfare of pupils and the competence of the staff, but decisions about day-to-day running of the school are normally made by the Head. The Head is responsible for the appointment of staff, selection of pupils, supervision of all activities

and arrangements, and is the final arbiter on any question, from academic decisions to the suspension of a pupil. Most Heads find time to continue teaching and make every effort to get to know all the pupils individually.

The Bursar

The Bursar is a key member of the school's management team, responsible to the Head for the non-academic administration of the school in activities such as catering and maintenance. In addition, the Bursar, in conjunction with the Governors, is responsible for the overall financial management of the school and it will be the Bursar's office which sends you the termly bill!

Director of Studies

With the curriculum growing more complex many schools now have a senior teacher responsible for ensuring that the school is up-to-date with developments. The Director of Studies will normally supervise the timetable and is responsible to the Head for arrangements for university entrance. The Head, Deputy and Director of Studies usually form the core management team of a school.

Housemaster/Housemistress

A Housemaster or Housemistress is responsible for the welfare and development of the pupils in a House. These are the staff who will maintain an overall view of your child's development both in academic and non-academic matters and relay information to and from the school. They are responsible for day-to-day discipline but will refer serious matters to the Head. The Housemaster or mistress plays a key

role in your child's school life and is normally the first point of contact for parents.

Subject teacher

Subject teachers are responsible for the progress of pupils in the class and will provide a termly subject report. Formal meetings also provide an opportunity for parents to discuss progress directly with teaching staff.

Chaplain

The Chaplain is responsible for the religious life of the school and is a valuable member of the pastoral care staff. Unlike the Housemaster or mistress he is not identified with discipline and can provide support and a 'listening ear' for both staff and pupils.

Matron

Matron is responsible for the housekeeping aspects including boarding accommodation and laundry, but is also a key figure for the pupils and will often know them well individually. She can be a great source of strength to harassed staff and to (temporarily) unhappy pupils!

Sister

The Sister is responsible for medical arrangements and is in charge of the sanatorium. She can also provide valuable insights into the development of your child.

Prefects

Senior pupils who exercise responsibility for some of the daily routines in school. They may have disciplinary powers but are now much more likely to encourage and lead by example than by the threat of sanctions. Most schools will offer pupils opportunities for posts of responsibility, but because many prefer their second year sixth-formers to devote more time to studies, it is quite usual to find boys and girls in the post of prefect at an earlier age than in the past.

Finding the Fees

by Chris Heyes *former Bursar of Rugby School*, and David Belchamber
former Bursar of King's College School, Wimbledon

Nobody should pretend that independent education is cheap. It never has been and never will be but succeeding generations of parents demonstrate their belief that good education is a priceless asset by continuing to send their children to independent schools.

Just under 600,000 pupils are currently being educated in over 2400 such schools in the UK with annual fees ranging from just under £3000 at the least expensive pre-prep schools to nearly £15,000 at the most expensive boarding schools, on top of which there are always some extras to be found. Additionally, increases in school fees tend to outstrip annual increases in the cost of living, so that the total fees bill (for day fees at middle cost schools) , taken over a 15 year period from the age of three to 18, could well equal the cost of another house.

Of course if the child then continues on to higher education, there will be a further period of fee-paying in prospect.

Methods of paying school fees

The four main ways in which fees are paid are:

> from fee plans that mature after a number of years
>
> from capital
>
> from immediate fee plans
>
> from income

These days many parents wishing to send their children to independent schools will predictably have three major items of expenditure to fund in the course of their working lives: the mortgage, school fees and a pension.

For this reason, it would seem prudent therefore to take advice from an Independent Financial Adviser (IFA) sooner rather than later to ensure that proper provision is being made that best value for money is being obtained.

School fee plans

Where school fees are concerned an IFA would, no doubt, advise on whether or not the setting up of a number of endowment policies to mature at yearly intervals would be appropriate (normally only if planning ten years or more ahead). If so, under present legislation, tax-free capital can be built up out of income.

Since independent education now starts so early, this option will only be appropriate in certain cases and the IFA might well advise that PEPs (soon to be replaced by ISAs), TESSAs, investment trusts or unit trusts might be more appropriate vehicles instead.

For many people high interest bearing investment accounts with banks, building societies or National Savings should ensure that savings beat inflation (although not neccesarily fees' inflation), though it must be remembered that some of these pay gross interest and tax will therefore have to be paid.

Sometimes grandparents are able to assist, either out of income or capital, but unfortunately they can no longer do so by transferring money under deeds of covenant, which used to attract tax relief.

Capital

If parents are fortunate enough to have enough capital available some years before fees become due, then the eventual costs can be substantially reduced.

Parents with capital available will no doubt have professional advisers who will suggest appropriate investments after taking into account all the factors affecting such decisions, for instance the investment period, tax position and other possible calls on the same funds.

Many schools operate their own Composition Fees scheme by which fees for a specified number of years (or termly credits) can be secured by the payment of a lump sum payment in advance. Parents should enquire from the bursar of the intended school for details; since interest rates vary greatly from school to school and there could sometimes be problems if the child did not eventually go to the school where the composition fee had been taken out, it would again be prudent to take professional advice on such schemes.

Immediate fee plans

An increasing number of parents are new to independent education and have not had the opportunity to make advance provision for fees.

In such cases, some banks such as The Royal Bank of Scotland, or a broker such as Mason & Mason Ltd, which have been endorsed by ISIS, offer drawdown facilities, by way of loans secured by a life assurance policy or perhaps, in the case of a larger loan, secured on the house itself. This can allow the fee commitment to be spread over a longer period of time than the actual schooling and might therefore suit parents prepared to make that long-term pledge.

Payment from income

At the other end of the scale, for parents who wish to keep their school fee borrowing to a minimum, credit schemes are now available which allow parents to budget for school fees on a monthly basis. Instead of having to pay the whole amount in advance, as is still the requirement in most schools, parents are enabled to spread the payment of fees over the whole term, the charge for which facility being typically 3% or 4%.

Many schools now allow parents to pay monthly, either by running their own scheme or by offering one managed by an outside firm, such as Holmwoods Termtime Credit or Alliance and Leicester plc.

Holmwoods Termtime Credit also has a monthly payment scheme for parents to use direct, if the school cannot offer any such scheme.

More detailed information can be obtained from

General

The Independent Schools Information Service (tel 0171 630 8793/4)

Publishes a helpful leaflet *School Fees* which notes a number of companies that specialise in school fee planning and suggests a number of IFAs.

Unit Trusts and Investment Trusts

The following have published leaflets on helping to meet school fees:

The Association of Investment Trust Companies (tel 0171 431 5222)

Association of Unit Trusts and Investment Funds (tel 0181 207 1361)

Immediate fee plans

The Royal Bank of Scotland Education Expenses Plan (tel 0131 523 2147)

Mason & Mason Ltd (tel 01625 529 536)

Monthly payment schemes

Holmwoods Termtime Credit (tel 01372 746 006)

Alliance and Leicester plc (tel 0131 451 5183)

Section One:
Pre-Preparatory & Preparatory Schools
Age range up to 14

Abbot's Hill Junior School St Nicholas House

Bunkers Lane, Hemel Hempstead, Hertfordshire HP3 8RP
Co-educational Boarding & Day

See Section Two

Ashford School

East Hill, Ashford, Kent TN24 8PB
Girls Day & Boarding

See Section Two

Bedgebury School

Bedgebury Park, Goudhurst, Cranbrook, Kent TN17 2SH
Girls Boarding & Day

See Section Two

Bredon School

Pull Court, Bushley, Tewkesbury, Gloucestershire GL20 6AH
Co-educational Boarding & Day

See Section Two

Ardvreck School

(Founded 1883)

Gwydyr Road, Crieff, Perthshire PH7 4EX

Tel: 01764 653112 Fax: 01764 654920
e-mail: headmaster@ardvreck.powernet-int.co.uk

Head: N W Gardner BA, CertEd(Dunelm)

Date of appointment: 1995

Member of: IAPS, BSA

Co-educational Boarding & Day

Religious affiliation: Christian - Interdenominational

Age range of pupils: 3 – 13

Boarders from 7 years

No. of students enrolled as at 1.9.98: 166

Average size of class: 12

Teacher/Pupil ratio: 1:10

Curriculum: Pupils are prepared for all major public schools through Common Entrance and scholarship examinations. Ardvreck has a long tradition of providing academic, sporting and musical excellence.

Entry requirements: Assessment and interview with Headmaster. Entry Scholarships are awarded each year following a competitive examination in February.

Range of fees per annum as at 1.9.98:

Day: £2730 – £5865

Boarding: £9045 – £9465

Nursery: £420 Mornings £325 Afternoons

Ardvreck stands in extensive grounds on the edge of the picturesque town of Crieff in the heart of Perthshire. It enjoys breathtaking views.

Ardvreck School is a Registered Charity in Scotland. It exists to provide quality education for boys and girls.

Cottesmore School

(Founded 1894)

Buchan Hill, Pease Pottage, West Sussex RH11 9AU

Tel: 01293 520648 Fax: 01293 614784

e-mail: 106750,276@compuserve.com

Cottesmore is one of very few all boarding schools in England. The Headmaster and his wife run the school as a family, making sure that weekends in are busy and happy. Within a warm and secure atmosphere, the children are encouraged to work hard, play hard, and strive for success.

Head: Mr M A Rogerson MA(Cantab)

Date of appointment: 1971

Member of: IAPS

Co-educational Boarding

Religious affiliation: Church of England

Age range of pupils: 7 – 13

No. of students enrolled as at 1.9.98: 145

Boys: 100 Girls: 45

Average size of class: 14

Teacher/Pupil ratio: 1:9

Curriculum: All the usual Common Entrance subjects are taught, plus Art, Music, Computer Studies, CDT, Dance and Drama.

Entry requirements: By interview.

Range of fees per annum as at 1.9.98:

Boarding: £10,110

Academic & leisure facilities: Music School, Computer Room, Laboratory, Art, Pottery, Trains, Printing, Woodwork, Gardens, Theatre. Tennis, Squash, Indoor Heated Swimming Pool, Shooting Range, Bowling Alley, Golf, Fishing, Canoeing, Boating, Windsurfing. New Technology Centre under construction.

Cottesmore School stands in 40 acres, one mile from the Pease Pottage exit of the M23, within easy reach of London, Gatwick Airport and the coast.

Dean Close Junior School

(Founded 1886)

Lansdown Road, Cheltenham, Gloucestershire GL51 6QS

Tel: 01242 512217 Fax: 01242 258005

Head: Mr Stephen W Baird BA

Date of appointment: 1997

Member of: IAPS, ISIS

Co-educational Day & Boarding

Religious affiliation: A Christian school with an evangelical Anglican foundation

Age range of pupils: 3 – 13

Boarders from 7+ years

No. of students enrolled as at 1.9.98: 303

Boys: 167 Girls: 136

Average size of class: 15

Teacher/Pupil ratio: 1:10

Curriculum: The School follows Common Entrance requirements and fully embraces the National Curriculum.

Entry requirements: A test in English, Mathematics and Verbal Reasoning.

Range of fees per annum as at 1.9.98:

Day: £6975

Boarding: £10,245

The School is a registered Charity (No. 311721), a Christian family school with outstanding facilities and caring staff committed to the development of the individual child in all aspects of education.

Dean Close Senior School, see page 60

Dragon School

(Founded 1877)

Bardwell Road, Oxford OX2 6SS

Tel: 01865 315400 Fax: 01865 311664
e-mail: dragon@rmplc.co.uk
Internet: http://www.rmplc.co.uk/eduweb/sites/
dragon/index.html

Head: Mr R S Trafford MA(Oxon)

Member of: IAPS

Co-educational Boarding & Day

Religious affiliation: Church of England

Age range of pupils: 3 – 13

Boarders from 8 years

No. of students enrolled as at 1.9.98: 815

Boys: 615 Girls: 200

Average size of class: 19

Teacher/Pupil ratio: 1:10

Curriculum: The curriculum is based on the Scholarship requirements of the major Public Schools (28 is the recent average number of Scholarships) and the Common Entrance syllabus.

Entry requirements: Those entering the School at 7 or 8 are required to be able to read up to a good standard for their age group and to have a basic knowledge of arithmetic. Assessment days are held 9-18 months ahead of entry. Early registration is advisable.

Range of fees per annum as at 1.9.98:

Day: £4290 – £7545

Boarding: £11,235

The School is situated in North Oxford close to the River Cherwell. The 260 boarders are placed in eight boarding houses, three with about 20 boys in each for the younger boarders (8 and 9 year olds), two middle houses (10 year olds), two senior houses (11 and 12 year olds), and a girls' boarding house. A wide range of activities is on offer and more than half the children represent the school in a variety of games, where they are very successful.

The Dragon School Trust Ltd, a registered charity, aims to provide education for boys and girls between the ages of 3 and 13.

Dulwich Preparatory School

(Founded 1939)

Coursehorn, Cranbrook, Kent TN17 3NP

Tel: 01580 712179 Fax: 01580 715322
e-mail: jchuter@dcpscran.demon.uk

Head: Mr M C Wagstaffe BA(Hons), PGCE

Date of appointment: April 1990

Member of: ISIS, IAPS

Co-educational Day & Boarding

Religious affiliation: Christian

Age range of pupils: 3 – 13

Boarders from 8 years

No. of students enrolled as at 1.9.98: 536

Boys: 288 Girls: 248

Average size of class: 18-20

Teacher/Pupil ratio: 1:11

Curriculum: Emphasis is placed on the basic skills whilst following the National Curriculum. Children are treated as individuals and helped to reach their full potential.

Entry requirements: Testing from seven years.

Range of fees per annum as at 1.9.98:

Day: £2250 – £6510

Boarding: £9660 – £9900

Lovely 40 acre grounds with excellent facilities. Three boarding houses. There is a happy relaxed, homely atmosphere for the boarders in three separate houses.

Dulwich Preparatory School Charitable Trust exists for the provision of high quality education in a Christian environment.

Dulwich College

London, SE21 7LD
Boys Day & Boarding

See Section Two

Eltham College

Grove Park Road, Mottingham, London SE9 4QF
Boys Day & Boarding

See Section Two

Farlington School

Strood Park, Horsham, West Sussex RH12 3PN
Girls Day & Boarding

See Section Two

Framlingham College

Framlingham, Woodbridge, Suffolk IP13 9EY

***Junior School -** Brandeston Hall*
Brandeston, Woodbridge, Suffolk IP13 7AQ

Co-educational Boarding & Day

See Section Two

Farringtons & Stratford House Junior School

(Founded 1911)

Perry Street, Chislehurst, Kent BR7 6LR

Tel: 0181 467 0256/0395

Head: Mrs Catherine James MA

Date of appointment: January 1999

Member of: GSA, GBSA, BSA

Girls Boarding & Day

Religious affiliation: Methodist

Age range of pupils: 2 – 11

Boarders from 7 years

No. of students enrolled as at 1.9.98: 212

Girls: 212

Average size of class: 15

Teacher/Pupil ratio: 1:12

Curriculum: In addition to the National Curriculum, we also offer French and many extra-curricular activities.

Entry requirements: If possible, a day spent in school and an informal assessment.

Range of fees per annum as at 1.9.98:

Day: £4230

Weekly Boarding: £10,320

Boarding: £10,770

Farringtons & Stratford House is situated within 25 minutes of London and short travelling distance for London airports. It has extensive sports grounds with swimming pool, full size sports hall and new Technology Centre and computer room.

Registered Charity No. 307916, Farringtons School exists solely to provide a high quality, caring education for girls.

Farrington & Stratford House Senior School – see page 66

Frensham Heights School

Rowledge, Farnham, Surrey GU10 4EA
Co-educational Boarding & Day

See Section Two

Giggleswick School

Giggleswick, Settle, North Yorkshire BD24 0DE
Co-educational Boarding & Day

See Section Two

Kirkham Grammar School

Ribby Road, Kirkham, Preston, Lancashire PR4 2BH
Co-educational Day & Boarding

See Section Two

Leaden Hall School

(Founded 1948)

70 The Close, Salisbury, Wiltshire SP1 2EP

Tel: 01722 334700 Fax: 01722 410575

e-mail: leaden.hall@virgin.net

Head: Mrs Diana Watkins MA

Date of appointment: September 1993

Member of: IAPS, BSA

Girls Day & Boarding

Religious affiliation: Christian

Age range of pupils: 3 – 13

Boarders from 7+

No. of students enrolled as at 1.9.98: 227

Entry requirements: Interview/assessment.

Range of fees per annum as at 1.9.98:

Day: £2634 – £4515

Weekly Boarding: £6885

Boarding: £8070

Leaden Hall girls will become "successful women of the 21st Century" because we encourage them to become confident, independent learners.

We help them prepare for change and give them vital skills to adapt, enabling them to enter 11+, 12+, 13+ Common Entrance and Scholarship Examinations as

well as the County Grammar School

The historic Cathedral Close is the perfect setting, giving inspiration to both the staff and the children who work here.

We specialise in preparing preparatory school girls for boarding in their senior secondary schools and have opened a new boarding house especially for girls to enjoy the independence of preparing for senior transfer.

We believe boarding should be comfortable, fun and stimulating. After school and weekend activities are action packed to allow the children to experience the very best in school life.

Full, weekly and day boarding options give parents the flexibility to enable their daughters to take part in the many extra curricular activities.

Leaden Hall School Ltd is a charitable trust which exists to provide quality education for girls aged three to 13 years.

Lime House School

Holm Hill, Dalston, Carlisle, Cumbria CA5 7BX
Co-educational Boarding & Day

See Section Two

New Hall School

Chelmsford, Essex CM3 3HT
Girls Boarding & Day

See Section Two

Newlands School

(Founded 1854)

Eastbourne Road, Seaford, East Sussex BN25 4NP

Tel: 01323 490000 Fax: 01323 898426
e-mail: newlands1@msn.com
Internet: http://www.interbd.com/newlands-school

Let us unlock you child's potential

Head of Preparatory School: Mr Oliver T Price BEd(Hons)

Head of Senior School: Mr Roland Miles BA(Hons)

Member of: IAPS, ISA

Co-educational Boarding & Day

Religious affiliation: Non-denominational

Age range of pupils: 2½ – 18

Boarders from 7 years

No. of students enrolled as at 1.1.99: 568

Boys: 358 Girls: 210 VIth Form: 68

Range of fees per annum as at 1.9.98:

Day: £4650 – £6450

Boarding: £8985 – £11,325

Our School

Newlands is a friendly, happy school with a strong academic tradition. Situated on one campus, Newlands offers an opportunity for educational continuity from nursery to university entrance. Classes are small and each pupil's progress is monitored carefully.

Location

Newlands is situated in a 21 acre campus in a pleasant coastal town surrounded by an area of outstanding natural beauty. Good communication links with Gatwick (37 miles), Heathrow (78 miles) and London (65 miles).

High Academic Standards

At Newlands we expect pupils to attain optimum results in external examinations, as is evident by our strong academic record. For the past few years pupils have won prizes awarded by the Independent Schools Association for outstanding academic results. Examination results are well above average, particularly in Mathematics, the Sciences, Art, and Computing.

At Newlands we also place an emphasis on fully developing your child's potential. The wide range of activities available makes it possible for every pupil to achieve success and confidence in one field or another.

Entry requirements

An interview and school report are required for the Junior School.

An interview and school reports are also needed for the Senior School.

Curriculum and Scholarships

We follow the National Curriculum whilst also preparing your child for Scholarships to Senior Schools. The Senior School offers all the usual subjects leading to GCSE and A level for university entrance.

The arts flourish with thriving music, drama and art departments. There is a strong choral tradition and several annual dramatic productions. Academic and music scholarships are available and there is a generous discount for Service families.

Academic and sports facilities

Our facilities include five high-tech computer rooms, access to the Internet, science laboratories, a large art studio, a design technology workshop, an assembly hall/theatre and music room.

There are the equivalent of eight football pitches, a heated indoor swimming pool, a hard playing surface for three tennis/netball courts, a new multi-purpose hall which is appropriate for most indoor games as well as other activities and .22 rifle range. There are opportunities for many sports including soccer, hockey, rugby, netball, cricket, athletics, volleyball, basketball, squash, rounders, badminton, tennis, golf and cross-country running.

Support learning

Dyslexic pupils and those learning English as a foreign language are taught by specialist staff in our well-equipped, purpose built centre. Staff provide individual programmes of learning on a one-to-one basis. Approved by the Council for the Registration of Schools Teaching Dyslexics.

Transport

When required, pupils are escorted to Gatwick, Stansted and Heathrow airports and met on in coming flights. Newlands' minibuses provide transport to Victoria Station and along the south coast as far as Romsey, Aldershot and Maidstone.

Newlands School exists to provide quality education

Old Buckenham Hall School

(Founded 1862)

Brettenham, Ipswich, Suffolk IP7 7PH

Tel: 01449 740252 Fax: 01449 740955
e-mail: obh@old-buck.demon.co.uk
Internet: http://www.old-buck.demon.co.uk

Head: Mr M A Ives BEd(Hons)

Date of appointment: 1997

Member of: IAPS, ISIS

Co-educational Day & Boarding

Religious affiliation: Church of England, welcoming other denominations.

Age range of pupils: 2 – 13

No. of students enrolled as at 1.9.98: 182

Average size of class: 12

Teacher/Pupil ratio: 1:9

Entry requirements: Interview, report from previous School, if over seven.

Range of fees per annum as at 1.9.98:

Day: £3750 – £7800

Weekly Boarding: £9750

Boarding: £9900

The School, founded in Lowestoft as South Lodge in 1862, moved in 1937 to Old Buckenham Hall, Norfolk and in 1956 to Brettenham Park, four miles from Lavenham and 18 miles from Ipswich. It became an Educational Trust in 1967.

The pupils go on to a wide range of, mostly boarding, Senior Independent Schools via Common Entrance and Scholarship Examinations. (Usual subjects plus German as a second modern language.)

The staff/pupil ratio is approximately 1:9, giving an average class-size of 12. All members of staff, including part-time staff, contribute to the provision of a wide range of extra-curricular activities in which every child has a chance to participate. The major sports are Rugby, Hockey, Soccer, Netball, Cricket and Rounders, but all pupils also take part in Athletics and Swimming. In addition there are opportunities for Tennis (six courts), Golf (nine hole course), Squash (two courts), Table-Tennis, Woodwork, Metalwork, Pets, Shooting and Photography. Art, Music and Drama particularly flourish.

The Main Building, an 18th Century mansion, stands in its own grounds of 75 acres of which some 25 are playing fields and six are woodland. In the past few years many building alterations and additions have been completed. A Music and Drama Centre was opened in 1986 and in 1989 a DT Centre was established. In 1990 two new Science Laboratories were completed and in 1995 the Computer Room was fully upgraded. In 1997 astro-turf tennis courts were created and a new girls' boarding house was refurbished. A purpose built Pre-Prep Department opened in September 1998.

Academic and Music Awards are available each year, details of which, along with a School Prospectus, can be obtained on application to the Headmaster's Secretary.

Old Buckenham Hall (Brettenham) Educational Trust Ltd, a registered charity, exists to provide boarding and day education for boys and girls.

Orwell Park School

(Founded 1867)

Nacton, Ipswich, Suffolk IP10 0ER

Tel: 01473 659225 Fax: 01473 659822
e-mail: headmaster@orwellpark.demon.co.uk Internet: http://www.ukschools.com/schools/orwell/

Head: Mr Andrew H Auster BA(Hons), DipEd(Cantab), Hon FLCM, FRSA

Date of appointment: September 1994

Member of: IAPS, ISIS
Co-educational Boarding & Day
Religious affiliation: Interdenominational

Age range of pupils: 3 – 13

Boarders from 7

No. of students enrolled as at 1.9.98:

Boys: 156 Girls: 89

Average size of class: 12

Teacher/Pupil ratio: 1:9

Curriculum: Full Common Entrance and Scholarship subjects plus Art, Computing, Current Affairs, CDT, Drama, superb Music and Public Speaking. 15 Sports plus 50 hobbies including active week-end programme.

Entry requirements: Children are accepted, after interview (and placement test).

Range of fees per annum as at 1.9.98:

Day: £2805 – £7830

Weekly Boarding: £9420 – £10,590

Boarding: £9420 – £10,590

Music tuition: £110 per term for a course of ten lessons.

Termly charges are also made for outside professional tuition in a number of voluntary activities for which written parental permission is always required.

This purposeful and successful school has a happy atmosphere and superlative facilities set in 105 beautiful acres. Easy access from London (60 minutes by train). Experienced at organising international travel arrangements.

As a registered charity Orwell Park Educational Trust exists to provide an excellent boarding school environment for both boys and girls.

Packwood Haugh

(Founded 1882)

Ruyton XI Towns, Shrewsbury, Shropshire SY4 1HX

Tel: 01939 260217 Fax: 01939 260051
Internet: http://www.packwood-haugh.co.uk

We put great store on academic matters as our scholarship success record shows, but also set out to achieve the right balance between work, sport, music and art. At the same time good manners, good behaviour, friendliness and consideration are the hallmarks of all Packwood children.

Head: Mr P J F Jordan MA(Cantab)

Date of appointment: September 1988

Member of: IAPS

Co-educational Boarding & Day

Religious affiliation: Church of England

Age range of pupils: 7 – 13

Boarders from 7 years

No. of students enrolled as at 1.9.98: 226

Boys: 144 Girls: 82

Average size of class: 14

Teacher/Pupil ratio: 1:10

Curriculum: The usual Common Entrance subjects are taught plus CDT, Art, and Music in the purpose-built Music School. Specialist assistance for dyslexia is available.

Entry requirements: Assessment Test only.

Range of fees per annum as at 1.9.98:

Day: £3150 – £7362

Boarding: £9468

Situated in 65 acres of North Shropshire countryside. In addition to extensive playing fields and grounds there is an Astroturf pitch, a swimming pool and a golf course. There is an extensive range of activities on offer.

Packwood Haugh School Ltd Charitable Trust exists to provide high quality education for boys and girls. Twenty scholarships won in 1994.

Papplewick

(Founded 1947)

Windsor Road, Ascot, Berkshire SL5 7LH
Tel: 01344 621488 Fax: 01344 874639
e-mail: LizzieS@aol.com

Head: Mr D R Llewellyn BA, DipEd

Date of appointment: 1991

Member of: IAPS

Boys Boarding & Day

Religious affiliation: Christian

Age range of pupils: 7 – 13

Boarders from 7

No. of students enrolled as at 1.9.98: 186

Boys: 186

Average size of class: 12

Teacher/Pupil ratio: 1:8

Curriculum: All main subjects are studied. Computing is taught throughout the School as is Art, Design and Technology. Steady work towards scholarships and CE passes is balanced with Music, PE and a wide range of competitive sports and games. Magnificent new Sports Hall and Music School.

Entry requirements: Parental choice and interview followed by placing test. It is essential to register boys well in advance of their sixth birthday.

Range of fees per annum as at 1.9.98:

Day: £8388

Boarding: £10,920

Papplewick enjoys a spacious rural location on the edge of Windsor Great Park. Convenient links with M4, M3, M25, Heathrow and Gatwick. The quality of care provided and the dedication of staff are outstanding and remain Papplewick's special hallmark.

The Papplewick Charitable Trust is justly proud of its academic, cultural and sporting success; yet it is equally aware that these can become inflated in importance and may be blazoned abroad in gilt lettering in a way that is not used for essential human virtues: after all, its chief responsibility is to ensure that all the boys in its care grow up to be kind and honest.

Pipers Corner School

Great Kingshill, High Wycombe,
Buckinghamshire HP15 6LP
Girls Boarding & Day

See Section Two

Pocklington School

West Green, Pocklington, York,
North Yorkshire YO42 2NJ
Co-educational Boarding & Day

See Section Two

Rannoch School

Rannoch, By Pitlochry,
Perthshire PH17 2QQ
Co-educational Boarding & Day

See Section Two

Rishworth School

Rishworth, Halifax, West Yorkshire HX6 4QA
Co-educational Boarding & Day

See Section Two

Rookesbury Park School

(Founded 1929)

Wickham, Hampshire PO17 6HT

Tel: 01329 833108 Fax: 01329 835090
e-mail: aj.cook@ukonline.co.uk
Internet: http://www.web.ukonline.co.uk
/aj.cook/index/html

Head: Mrs S M Cook BA(Hons), PGCE

Date of appointment: 1997

Member of: IAPS, BSA

Girls Day & Boarding

Religious affiliation: Church of England

Age range of pupils: Boys 3 – 7 Girls 3 – 13

Boys 3-7. Boarders from 7.

No. of students enrolled as at 1.9.98: 135

Girls: 135

Average size of class: 12-18

Teacher/Pupil ratio: 1:11

Curriculum: The girls are prepared for the Common Entrance Examination to Independent Schools and for Independent Senior School Scholarships. There is a large, well qualified staff and the average class size is 12-18 pupils. Games played include netball, lacrosse, tennis, rounders, athletics and swimming.

Entry requirements: Acceptance is conditional on an interview with the Headmistress and a satisfactory previous school report if appropriate.

Range of fees per annum as at 1.9.98:

Day: £1740 – £5985

Boarding: £7425 – £8730

Rookesbury Park School occupies the former Manor House in the village of Wickham, in an unrivalled setting of 14 acres overlooking farmland. The School was founded in 1929 and in 1961 it became an Educational Trust, administered by a Board of Governors. It is a friendly and flourishing school with an established nursery department offering small classes and a balanced curriculum. Well equipped with science laboratory, swimming pool, tennis courts, athletics field, computer room and technology room. There are approximately 135 girls and boys in school which includes both day and boarding. The School has a very busy and stimulating extra-curricular programme in which all children are encouraged to participate. Activities range from judo and archery to chess and drama. Cookery is taught in French.

Registered as a Charity for the Education of Children.

St Edmund's College

Old Hall Green, Near Ware, Hertfordshire SG11 1DS
Co-educational Boarding & Day

See Section Two

Sidcot School

Winscombe, North Somerset BS25 1PD
Co-educational Boarding & Day

See Section Two

St Mary's Hall

Eastern Road, Brighton, East Sussex BN2 5JF
Girls Boarding & Day

See Section Two

St Bede's School

The Dicker, Hailsham, East Sussex BN27 3QH
Co-educational Boarding & Day

See Section Two

St Mary's Westbrook

Ravenlea Road, Folkestone, Kent CT20 2JU
Co-educational Boarding & Day

See Section Two

St Catherine's School

Bramley, Guildford, Surrey GU5 0DF
Girls Boarding & Day

See Section Two

St Paul's Cathedral School

(Founded 12th Century or earlier)
2 New Change, London EC4M 9AD
Tel: 0171 248 5156 Fax: 0171 329 6568

Head: Mr Stephen S Sides BEd(Oxon), CertEd

Date of appointment: 1995

Member of: CSA, IAPS

Boys Boarding & Day

Religious affiliation: Anglican

Age range of pupils: Boys 4 – 13 Girls 4 – 7

Boarders from 7

No. of students enrolled as at 1.9.98: 142

Average size of class: 15

Teacher/Pupil ratio: 1:8

Curriculum: A broadly based curriculum leading to Scholarship and Common Entrance Examinations is supported by a strong musical component. Choristers are members of St Paul's Cathedral Choir.

Entry requirements: Choristers: Voice Trial and Entrance Tests, three times a year. Day Boys: Entrance Tests in February. Pre-Prep assessments October/November.

Range of fees per annum as at 1.9.98:

Day: £5100 – £5580

Boarding: £3360

The School at the east end of the cathedral is a modern building at the centre of the City but with many sports facilities nearby.

St Richard's School

(Founded 1921)
Bredenbury Court, Bromyard,
Herefordshire HR7 4TD
Tel: 01885 482491 Fax: 01885 488982

Head: Mr R E H Coghlan MA(Cantab)

Date of appointment: 1982

Member of: IAPS, ISIS

Co-educational Boarding & Day

Religious affiliation: Roman Catholic

Age range of pupils: 4 – 13

Boarders from 7 years

No. of students enrolled as at 1.9.98: 138

Boys: 73 Girls: 65

Average size of class: 13

Teacher/Pupil ratio: 1:9

Curriculum: Pupils are prepared for their Common Entrance exams to their Secondary Schools.

Entry requirements: Interview or scholarship examination.

Range of fees per annum as at 1.9.98:

Day: £1980 – £5475

Boarding: £7500 – £8025

St Richard's is situated in beautiful Herefordshire countryside. Set in 35 acres of parkland, it combines a homely atmosphere with academic excellence.

Stamford High School

St Martin's, Stamford, Lincolnshire PE9 2LJ
Girls Boarding & Day

See Section Two

Stamford School

St Paul's Street, Stamford, Lincolnshire PE9 2BS
Boys Boarding & Day

See Section Two

The International School of Choueifat UK

Ashwicke Hall, Marshfield, Wiltshire SN14 8AG
Co-educational Boarding

See Section Two

The King's School Ely

Ely, Cambridgeshire CB7 4DB
Co-educational Boarding & Day

See Section Two

The Royal Masonic School for Girls

Rickmansworth Park, Rickmansworth, Hertfordshire WD3 4HF
Girls Boarding & Day

See Section Two

The Royal School, Hampstead

65 Rosslyn Hill, Hampstead, London NW3 5UD
Girls Boarding & Day

See Section Two

The Royal Wolverhampton School

Penn Road, Wolverhampton, West Midlands WV3 0EG
Co-educational Boarding & Day

See Section Two

Truro High School for Girls

Falmouth Road, Truro, Cornwall TR1 2HU
Girls Boarding & Day

See Section Two

Windlesham House

(Founded 1837)

Washington, Pulborough, West Sussex RH20 4AY

Tel: 01903 873207 Fax: 01903 873017

Head: Philip J Lough MA(Oxon), PGCE(Dunelm)

Date of appointment: 1996

Member of: IAPS, BSA

Co-educational Boarding

Religious affiliation: Church of England

Age range of pupils: 4 – 13

All-boarding from 9

No. of students enrolled as at 1.9.98: 285

Boys: 160 Girls: 125

Average size of class: 15

Teacher/Pupil ratio: 1:8

Curriculum: Usual Common Entrance and Scholarship subjects with the emphasis on as broad a curriculum as possible. Spanish, Drama, Design Technology, Art, Pottery, Music and PSE (Personal and Social Education) in the timetable for all pupils. Latin and Greek options and German and Mandarin Chinese are also available.

Entry requirements: Interview only.

Range of fees per annum as at 1.9.98:

Boarding: £10,350

Pre-prep: £1350 - £1550

History dating back to 1837. First co-ed IAPS boarding school in Britain (1967). Queen Anne house with modern additions set in 60 acres of Sussex Downs country. Innovative, forward-thinking school where individuals thrive. Strong family atmosphere and House-based tutorial system.

The School has almost 100 expatriate children, including 40 from Foreign Office families, and will organise travel arrangements to airports. Strong weekend programme with imaginative and varied activities. This is a real boarding school, which believes in education of the whole person.

Windlesham House School a registered charity (The Malden Trust Ltd) exists to provide boarding education for girls and boys.

Section Two:
Senior Independent Schools

Abbot's Hill School

(Founded 1912)

Bunkers Lane, Hemel Hempstead, Hertfordshire HP3 8RP

Tel: 01442 240333 Fax: 01442 269981

Headmistress: Mrs K Lewis MA(Cantab), BSc(Open), PGCE, FRSA, MIMgt

Girls Boarding & Day

Religious affiliation: The School follows the principles of the Church of England and has a daily service in the Chapel. Abbot's Hill also welcomes girls of other religious beliefs.

Age range of pupils: 11 – 16

No. of students enrolled as at 1.9.98: 165

Girls: 165

Range of fees per annum as at 1.9.98:

Day: £7050

Weekly Boarding: £11,745

Boarding: £11,820

Abbot's Hill is an Independent Full/Weekly Boarding and Day School for girls aged 11-16 years. There are 165 pupils. The School is situated in parkland which extends to over 70 acres, under three miles from M1/M25, all major road/rail networks and international airports. The main accommodation is located in a spacious and comfortable late Georgian House. The teaching blocks are in the grounds with a new Science and IT and Technology building recently completed.

There is a modern and well equipped gymnasium, lacrosse pitches, a heated swimming pool, four grass and five hard tennis courts with the use of two indoor courts. The main sports are lacrosse and netball in winter and tennis, athletics and swimming during the summer. Tennis coaching is available throughout the year and there is a strong competitive Ski Team. Other sports include badminton, squash and riding. A wide range of extra curricular activities is offered, which is enhanced by the School's easy proximity to London.

With a staff ratio of 1:8, girls are taught in small subject classes to GCSE. Outstanding results are achieved commensurate with pupils' ability. At Abbot's Hill, girls are encouraged to consider their future prospects and are very well prepared to choose from a wide range of A level and GNVQ courses offered to them when they leave. There is a comprehensive careers programme available in the Fifth Year to further enhance their decisions. Girls are individually coached for music, dance, speech and drama examinations. Details of Scholarships and Bursaries are available on request.

The Abbot's Hill Charitable Trust No. 3110533 is dedicated to providing high quality education for children.

St Nicholas House

Headmistress: Mrs B Vaughan CertEd(Reading)

School foundation: 1923

Independent Preparatory School, Day & Boarding

Religious affiliation: The School follows the principles of the Church of England and has regular religious assemblies. St Nicholas House welcomes children of other religious denominations

Age range of pupils: Boys 3 – 7 Girls 3 – 11

Boarders from 8 years

No. of students enrolled as at 1.9.98: 280

Boys: 130 Girls: 150

Range of fees per annum as at 1.9.98:

Day: £3810 – £4710

Situated in the grounds of Abbot's Hill is the Junior School, St Nicholas House. The School is run by a fully qualified staff under the direction of the Headmistress, Mrs B Vaughan. At St Nicholas House teaching groups are small, and classroom assistants help with the younger children. Lessons based on the National Curriculum are carefully planned. The curriculum is further enriched with specialist subject teaching in Latin, French, Music, Dance and Drama.

Older girls have the benefit of a timetable in which they spend half of their time with their own form teacher, who has overall responsibility for academic success, pastoral care and subject continuity. The remainder of their time is allocated to specialist subject teaching.

The facilities of the School are shared with Abbot's Hill which enables pupils to have access to a first class Science, IT and Technology block, gymnasium, sports field, tennis courts and swimming pool.

Little Saints Nursery is an integral part of St Nicholas House with its own safe play area, professionally qualified staff and happy environment.

The Abbot's Hill Charitable Trust No. 3110533 is dedicated to providing high quality education for children.

Abingdon School

(Founded 1256)

Park Road, Abingdon, Oxfordshire OX14 1DE

Tel: 01235 531755 Fax: 01235 536449

Head: M St John Parker MA

Date of appointment: 1975

Member of: HMC

Boys Boarding & Day

Religious affiliation: Church of England

Age range of pupils: 11 – 18

No. of students enrolled as at 1.9.98: 795

Boys: 795 VIth Form: 270

Average size of class: 21

Teacher/Pupil ratio: 1:11

Curriculum: Broad course of studies to 16, average ten good GCSE passes per boy. Over 20 A level choices, plus AS and General Studies. Almost all leavers enter university.

Entry requirements: School's examination at 11, Common Entrance at 13, GCSE results for sixth form.

Other age entries considered. Means-tested academic, music, art scholarships.

Range of fees per annum as at 1.9.98:

Day: £6246

Boarding: £11,511

In market town near Oxford. Noted for academic, musical and artistic excellence, wide sporting and leisure opportunities, friendly unpretentious and positive atmosphere. Weekly boarding very popular. Excellent sixth form study bedrooms. Merged with Josca's Prep School September 1998.

Abingdon School is a registered charity which exists to provide educational opportunities open to talented boys without regard to their families' economic standing. Its curriculum is designed to promote intellectual rigorousness, personal versatility and social responsibility.

Ashford School

(Founded 1898)

East Hill, Ashford, Kent TN24 8PB

Tel: 01233 625171/2 Fax: 01233 647185

e-mail: registrar@ashford.kent.sch.uk

Headmistress: Mrs J Burnett BEd(Durham), MA(Bristol)

Date of appointment: 1997

Member of: GSA

Girls Day & Boarding

Religious affiliation: Inter-denominational

Age range of pupils: 3 – 18

Boarders from 8

No. of students enrolled as at 1.9.98: 525

Girls: 525 VIth Form: 111

Average size of class: 17

Teacher/Pupil ratio: 1:9

Curriculum: All the usual academic subjects including Latin, A level Business Studies and History of Art, Art, Music, Food Studies, Technology, Drama; Careers Advice, Health Education and Study Skills; Physical Education activities include gymnastics, dance, hockey, netball, tennis, badminton, rounders and swimming. Wide GCSE and A level choice.

Entry requirements: 11+, our own tests in Maths, English, Science. Other stages, Maths, English, French, interview (pref). Sixth Form, GCSE results, previous School's report, tests in three subjects and interview.

The amount needed for educational extras is very variable. All basics are included in fees. This applies to stationery and use of text books, but not cost of Field Trips, visits *etc*. Fifth and Sixth Forms buy specialist books; laboratory fees for Sixth Form Scientists (£15 per term). Academic and Music Scholarships available.

Range of fees per annum as at 1.9.98:

Day: £1167 – £8541

Boarding: £10,674 – £12,897

Examinations offered including boards: GCSE: LEAG, MEG, NEAB, SEG. City & Guilds. GCE Advanced Level: London; AEB and Oxbridge.

Subject specialities and academic track record: all round, very sound Maths and Science. The GCSE level pass rate was 98.1% in 1998, A level was 94%. We have about six Oxbridge entrants per year.

Most students go on to Higher Education before professions, which include: medicine, engineering, journalism, law, teaching, advertising, banking, management, the Media. Degree subjects range from A(rchaeology) to Z(oology).

Academic & leisure facilities: Language Laboratory, nine Laboratories, Music wing, Art and Craft block, Technology Centre, Sixth Form centre, good

Information Technology facilities, heated indoor Swimming pool, Hockey pitches, 11 Tennis/Netball courts, purpose-built Refectory, Hall with Stage and Organ. Large Library, plus House libraries. Sanatorium (SRN).

Three Boarding Houses and a strong Duke of Edinburgh Award Scheme.

Ashford School is set in 23 acres bordering the River Stour, an enclave in Ashford Town. Only an hour from London by train, 20 minutes from Dover, 2 1/4 hours from Paris and from Brussels. Full escort service available.

The International Station offers direct rail link, through the Channel Tunnel, to the Continent. Eurostar International Station is five minutes away, making weekly boarding convenient for girls, as they can be home with their families in: Lille (1 hour), Bruxelles (1 hour 40 minutes) and Paris (2 hours).

The Ashford School Charitable Trust exists to provide high quality education for girls.

For further information about independent and non-maintained special schools, why not consult
Which School ? for Special Needs,
also published by John Catt Educational Ltd

Bedgebury School

(Founded 1860)

Bedgebury Park, Goudhurst, Cranbrook, Kent TN17 2SH

Tel: 01580 211221/211954 Fax: 01580 212252
e-mail: info@bedgebury.ndirect.co.uk
Internet: www.bedgebury.ndirect.co.uk

Headmistress: Mrs L J Griffin BA, BPhil
Date of appointment: April 1995
Member of: GBGSA and GSA

Girls Boarding & Day

Religious affiliation: Church of England

Age range of pupils: Boys 3 – 7 Girls 3 – 18

Boarders from 7+

No. of students enrolled as at 1.9.98: 360

Boys: 9 Girls: 360 VIth Form: 81

Average size of class: 12

Teacher/Pupil ratio: 1:8.6

Curriculum: A broad programme to GCSE. Exceptionally wide range of A levels including Theatre Studies, Communications, Business Studies and Computing; Interior Design and Product Design. Sixth Form vocational courses include Fashion, Ceramics, Jewellery, RSA Secretarial, GNVQ Leisure and Tourism, BHSAI and BTEC Business and Finance (Equestrian).

Entry requirements: Common Entrance or Bedgebury's own examinations as appropriate. Open entry Sixth Form but proven willingness to work essential. Details from The Registrar 01580 211954.

Range of fees per annum as at 1.9.98:

Day: £1830 – £7806

Boarding: £8286 – £12,570

Academic & leisure facilities: Own BHS approved Equestrian Centre, heated swimming pool, lake with several watersports, 15 stage assault course, abseil tower, climbing wall. Specialist Arts Centre and Sixth Form boarding house with 60 single study bedrooms. Convenient M25, airports, Channel ports and tunnel, London. Magnificent country house, 250 acre estate.

Bedgebury School is a registered charity providing a widely based Christian education.

Bredon School

(Founded 1962)

Pull Court, Bushley, Tewkesbury, Gloucestershire GL20 6AH

Tel: 01684 293156 Fax: 01684 298008

Bredon has established a successful reputation based on academic endeavour, individual attention and an innovative approach to the curriculum. Determined to achieve the right balance between academic studies and the development of personal qualities, Bredon has a rich and varied curriculum including traditional academic and vocational courses, as well as a modern learning support centre.

Head: Mr Colin E Wheeler BEd, MIMgt

Date of appointment: 1994

Member of: ISA

Co-educational Boarding & Day

Religious affiliation: Church of England

Age range of pupils: 3 – 18

Boarders from 7

No. of students enrolled as at 1.9.98: 253

Average size of class: 10 to 12

Teacher/Pupil ratio: 1:7

Curriculum: Broad-based curriculum containing a practical element. National Curriculum has been introduced for all Key Stages, with specialist facilities and full range of subjects to GCSE.

Specialist Post-16 courses include: BTEC/GNVQ Intermediate and/or Advanced programmes in Business, Design, Health and Social Care, Leisure and Tourism, Engineering, Land Based Industries (Agriculture) as well as A levels. Specialist tuition is offered in Literacy and Numeracy through the Learning Support Department.

Entry requirements: Acceptance is subject to interview with the Headmaster and preliminary academic assessment. Also satisfactory report from the pupil's previous Headmaster.

Range of fees per annum as at 1.9.98:

Day: £2940 – £8550

Weekly Boarding: £8820 – £13,320

Boarding: £9000 – £13,500

Bredon School is rurally situated near the River Severn, bordering Worcestershire and Gloucestershire. It stands within 82 acres and has its own school farm.

Information about day schools can be found in *Which School?* also published by John Catt Educational Ltd

d'Overbroeck's College

(Founded 1977)

Beechlawn House, Park Town, Oxford, Oxfordshire OX2 6SN

Tel: 01865 310000 Fax: 01865 552296
e-mail: mail@doverbroecks.oxon.sch.uk
Internet: http://www.doverbroecks.oxon.sch.uk

Principals: Mr S Cohen BSc & Dr R Knowles MA, DPhil(Oxon)

Co-educational Day & Boarding

Religious affiliation: Non-denominational

Age range of pupils: 13 – 19

No. of students enrolled as at 1.9.98: 270

Boys: 130 Girls: 140

Average size of class: 6

Teacher/Pupil ratio: 1:4

Range of fees per annum as at 1.9.98:

Day: £6750 – £10,215

Boarding: £10,350 – £15,315 (Sixth Form)

d'Overbroeck's offers a truly distinctive and successful environment in which to study. There is no uniform, no assemblies and no compulsory sport in the Sixth Form. What there is is a strong commitment to academic success, teachers who are always willing to listen and a refreshingly positive approach. The teaching is highly interactive, profoundly stimulating and in small groups where everyone can receive the personal attention they need (in the Sixth Form, for example, there is a maximum of eight students in a group). The College also offers an unusual degree of flexibility both in terms of the choice and combinations of subjects which are available. You can study almost everything from the traditional Classical Civilisation to the more modern Communication Studies and Theatre Studies – and there is no restriction on choice. There is also a full and lively extra curricular programme – participation is voluntary but there are so many activities organised that everyone should find something they like!

Throughout the College there is a tremendous sense of dynamism, energy and fun which complements and contributes to students' academic achievements. The exam results are excellent with a strong entry to university including Oxford and Cambridge, Law, Medical and Veterinary schools as well as a superb track record of students gaining places at their first choice Art school. The College is fully accredited by the ISC and is a member of the ISA.

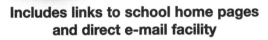

Dauntsey's School

(Founded 1542)

High Street, West Lavington, Devizes, Wiltshire SN10 4HE

Tel: 01380 818441 Fax: 01380 813620

Head: Mr Stewart B Roberts MA

Date of appointment: 1997

Member of: HMC

Co-educational Day & Boarding

Religious affiliation: Inter Denominational

Age range of pupils: 11 – 18

No. of students enrolled as at 1.9.98: 665

Boys: 364 Girls: 301 VIth Form: 236

Average size of class: 20; 12 in Sixth Form

Teacher/Pupil ratio: 1:9

Curriculum: Full range of Sciences, Mathematics, Humanities, Languages, practical and aesthetic subjects, Music, Drama, Sailing, virtually all sports.

Entry requirements: Own exam for Year 7 (aged 11+); Common Entrance (or own exam) for Year 9 (aged 13+); Interview and GCSE results for Sixth Form. Scholarships available at all stages.

Range of fees per annum as at 1.9.98:

Day: £7512

Boarding: £12,318

Founded in 1542. Fully co-educational school in 100 acres, ten minutes from Devizes. Good rail/road links to London, Heathrow, Salisbury, Bath.

The Dauntsey School Foundation, which is a registered charity, exists to educate girls and boys.

Dean Close School

(Founded 1886)

Cheltenham, Gloucestershire GL51 6HE

Tel: 01242 522640 Fax: 01242 258003

e-mail: dcscomp@rmplc.co.uk

Head: Rev Timothy M Hastie-Smith MA

Member of: HMC

Co-educational Boarding & Day

Religious affiliation: Church of England

Age range of pupils: 12 – 18

Boarders from 12 years

No. of students enrolled as at 1.9.98: 432

Boys: 249 Girls: 183 VIth Form: 180

Range of fees per annum as at 1.9.98:

Day: £9810

Boarding: £14,055

Strong emphasis is placed on personal faith, mutual respect, service, integrity, friendship and the need to discover and develop individual talents. We endeavour to find and enhance these talents, whether they are creative, intellectual or athletic, employing the skills of a versatile and professional staff and our extensive facilities. We expect to see self-discipline, leadership and the use of personal initiative in every scholar. A co-educational system throughout the School provides a realistic and stable environment in which to mature.

Everyone – day and boarding – has a workroom or study, and the boarders are placed in small-sized houses with substantial study bedroom accommodation for the seniors. Impressive facilities include a superb 25m indoor swimming pool, sports hall, two artificial grass pitches, a fine theatre/concert hall, a new art and design centre as well as a brand new, purpose built music school. A wide range of A levels is available. Ninety-eight per cent of scholars go on to higher education with the best of these achieving Oxbridge places. Generous scholarships and bursaries are available.

Dean Close School Charitable Trust was founded on a Church of England and Evangelical basis to provide education for children of professional classes.

Downe House School

(Founded 1907)

Cold Ash, Thatcham, Berkshire RG18 9JJ

Tel: 01635 200286 Fax: 01635 202026

Head: Mrs E McKendrick BA(Liverpool)

Date of appointment: September 1997

Member of: GSA

Girls Boarding & Day

Religious affiliation: Church of England

Age range of pupils: 11 – 18

Boarders from 11

No. of students enrolled as at 1.9.98: 554

Girls: 554 VIth Form: 166

Average size of class: 18

Teacher/Pupil ratio: 1:6

Curriculum: A wide selection of subjects is available for study at GCSE and A level. Girls are also prepared for University entrance.

Entry requirements: Common Entrance and assessment. Five passes at Grade C or above at GCSE level for an A level course.

Range of fees per annum as at 1.9.98:

Day: £10,275

Boarding: £14,175

Five miles from Newbury with easy access to motorway and London. The School has an excellent academic record with nearly all going on to University.

Duke of York's Royal Military School

(Founded 1803)

Guston, Dover, Kent CT15 5EQ

Tel: 01304 245024 Fax: 01304 245019

Head: Col G H Wilson BA, DipEd, MEd, FRSA

Date of appointment: September 1992

Member of: GBA, BSA, SHMIS, ISIS

Co-educational Boarding

Religious affiliation: Church of England

Age range of pupils: 11 – 18

No. of students enrolled as at 1.9.98: 500

VIth Form: 110

Average size of class: 16

Teacher/Pupil ratio: 1:10

Curriculum: National Curriculum to GCSE/KS4. A level and Advanced GNVQ Course in Business in Sixth Form. French/German for all Sixth Form. Strong academic emphasis.

Entry requirements: One parent must have four years Service in the RN, RM, Army or RAF. Own entrance tests in English and Mathematics plus report from present school.

Range of fees per annum as at 1.9.98:

Boarding: £855

Independent, total boarding. Estate: 150 acres of parkland estate on Dover outskirts.

Dulwich College

(Founded 1619)

London, London SE21 7LD

Tel: 0181 693 3601 Fax: 0181 693 6319

Head: G G Able MA, MA

Date of appointment: 1st January 1997

Member of: HMC

Boys Day & Boarding

Religious affiliation: Church of England

Age range of pupils: 7 – 18

Boarders from 10

No. of students enrolled as at 1.9.98: 1396

Boys: 1396 VIth Form: 391

Average size of class: 17

Teacher/Pupil ratio: 1:12

Curriculum: Full range of subjects to GCSE. Sixth Form students follow a General Studies programme and study a wide range of A and AS level subjects.

Entry requirements: Informal assessment and testing (age 7), Dulwich College Entrance and Scholarship Examination (ages 8-11, 13) or Common Entrance Examination (age 13). Entry at age 16 is dependent on GCSE results.

Range of fees per annum as at 1.9.98:

Day: £6705 – £7080

Boarding: £13,410 – £13,965

Dulwich has a fine record of academic, musical and sporting achievements, offering full and weekly boarding with easy access to rail, road and air links.

Dulwich College Charitable Trust exists to provide education for children.

Eltham College

(Founded 1842)

Grove Park Road, Mottingham,
London SE9 4QF

Tel: 0181 857 1455 Fax: 0181 857 1913

The School enjoys an outstanding reputation for academic success and effective pastoral care. It has very high standards of expectation and achievement in cultural and extra-curricular activities. Centred on an 18th Century mansion set in 25 acres of playing fields, its facilities are superb.

Headmaster: Mr D M Green MA, FRSA

Date of appointment: 1990

Member of: HMC

Boys Day & Boarding

Religious affiliation: Christian (Non-denominational)

Age range of pupils: Boys 7 – 18 Girls 16 – 18

Boarders from 11

No. of students enrolled as at 1.9.98: 774

Boys: 734 Girls: 40 VIth Form: 189

Average size of class: 25 (12 in Sixth Form)

Teacher/Pupil ratio: 1:12

Curriculum: Pupils follow a wide ranging curriculum leading to 10 GCSs and three or four A levels. It is well balanced and diverse.

Entry requirements: Tests in English, Maths, Verbal and Numerical Reasoning and interview.

Range of fees per annum as at 1.9.98:

Day: £5300 – £6400

Boarding: £12,625 – £13,225

The School, with its small boarding house, is set in expansive grounds in Mottingham, south-east London. It is within easy reach of bus routes and London South-East railway.

Eltham College is a leading charitable school in the field of Junior and Secondary education.

Don't forget to read the articles which appear at the front of this book.
They may save you a lot of time and trouble

Farlington School

(Founded 1896)

Strood Park, Horsham, West Sussex RH12 3PN

Tel: 01403 254967 Fax: 01403 272258

Headmistress: Mrs P M Mawer BA

Date of appointment: 1992

Member of: GSA, BSA, IAPS

Girls Day & Boarding

Religious affiliation: Church of England

Age range of pupils: 4 – 18

Boarders from 9-18

No. of students enrolled as at 1.9.98: 370

VIth Form: 60

Average size of class: 12

Curriculum: We aim to provide a broad and balanced curriculum for all age groups. Our academic standards are high, and we encourage girls to raise their own expectations of achievement.

Subject specialities and academic track record: 1998 results: GCSE-98.6% A*-C pass rate; 55.5% A*-A; A level pass rate 95.5%; 67.1% A & B grades.

Entry requirements: Entry is by our own examination and interview. A wide range of bursaries and scholarships are available including Sixth Form and Music.

Range of fees per annum as at 1.9.98:

Day: £3045 – £6795

Boarding: £8745 – £11,040

Examinations offered including boards: Girls work to GCSE examinations using SEG, EDEXCEL(London) and MEG syllabuses, and A, AS and S levels with AEB, OCEAC and EDEXCEL(London), in a wide variety of subjects.

Destination/career prospects of leavers: 95% go on to university. Wide-ranging subjects - engineering, psychology, business studies, history of art, natural sciences, vet science, medicine, sports science, politics, drama, accountancy.

Academic & leisure facilities: Girls are mainly taught in a purpose built classroom block. There is also a Music and Drama specialist area and a new science building. Sports facilities include an all weather astroturf pitch which provides hockey pitches, tennis courts and a 200m athletics track, and a heated swimming pool. Our Riding Squad has been the National Schools' Champions for six consecutive years. We place great emphasis on extra curricular activities and encourage each girl to develop her interests in a wide variety of ways.

Set in 32 acres of parkland, 30 minutes from Gatwick Airport.

Farlington School Trust, a charitable trust for the purpose of educating girls.

Farringtons & Stratford House

(Founded 1911)

Perry Street, Chislehurst, Kent BR7 6LR

Tel: 0181 467 0256 Fax: 0181 467 5442
Internet: http://www.darch.co.uk

Headmistress: Mrs Catherine James MA

Date of appointment: January 1999

Member of: GSA, GBSA, BSA

Girls Day & Boarding

Religious affiliation: Methodist

Age range of pupils: 11 – 18

No. of students enrolled as at 1.9.98: 285

Girls: 285 VIth Form: 60

Average size of class: 20; Sixth Form teaching groups (average): 6

Teacher/Pupil ratio: 1:12

Curriculum: In the Senior School all girls follow, for the first three years, a common curriculum which includes basic subjects plus German, Spanish, Food and Nutrition, Texiles, Ceramics, Design and Technology, Computing and Music. At 14+ girls take a core curriculum of five subjects plus 3-5 options. A levels are offered in 19 subjects with specialist areas being Modern Languages, Music, Sciences and English. 81% of all GCSE passes in 1998 were A*-C grades. Excellent A level results from a wide-ability intake.

Entry requirements: Senior: Entrance Examination and interview. Account is taken of boarding need. No entrance examination for girls transferring from our Junior School.

Range of fees per annum as at 1.9.98:

Day: £6030

Weekly Boarding: £11,490

Boarding: £11,880

Examinations offered including boards: OCR, AQA, Edexcel.

Academic facilities include newly-equipped Computer Rooms and Science block, satellite TV for modern language learning and a new Technology Centre. The Duke of Edinburgh Award Scheme is very active as is Young Enterprise for LVI girls. Badminton, Trampolining, Ballet, Fencing, Drama, Jazz Dance, Aerobics and Modern Dance are all popular, and many other activities are available.

Farringtons & Stratford House is a Girls' Weekly and Full Boarding and Day School situated in 25 acres of its own beautiful grounds, 25 minutes from central London within easy reach of the M25 motorway and London's airports. It has extensive playing fields, hard and grass tennis courts, a swimming pool and a large Sports Hall with weights room and dance studio.

Farringtons & Stratford House School is a Charitable Trust which exists solely to provide a high quality, caring education for girls.

**Information about day schools can be found in *Which School ?*
also published by John Catt Educational Ltd**

Framlingham College

(Founded 1864)

Framlingham, Woodbridge, Suffolk IP13 9EY

Tel: 01728 723789 Fax: 01728 724546

Junior School - Brandeston Hall

Brandeston, Woodbridge, Suffolk IP13 7QA
Tel: 01728 685331 Fax: 01728 685437

Head: Mrs G M Randall BA

Date of appointment: 1994

Master of Junior School: Mr N Johnson BA

Member of: HMC, IAPS

Co-educational Boarding & Day

Religious affiliation: Church of England but all denominations welcome.

Age range of pupils: 4 – 18

Boarders from 7

No. of students enrolled as at 1.9.98: 700

Boys: 432 Girls: 268

Curriculum: The curriculum at Framlingham and its Junior School, Brandeston Hall is carefully co-ordinated to give a broadly-based, well rounded, seamless education from 4 to 18 years of age. Pupils are prepared for Common Entrance, GCSE, A level and Oxbridge. The College has high expectations of its pupils and is committed to identifying, unlocking and developing the unique potential of each one. We aim to provide our students with the best academic passport possible, a zest for life, and a sense of responsibilty for each other.

The school has a dynamic development programme, and both academic and sports facilities are first-class. An exciting new humanities complex and greatly expanded library have recently been completed. A brand new girls' boarding house opened its doors in September, and plans are in hand to enhance all the remaining houses.

Entry requirements: Entry to the Junior School is by test and interview. Common Entrance, scholarship examination and/or interview form the normal means of entry to the College at 13+, GCSE results and interview at 16+. Overseas students apply initially on the basis of a current Principal's report. Enquiries regarding scholarships are invited.

Range of fees per annum as at 1.9.98:

Day: £7299

Boarding: £11,373

Framlingham College is a registered charity which exists to provide quality education to children.

Frensham Heights School

(Founded 1925)

Rowledge, Farnham, Surrey GU10 4EA

Tel: 01252 792134 Fax: 01252 794335
e-mail: Headmaster@frensham-heights.org.uk
Internet: http://www.demon.co.uk/frensham-heights

Head: Peter M de Voil MA, FRSA

Date of appointment: 1993

Member of: HMC

Co-educational Boarding & Day

Religious affiliation: Non-denominational

Age range of pupils: 4 – 18

Boarders from 11

No. of students enrolled as at 1.9.98: 342

Boys: 160 Girls: 176 VIth Form: 90

Average size of class: 16

Teacher/Pupil ratio: 1:8

Curriculum: The school follows the essentials of the National Curriculum where appropriate. The following subjects are offered at GCSE: English, Mathematics, Sciences, History, Geography, PE, Outdoor Education, Photography, Economics, French, German and Spanish. In addition, all pupils study creative and performing arts, choosing two of the following to GCSE: Art, Ceramics, Design and Technology, Music, Dance and Drama. English as a second language is available for international pupils and support for the mildly dyslexic.

Academic results are excellent: average A level pass rates: 95%; GCSE A*-C: 86%.

The school has a national reputation for the quality of its choral and orchestral music. Scholarships are available for talented musicians.

Entry requirements: 11-14 year olds: examination, assessment, reports, interview. Sixth Form: five GCSE grades A-C, reports and interview.

Range of fees per annum as at 1.9.98:

Day: £8100 – £9150

Boarding: £12,600 – £13,800

Founded in 1925 as part of a liberal movement to promote co-education and less formal relationships between teachers and pupils, Frensham Heights has always been a genuinely co-educational school, and believes in the equality of the sexes. It sees the pursuit of enlightenment and liberal values as a fundamental aim. It opposes all forms of prejudice, racial, religious or social, and every effort is made to deepen understanding of human nature and behaviour and develop self-esteem. The School has a dress code but no school uniform.

The site comprises 100 acres of beautiful woodland and parkland. Boarding accommodation is comfortable and the school is spacious, well-equipped and deliberately small enough for everyone to be known as a person. It has a new art and design centre, a sports hall, an outdoor education centre and a sixth form centre. The IT Centre is equipped with the latest PCs.

The School is 50 minutes from London by rail and 40 minutes from Heathrow and Gatwick airports.

Frensham Heights Educational Trust Ltd is a registered charity and exists to provide high quality education for boys and girls.

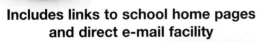

Giggleswick School

(Founded 1512)

Giggleswick, Settle, North Yorkshire BD24 0DE

Tel: 01729 823545 Fax: 01729 824187
e-mail: office@giggleswick-n-yorks.sch.uk
Internet: www.giggleswick.n-yorks.sch.uk

Head: Mr A P Millard BSc(Econ), FRSA

Date of appointment: September 1993

Member of: HMC

Co-educational Boarding & Day

Religious affiliation: Church of England

Age range of pupils: 7 – 18

Boarders from 7 years

No. of students enrolled as at 1.9.98: 440

Boys: 289 Girls: 151 VIth Form: 157

Average size of class: 17 (3rd-5th Form), 8 (L6/U6)

Teacher/Pupil ratio: 1:7.5

Curriculum: English, Maths, Classics, Business Studies, History, Geography, Biology, Physics, Chemistry, Economics, Politics, Art, Design & Technology, Home Economics, Music, Religious Education, Physical & Health Education, Modern Languages - (French, German, Spanish), and Theatre Studies.

Entry requirements: 3rd Form via CE, interview, satisfactory report from current headmaster. L6: minimum of five GCSEs Grade C or better. Giggleswick 2000: interview and satisfactory report from present headmaster.

Range of fees per annum as at 1.9.98:

Day: £6870 – £8970

Boarding: £10,269 – £13,515

Leading co-educational boarding school in the North of England, Giggleswick offers a happy, secure and challenging environment for young people in the beautiful setting of the Yorkshire Dales. Yet it is close to M1/M6 and the international airports of Leeds and Manchester.

"Giggleswick 2000" is a one year post GCSE course which will appeal to pupils who wish to experience the very best of British Boarding.

Giggleswick School Charitable Trust exists to provide high quality education for boys and girls.

Glenalmond College, Perth

(Founded 1841)

Glenalmond, Perth, Perthshire & Kinross PH1 3RY

Tel: 01738 880442 Fax: 01738 880410
e-mail: registrat@glencollege.demon.co.uk Internet: http://metro.turnpike.net/j/jules/glenalmond

Head: I G Templeton MA, BA

Date of appointment: September 1992

Member of: GBA, HMC, BSA

Co-educational Boarding & Day

Religious affiliation: Episcopal Church of Scotland

Age range of pupils: 12 – 18

Main entry at 13

No. of students enrolled as at 1.9.98: 367

Boys: 257 Girls: 110 VIth Form: 153

Entry requirements: Common Entrance Examination at 13+ and own Entrance Examination at 12+, and for the L6 Scholarships are offered for academic excellence, Music or Art.

Range of fees per annum as at 1.9.98:

Day: £6900 – £9195

Boarding: £10,335 – £13,785

Glenalmond College, set in spectacular Highland scenery, is 15 minutes from Perth and about an hour from airports.

Predominantly boarding, it also has day pupils brought by bus. The College is now fully co-educational.

There is a strong tradition of academic success at A level and Scottish Higher. Facilities for Technology are superb, Art and Drama flourish, and Music enjoys a national reputation.

With a golf course, artificial ski-slope and salmon river in the grounds, the school offers an unrivalled range of outdoor activities.

There are frequent cultural and sporting excursions as well as overseas trips and tours.

New in September 1998 a second girls' house. New artificial grass surface.

Glenalmond College is a charitable trust which exists to provide quality education for boys and girls in a rural setting.

Harrow School

(Founded 1572)
1 High Street, Harrow, Middlesex HA1 3HW
Tel: 0181 869 1200 Fax: 0181 864 5352

Head: Mr Nicholas R Bomford MA, FRSA
Date of appointment: 1991
Member of: HMC
Boys Boarding
Religious affiliation: Church of England
Age range of pupils: 13 – 18
Boarders from 13
No. of students enrolled as at 1.9.98: 790
Boys: 790 VIth Form: 320
Teacher/Pupil ratio: 1:9.5
Curriculum: GCSE; A level.
Entry requirements: Scholarship or Common Entrance.
Range of fees per annum as at 1.9.98:
Boarding: £15,150
Fully boarding boys' school in village setting on Harrow Hill.

Heathfield School

(Founded 1899)

London Road, Ascot, Berkshire SL5 8BQ

Tel: 01344 882955 Fax: 01344 890689

At Heathfield we educate our girls academically, socially and pastorally in an environment that can only exist in a full-boarding school. Emphasis on the individual, small classes, streaming, study skills and a highly qualified staff combine to achieve the excellent results, including Oxbridge entry, for which Heathfield is noted.

Headmistress: Mrs J M Benammar BA, MËsL

Date of appointment: September 1992

Member of: GSA, BSA

Girls Boarding

Religious affiliation: Church of England

Age range of pupils: 11 – 18

Boarders from 11 years

No. of students enrolled as at 1.9.98: 215

Girls: 215 VIth Form: 54

Average size of class: Juniors 14, Seniors 8

Teacher/Pupil ratio: 1:7

Curriculum: With 20 subjects offered at GCSE and 24 at A level, including usual subjects plus Law, Economics, Photography, the range of options is unique for a small school.

Entry requirements: Girls attend an internal Assessment in the October preceding entry, followed by the appropriate Common Entrance Examination. Scholarships are available for academic excellence, Music and Art.

Range of fees per annum as at 1.9.98:

Boarding: £14,625

The original Georgian house, set in 38 acres, has been much extended and facilities, both academic and boarding, are excellent. London: 40 minutes; Heathrow: 25 minutes.

Heathfield School is a registered charity and exists to provide a high quality education for girls.

King Edward's School Witley

(Founded 1553)

Petworth Road, Wormley, Godalming, Surrey GU8 5SG

Tel: 01428 682572 Fax: 01428 682850

New sports hall, lecture theatre, maths and computing block. 100 acres of games fields, indoor swimming pool, new Sixth Form centre.

Head: R J Fox MA, CMath, FIMA

Date of appointment: 1988

Member of: HMC

Co-educational Boarding & Day

Religious affiliation: Church of England

Age range of pupils: 11 – 18

Boarders from 11 years

No. of students enrolled as at 1.9.98: 472

Boys: 282 Girls: 190 VIth Form: 127

Average size of class: 20

Teacher/Pupil ratio: 1:8

Curriculum: English Literature/Language, Biology, CDT, Chemistry, Physics, French, German, Latin, Geography, History, Home Technology, Economics, Maths, Religious Studies, IT, Art, Music, Theatre Studies, Classical Civilisation.

Entry requirements: Own entrance tests.

Range of fees per annum as at 1.9.98:

Day: £7320

Boarding: £10,695

Founded by King Edward VI in rural countryside on Surrey, Sussex, Hampshire borders. Generous bursaries and Assisted Places available to children with a genuine need for boarding.

King Edward's School Witley is a registered charity which exists to provide high quality education for both girls and boys.

Kirkham Grammar School

(Founded 1549)

Ribby Road, Kirkham, Preston, Lancashire PR4 2BH

Tel: 01772 671079 Fax: 01772 672747

Head: B Stacey MA, DipEd(Oxon), FRSA

Date of appointment: 1991

Member of: SHMIS, GBA, BSA, AGIS, ISC

Co-educational Day & Boarding

Religious affiliation: Non-denominational

Age range of pupils: 4 – 18

Boarders from 11 years

No. of students enrolled as at 1.9.98: 867

Boys: 439 Girls: 428 VIth Form: 179

Average size of class: 20

Teacher/Pupil ratio: 1:12

Curriculum: The academic aim of the School is to enable every individual pupil to achieve his/her potential. A traditional GCSE and A level curriculum is followed, offering a broad range of subjects, delivered by a well qualified staff. Subject specialities: Very strong Mathematics, Science, English, Art and Humanities Departments. International Centre of Excellence for Technology.

Excellent GCSE and A level results. Special provision for Oxbridge candidates. GCSE and A level Drama. A level Psychology and Sports Science.

Kirkham Grammar School was founded in 1549 and has traditionally adopted a holistic approach to education, being concerned with the development of the whole person. Though good academic results are the School's top priority, a great deal of effort goes into the provision of a broad and balanced education which seeks to enhance personal development. Academic results have improved consistently in recent years to reach a very high standard. In 1998 98% of all GCSE candidates achieved five or more passes at Grades A-C and in 1996 the A level pass rate reached 93% with 65% Grades A, B or C. No less than 16 A level subject areas achieved 100% pass rates, including English and Mathematics.

The School is renowned for its sporting prowess and its rugby and hockey teams are among the most prominent in the country. The school 1st XV reached the final of the *Daily Mail* England Schools' Rugby Championships at Twickenham in 1997 and the girls' hockey teams have participated in several national finals in recent years. Athletics, cricket, tennis and swimming are all strong, and there are many county, regional and some international sportsmen and women in the School. Kirkham Grammar School also enjoys an enviable reputation for music, art and drama and there is a strong and popular Combined Cadet Force with Army and Air Force sections. A flourishing House system brings most pupils into contact with many activities and competitions, as do the School's clubs, societies and trips abroad.

Destination/career prospects of leavers: Most (90%+) leavers enter Universities. Some go on to Art, Drama and Music Schools and others into careers in HM Armed Forces and the Professions.

Range of fees per annum as at 1.9.98:

Day: £3255 – £4335

Boarding: £8463

Ne educational extras are required. Scholarships and Bursaries are available. Fee reductions for siblings and Armed Forces personnel.

Academic & leisure facilities: Both the Senior and Junior Schools have been designated as International Centres of Excellence for Technology, and Kirkham Grammar School is the flagship of the British Aerospace Schools' Network. Outstanding, leading edge technology facilities include; Computer Assisted Design and Manufacture, Robotics, Pneumatics, Electronics, Multi Media Manufacturing Workshop, three large IT Suites, video conferencing equipment and interactive whiteboards. New Sixth Form Centre. Excellent sporting facilities include sports hall, gymnasium, extensive playing fields, on site floodlit astro-turf pitch for hockey and tennis.

A warm, friendly school, pleasantly situated in semi-rural surroundings on the Fylde - five miles east of Lytham St Anne's. Excellent road and rail links to all parts of the country.

The Kirkham Educational Foundation exists to provide a high quality academic education with breadth and balance within a strong Christian framework and tradition. The School's most attractive feature in the eyes of many parents is its uniquely friendly and cheerful family ethos, within which pupils are able to feel secure and enjoy their education. There is a great deal of pride in the School's achievements which is shared by pupils, staff and parents, and a deliberate attempt is made to foster self-discipline, leadership skills and a real sense of responsibility and community.

Kirkham Grammar School is a registered charity which exists to provide education for children, educating the whole person to standards of excellence.

Langley School

(Founded 1910)

Langley Park, Loddon, Norwich, Norfolk NR14 6BJ

Tel: 01508 520210 Fax: 01508 528058
e-mail: langley.school@dial.pipex.com
Internet: www.langley.norfolk.sch.uk

Head: Mr J G Malcolm BSc, MA, CertEd

Date of appointment: 1997

Member of: SHMIS, GBA, ISIS, BSA

(Junior School IAPS)

Co-educational Boarding & Day

Religious affiliation: Non-denominational

Age range of pupils: 10 – 18

No. of students enrolled as at 1.9.98: 259

Boys: 192 Girls: 67 VIth Form: 73

Average size of class: 14

Teacher/Pupil ratio: 1:8

Curriculum: In addition to core subjects, students in the Lower School study Drama, Music, Design Technology, Information Technology, Art, Ceramics, and PE. All these subjects plus others are continued through GCSE to A level (22 subjects in total). Languages available include French, German, Spanish, Latin and Russian.

The School has extensive facilities, including a recently built 11 lab Science and Computing centre, 3D Arts centre, Technology workshops including CAD. and electronics rooms, and a centre for Performing Arts.

Sports provision includes a sports hall, 13 tennis courts, extensive playing fields and a nine-hole golf course.

Extra-curricular activities play an important part in the school day, with an average of 70 different activity choices offered each term, including most sports, drama, music, technological, scientific and esoteric pursuits. The school also has an active CCF and promotes the Duke of Edinburgh Award Scheme.

Entry requirements: Interview and detailed reports. CE at 13 and 5+ GCSE passes at Sixth Form. Valuable Entrance Scholarships are awarded for Academic ability, Music, Drama, Art, Technology and Sport. Discounts for family and Forces children.

Range of fees per annum as at 1.9.98:

Day: £5190 – £6330

Weekly Boarding: £9405 – £11,415

Boarding: £10,065 – £12,195

Junior School: £3300 - £4890
  Nursery rates available on request from Junior School

Langley School is a Charitable Trust for the purpose of educating children.

Langley School

1. Rifle Range,
2. Sports Hall,
3. Playing Fields,
4. Boys' Boarding Facility,
5. Dining Hall,
6. Reception,
7. Library & Ballroom,
8. Golf Course,
9. Lawn Tennis Courts,
10. Headmasters' House,
11. Performing Arts Centre,
12. Girls' Boarding Facility,
13. Day Pupil Centre,
14. Specialist Classrooms,
15. Art & Design Technology,
16. Pottery Studio,
17. Science & Information Technology,
18. All Weather playing surface.

Lime House School

(Founded 1809)

Holm Hill, Dalston, Carlisle, Cumbria CA5 7BX

Tel: 01228 710225 Fax: 01228 710508
e-mail: NRice51711@aol.com
Internet: www.limehouse.u-k.org

Principal: Mr N A Rice BA, CertEd

Date of appointment: 1983

Member of: IAIS

Co-educational Boarding & Day

Religious affiliation: Inter-denominational

Age range of pupils: 5 – 18

Boarders from 5 years

No. of students enrolled as at 1.9.98: 185

VIth Form: 30

Average size of class: 11

Teacher/Pupil ratio: 1:10

Range of fees per annum as at 1.9.98:

Boarding: £3000 – £8850

Sixth Form Day: £4350

Sixth Form Boarding: £8850

Sited on the fringe of the Lake District our happy school offers continuity of education through Junior School to GCSE and A Level. Maximum class size is 20 with a dyslexic unit available, Army Cadet Force, school farm. Parents in HM Forces may be awarded bursaries.

Loughborough Grammar School

(Founded 1495)

6 Burton Walks, Loughborough, Leicestershire LE11 2DU

Tel: 01509 233233 Fax: 01509 218436

Principal: P B Fisher MA

Date of appointment: 1998

Member of: HMC, ISIS, ISCO

Boys Day & Boarding

Religious affiliation: Non-denominational. Christian, welcoming all faiths.

Age range of pupils: 10 – 18

Boarders from 10

No. of students enrolled as at 1.9.98: 970

Boys: 970 VIth Form: 280

Curriculum: At least the National Curriculum until the end of Key Stage 3, but then we allow a curriculum which allows pupils a wider choice at GCSE but which includes all the National Curriculum subjects. The Sciences continue to be taught as separate subjects.

Entry requirements: Entrance is by examination at 10+, 11+, 13+ and Common Entrance. Entry to the Sixth Form is dependent on GCSE results, interview

and school report. Entry at other age groups is by examination. Academic Scholarships and Music Scholarships are also awarded along with Assisted School places at 10+, 11+, 13+ and 16.

Range of fees per annum as at 1.9.98:

Day: £5148

Weekly Boarding: £8235

Boarding: £9369

Examinations offered including boards: GCSE: The traditional subjects plus German, Greek, Latin, Classical Civilisation, Religious Studies, CDT. Also, Spanish and Italian in the Sixth Form only.

A Level: All traditional subjects, including Business Studies, Economics, Computer Studies, Classical Studies, Latin, Music, CDT, Government and Political Studies, Religious Studies.

Also available A/S level in modular subjects and French, German, Latin, Greek, Further Mathematics.

Academic results: Awards to Oxford and Cambridge average 20 per year.

1998 A level: 135 candidates averaged 3.92 passes per candidate. 63% of all entries were at Grades A or B. 34 boys achieved three A Grades or higher.

1998 GCSE level: 148 candidates averaged nine passes each at Grades A*ABC (98%). 62% at Grades A* or A.

Academic & leisure facilities: The School views education in a traditional sense of academic, social, spiritual and physical development. It prides itself on having a family atmosphere and caters for day boys and boarders. It is exceptionally well equipped and academic results are excellent. Music and drama are strong, orchestras and productions running jointly with our sister School. A wide range of sports is available, with clubs and societies to cater for every need. A big emphasis on outdoor pursuits, including a large CCF, Scouts and Duke of Edinburgh Scheme.

Loughborough Grammar School is a Registered Charity which exists to provide high quality education for boys aged 10-18 years.

ERSKINE STEWART'S MELVILLE GOVERNING COUNCIL
(Principal: Mr P F J Tobin MA)

BOARDING WITH A DIFFERENCE

THE MARY ERSKINE SCHOOL
and
STEWART'S MELVILLE COLLEGE

are twinned Edinburgh Merchant Company
Schools for girls and boys respectively.
Each House offers comfortable and attractive
accommodation for up to 40 girls and 40
boys between the ages of 10 and 18.

ERSKINE HOUSE and DEAN PARK HOUSE

- are homely, not institutional
- are next door to each other, with shared dining room - ideal for brothers and sisters
- enjoy the superb facilities of the two schools
- are served by expert and caring house parents and staff
- are close to the heart of a lovely city
- offer remarkable value for money

Total fees, including Tuition: P6/P7 £2915 per term; Senior School £3270 per term

For prospectus and further details, or to arrange a visit, contact the Admissions secretary at:

The Mary Erskine School, Ravelston, Edinburgh EH4 3NT
Telephone 0131 337 2391 Fax 0131 346 1137

Stewart's Melville College, Queensferry, Edinburgh EH4 3EZ
Telephone 0131 337 7925 Fax 0131 343 2432

Leading independent school in the field of junior and secondary education.
Operated under the Edinburgh Merchant Company educational endowment Scheme 1960,
a registered charity.

Monmouth School

(Founded 1615)

Monmouth, Monmouthshire NP5 3XP

Tel: 01600 713143 Fax: 01600 772701

Head: Mr Timothy H P Haynes BA

Date of appointment: 1995

Member of: HMC

Boys Day & Boarding

Religious affiliation: Anglican
(Church of England/Church in Wales)

Age range of pupils: 11 – 18

Boarders from 11 or 13

No. of students enrolled as at 1.9.98: 735

VIth Form: 169

Average size of class: 18

Teacher/Pupil ratio: 1:11

Curriculum: Broadly-based curriculum. Classics from 11+. Pupils take at least nine GCSEs. Modern Languages include French, German, Spanish and Russian. Information Technology taught to all juniors. 27 subjects available at A level, 14 at AS level. Combined Sixth Form timetable allows shared teaching programme with Haberdashers' Monmouth School for Girls.

Entry requirements: Own exam at 11+; CEE or Scholarship at 13+; VI Scholarship or entry via GCSE/interview.

Subject specialities and academic track record: GCSE A, B, C grades (1997) 97.7%; A*, A, B grades 87%; A level passes (1997) 95.7%; A, B grades 63%; Oxbridge places (1997) 8 (70 in the past seven years).

Range of fees per annum as at 1.9.98:

Day: £5871

Boarding: £9780

Educational extras only include public examination fees, field-courses, etc. Books are not charged as extras.

Examinations offered including boards: GCSE (MEG, WJEC, NEAB). A level (OCSEB, UODLE, ULEAC, UCLES, AEB, NEAB); Oxford Entrance and Cambridge STEP Examinations.

Destination/career prospects of leavers: Some 98% of Sixth-Form leavers take up degree courses in Higher Education. In 97/98 all but one Sixth Form leaver entered degree courses.

Academic & leisure facilities: Recent buildings include £3m Sports Complex opened 1998, Library (1987), Music School (1989), Technology Centre (1991), Maths Centre (1994), IT Centre (1995). All boarding and day houses have been upgraded in recent years. The School Chapel was refurbished in 1996.

Located in historic border town of Monmouth, in the centre of the Wye Valley. Easy motorway access to London, Midlands, South West and South Wales.

The Jones Grammar School Charitable Trust, in association with the Haberdashers' Company, exists to support excellent all-round education for boys and girls in its two Monmouth Schools.

Moreton Hall

(Founded 1913)

Weston Rhyn, Oswestry, Shropshire SY11 3EW

Tel: 01691 773671 Fax: 01691 778552

Moreton Hall has a clear commitment to quality in all aspects of its education and pastoral care. The tutorial system, small class size and wide range of curricular and extra curricular opportunities ensure that each girl has the best possible chance to benefit from high class teaching and first rate facilities.

Head: Mr Jonathan Forster BA, FRSA

Date of appointment: 1992

Member of: SHA, GSA, GBGSA, ISIS, ISCO

Girls Boarding & Day

Religious affiliation: Church of England

Age range of pupils: 11 – 18

Boarders from 11

No. of students enrolled as at 1.9.98: 261

VIth Form: 90

Average size of class: 15

Teacher/Pupil ratio: 1:9

Curriculum: Moreton Hall offers throughout the school both traditional academic and practical subjects. Languages available include French, German, Spanish. A levels include History of Art, Business Studies and Theatre Studies. IT is compulsory. New GNVQ level 3 (BTEC) vocational A level course in Business.

Entry requirements: Girls are admitted to the school at the age of 11, 12 or 13 either by Common Entrance or School's entrance examination. Sixth Form entrance is by examination and interview.

Range of fees per annum as at 1.9.98:

Day: £9135

Boarding: £13,320

Fees include laboratory fees, stationery, materials *etc*.

Examinations offered including boards: GCSE: (MEG, SEG, NEAB, London); A level: (Oxford, JMB, London). RSA (Computer Literacy), ABRSM, LAMDA.

95% of second year Sixth Form students go on to University. 1998 three pupils to Oxbridge.

Moreton Hall, a charitable trust, exists to provide high quality education for girls. (Charity registration number 528409).

Mount St Mary's College

(Founded 1842)

Spinkhill, Near Sheffield, Derbyshire S21 3YL

Tel: 01246 433388 Fax: 01246 435511

The School combines learning with responsibility and seeks to produce young men and women 'for others'.

Head: Mr P G MacDonald MA(Oxon)

Date of appointment: September 1998

Member of: HMC, GBA

Co-educational Boarding & Day

Religious affiliation: Roman Catholic (Jesuit)

Age range of pupils: 11 – 19

Boarders from 11

No. of students enrolled as at 1.9.98: 302

Boys: 201 Girls: 101 VIth Form: 122

Average size of class: 15

Teacher/Pupil ratio: 1:9

Curriculum: National Curriculum core subjects: Maths, English, Science (Physics, Chemistry, Biology) and Foundation Subjects: History, Geography, Technology, Music, Art, Foreign Languages (French, Spanish, German) and Religious Studies. In addition Latin, Greek, Politics, Business Studies and Sports Studies may also be taken.

At Advanced level subjects are drawn up into blocks all standard combinations are possible.

Entry requirements: 13+: CE, 16+: 7 GCSEs

Range of fees per annum as at 1.9.98:

Day: £6150

Boarding: £10,200

All essential items are included in the fees.

Examinations offered including boards: GCSE is available in all subjects listed above using NEAB and MEG mainly. A, S, AS levels are all possible in the Sixth Form with preparation for Oxbridge also available. English for Overseas Students is offered.

Destination/career prospects of leavers: Most leavers go on to Universities and tertiary education.

Subject specialities and academic track record: All subjects are treated as specialities. Advanced level pass rate is between 76% and 86% over the last 10 years.

Over the last two years Mount St Mary's College has benefitted from a £1 million investment in facilities, resulting in first class teaching and living accomodation. These excellent provisions include: modern boarding accommodation with en-suite facilities, and modern science and language laboratories. The School's success in the teaching of art and music has been further strengthened by the modernisation of the Music Centre. The School enjoys an excellent reputation for sport and, in 1994, won the under 18 *Daily Mail* Cup for rugby at Twickenham. The finest sports equipment and facilities are available to all pupils, inluding an indoor swimming pool, gymnasia, all weather pitch, and redeveloped playing fields.

Catering at Mount St Mary's College is provided by a team of highly qualified and experienced chefs. Excellent teacher to student ratio results in increased pupil attention and consistent academic achievements.

Mount St Mary's College was founded in 1842, is a registered charity and exists to provide an education for children.

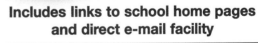

`New Hall School

(Founded 1642)

Chelmsford, Essex CM3 3HT

Tel: 01245 467588 Fax: 01245 464348

e-mail: admin@newhallschool

Headmistress: Sr Anne Marie CRSS, MA(Cantab)

Date of appointment: September 1996

Member of: GSA, GBGSA, ISIS

Girls Boarding & Day

Religious affiliation: Roman Catholic, others welcomed.

Age range of pupils: Boys 4 – 11 Girls 4 – 18

Boarders from 9 (girls only)

No. of students enrolled as at 1.9.98: 637

Boys: 85 Girls: 552 VIth Form: 115

Average size of class: 18 (Yrs I-V); 8 (Sixth Form)

Teacher/Pupil ratio: 1:10

Curriculum: Broadly based Years 7-9; Core + choice from 20+ GCSE options including, IT, Drama, all Sciences; 20 A-level subjects and a variety of non A-level Sixth Form subjects. 98% pass rate for A level.

Entry requirements: Suitability for mixed ability Christian Community; selected on Head's report, Interviews; Current school work and school's own examinations.

Range of fees per annum as at 1.9.98:

Day: £3900 – £7950

Weekly Boarding: £11,865

Boarding: £12,240

Situated in extensive grounds offering both space and peace, the School achieves high academic standards and encourages a full extra-curricular life. Excellent facilities include a purpose-built Performing Arts Centre with recording studio, three IT suites and six science laboratories. There is strong emphasis on a pastoral care based on small tutor groups and resident house staff. Girls are encouraged to develop self-motivation, good study skills and to take part in a wide ranging Voluntary Service Programme.

The Preparatory School welcomes both boys and girls from the ages of 4-11.

New Hall School is a registered charity for educational purposes, offering a broad-based Christian education for life.

Newlands School

(Founded 1854)

Eastbourne Road, Seaford, East Sussex BN25 4NP

Tel: 01323 490000 Fax: 01323 898420
e-mail: newlands1@msn.com
Internet: http://www.interbd.com/newlands-school

Let us unlock you child's potential.

Head of Preparatory School: Mr Oliver T Price BEd(Hons)

Head of Senior School: Mr Roland Miles BA(Hons)

Member of: IAPS, ISA

Co-educational Boarding & Day

Religious affiliation: Non-denominational

Age range of pupils: 2½ – 18

Boarders from 7 years

No. of students enrolled as at 1.1.99: 568

Boys: 358 Girls: 210 VIth Form: 68

Range of fees per annum as at 1.9.98:

Day: £4650 – £6450

Boarding: £8985 – £11,325

Our School

Newlands is a friendly, happy school with a strong academic tradition. Situated on one campus, Newlands offers an opportunity for educational continuity from nursery to university entrance. Classes are small and each pupil's progress is monitored carefully.

Location

Newlands is situated in a 21 acre campus in a pleasant coastal town surrounded by an area of outstanding natural beauty. Good communication links with Gatwick (37 miles), Heathrow (78 miles) and London (65 miles).

High Academic Standards

At Newlands we expect pupils to attain optimum results in external examinations, as is evident by our strong academic record. For the past few years pupils have won prizes awarded by the Independent Schools

Association for outstanding academic results. Examination results are well above average, particularly in Mathematics, the Sciences, Art, and Computing.

At Newlands we also place an emphasis on fully developing your child's potential. The wide range of activities available makes it possible for every pupil to achieve success and confidence in one field or another.

Entry requirements

An interview and school report are required for the Junior School.

An interview and school reports are also needed for the Senior School.

Curriculum and Scholarships

We follow the National Curriculum whilst also preparing your child for Scholarships to Senior Schools. The Senior School offers all the usual subjects leading to GCSE and A level for university entrance.

The arts flourish with thriving music, drama and art departments. There is a strong choral tradition and several annual dramatic productions. Academic and music scholarships are available and there is a generous discount for Service families.

Academic and sports facilities

Our facilities include five high-tech computer rooms, access to the Internet, science laboratories, a large art studio, a design technology workshop, an assembly hall/theatre and music room.

There are the equivalent of eight football pitches, a heated indoor swimming pool, a hard playing surface for three tennis/netball courts, a new multi-purpose hall which is appropriate for most indoor games as well as other activities and .22 rifle range. There are opportunities for many sports including soccer, hockey, rugby, netball, cricket, athletics, volleyball, basketball, squash, rounders, badminton, tennis, golf and cross-country running.

Support learning

Dyslexic pupils and those learning English as a foreign language are taught by specialist staff in our well-equipped, purpose built centre. Staff provide individual programmes of learning on a one-to-one basis. Approved by the Council for the Registration of Schools Teaching Dyslexics.

Transport

When required, pupils are escorted to Gatwick, Stansted and Heathrow airports and met on in coming flights. Newlands' minibuses provide transport to Victoria Station and along the south coast as far as Romsey, Aldershot and Maidstone.

Newlands School exists to provide quality education for boys and girls. Registered Charity No 297606.

Pangbourne College

(Founded 1917)

Pangbourne, Reading, Berkshire RG8 8LA

Tel: 01189 842101 Fax: 01189 845443

Head: Mr Anthony Hudson MA(Oxon), DipEd(London)

Date of appointment: 1988

Member of: HMC, SHMIS, GSA

Co-educational Boarding & Day

Age range of pupils: 11 – 18

Boarders from 11

No. of students enrolled as at 1.9.98: 354

VIth Form: 110

Average size of class: 15 in Lower School, 10 in Senior

Teacher/Pupil ratio: 1:9

Entry requirements: For Junior School: own Cognitive Ability Test and interview.

For Senior School: Common Entrance and Report.

For Overseas candidates: Posted Exam and Report.

For Sixth Form: Five GCSE passes at C or above.

Range of fees per annum as at 1.9.98:

Day: £6705 – £10,485

Boarding: £9240 – £13,197

Caring tuition in 250 acres of rolling parkland. The advantages of the small school combined with high standards. Focussing on leadership and teamwork, the College produces friendly, well mannered, rounded individuals. Particularly strong sport.

Pangbourne College is a registered charity (no. 309096. It was founded to train boys for a career at sea and subsequently developed into a fully-fledged public school preparing pupils for university and a wide range of careers. The College is now co-educational throughout the 11-18 age range.

Pipers Corner School

(Founded 1930)

Great Kingshill, High Wycombe, Buckinghamshire HP15 6LP

Tel: 01494 718255 Fax: 01494 719 806

e-mail: pipers@enterprise.net

Headmistress: Mrs V M Stattersfield MA(Oxon), PGCE

Date of appointment: 1996

Member of: GSA, GBGSA, AHIS, SHA

Girls Boarding & Day

Religious affiliation: Church of England

Age range of pupils: 4 – 18

Boarders from 7

No. of students enrolled as at 1.9.98: 350

Girls: 350 VIth Form: 60

Average size of class: 20

Entry requirements: Prep Department: Interview and report; Senior School: Entrance Examination, interview and report; Sixth Form: Interview and report.

Academic and service bursaries and Sixth Form scholarships are available.

Range of fees per annum as at 1.9.98:

Day: £3000 – £6588

Weekly Boarding: £9018 – £10,860

Boarding: £9147 – £11,010

Pipers Corner is situated in its own 36 acres of open country and is easily reached from London, and from Heathrow, Gatwick and Luton airports; overseas boarders can be escorted to and from airports. Weekly and short term occasional boarding are popular options. School coaches are available for day girls from a wide area.

In addition to girls chosen for academic ability, Pipers invites you to apply if you have an interest in the expressive arts and sport. A broad and balanced curriculum is followed, supported by expert careers advice. A full programme of extra-curricular activities is offered and experience of the wider community is gained through travel opportunities.

Pupils progress through the Prep Department to the Senior School. Girls are encouraged to achieve high standards and small classes ensure attention to individual growth.

We have a thriving Sixth Form which provides a wide range of A level courses and GNVQ Level 3 Advanced Business Studies. All girls are prepared for Higher Education in the friendly, lively challenging atmosphere which prevails.

Our resident nursing sister ensures high standards of health care. Housemistresses arrange weekend activities and give boarders a warm and secure environment.

Our aim is to provide a secure and happy environment in which each individual is helped to fulfil her potential and to emerge with maturity, confidence and a sense of independence.

Pipers Corner School is a charitable trust and exists to provide high quality education for girls.

**Don't forget to read the articles which appear at the front of this book.
They may save you a lot of time and trouble**

Plymouth College

(Founded 1877)

Ford Park, Plymouth, Devon PL4 6RN

Tel: 01752 203300 Fax: 01752 203246
e-mail: admin@plycol.co.uk
Internet: http://www.plycol.co.uk

Head: Mr A J Morsley BSc, ARCS, AFIMA, FRSA

Date of appointment: 1992

Member of: HMC, GBA

Co-educational Boarding & Day

Religious affiliation: Christian

Age range of pupils: 11 – 18

No. of students enrolled as at 1.9.98: 605

VIth Form: 179

Average size of class: Age 11 to 13 - 22, 14 to 16 - 24, Sixth Form 11

Teacher/Pupil ratio: 1:11

Curriculum: Broad academic curriculum 11 to 13 leads into setted option system for GCSE. Tweny A levels available in Sixth Form.

Entry requirements: Entry is by our own examination (English, Maths, Verbal Reasoning) at 11+. Common Entrance Examination at 13+. Occasional vacancies at other ages. GCSEs for Sixth Form.

Range of fees per annum as at 1.9.98:

Day: £5721

Boarding: £10,977

Plymouth College is situated centrally in a quiet area of Plymouth close to rail, motorway and airport links.

The Plymouth College Charitable Trust exists to provide high quality education to girls and boys.

Pocklington School

(Founded 1514)

West Green, Pocklington, York, East Yorkshire YO42 2NJ

Tel: 01759 303125 Fax: 01759 306366
e-mail: mainoffice@pocklingtonsch.org.uk
Internet: www.pocklingtonsch.org.uk

Head: Mr J N D Gray BA

Date of appointment: 1992

Member of: HMC, BSA

Co-educational Day & Boarding

Religious affiliation: Church of England

Age range of pupils: 7 – 18

Boarders from 9 years

No. of students enrolled as at 1.9.98: 751

Boys: 447 Girls: 304 VIth Form: 165

Average size of class: 18

Curriculum: The core subjects of English, Mathematics, French and Sciences are supplemented by Art, CDT, Music and IT up to GCSE level. Options are available in History, Geography, Latin, Spanish, German, PE and Religious Studies. A wide range of subjects are available at A level.

Entry requirements: Entry by examination at 7, 8, 9, 11 and 13 or by arrangement. Sixth Form candidates

are admitted after interview and on GCSE results.

Academic, Art and Music scholarships at 11, 13 and 16. Five local bursaries at age 11.

Range of fees per annum as at 1.9.98:

Day: £5127 – £5955

Boarding: £8526 – £9900

Set in 70 acres on the edge of a market town; noted for high academic achievement, music, sport, art and design; lively and friendly boarding community.

* Major extension and refurbishment to Lyndhurst Junior School, 1998.

* New girls boarding house for ages 9 upwards to open in September 1999.

* Performing Arts Centre to open in the year 2000.

Pocklington School is a registered charity and exists to provide a quality education for young people.

Prior's Field School

(Founded 1902)

Priorsfield Road, Godalming, Surrey GU7 2RH

Tel: 01483 810551 Fax: 01483 810180

e-mail: admin@priorsfield.demon.co.uk

Headmistess: Mrs J M McCallum BA(Hons)

Date of appointment: 1987

Member of: GSA

Girls Boarding & Day

Religious affiliation: Non-denominational

Age range of pupils: 11 – 18

Boarders from 11 years

No. of students enrolled as at 1.9.98: 234

Girls: 234 VIth Form: 56

Average size of class: 14

Teacher/Pupil ratio: 1:8

Curriculum: Our aim is to provide a varied education, to which end most girls take nine GCSE (MEG, SEG, ULEAC) subjects. We offer 20 subjects at A level (OCR, EDEXCEL, AEB), with a minority programme including Business Studies, IT, Sports, Current Affairs, Photography, Duke of Edinburgh Award and EFL.

Accommodation for Sixth Formers is in a purpose built house with single study bedrooms.

Entry requirements: Common Entrance or Prior's Field exam. Five GCSE at Grade C or above for Sixth Form (or equivalent). Scholarships are available.

Range of fees per annum as at 1.9.98:

Day: £7800

Boarding: £11,670

Academic & leisure facilities: Include Science and Technology Laboratories, Business Skills Centre, Model Office, Computer Room, Drama Studio, Home Economics Room, Library, Art and Craft block, Music Centre and Sixth Form House. We have ample sports facilities including Lacrosse, Netball, Hockey, Volleyball, Badminton, Tennis, Rounders, Athletics and Swimming.

Teaching is in small groups resulting in a great deal of individual attention, the objective being to achieve high academic results, at the same time developing self confidence for smooth transition to Higher education. Dyslexia support is provided on a 1:1 basis.

A weekend and evening programme of outings and activities is planned to fit the interests of the girls and includes drama, craft, music and sports both on and off site at the local leisure centres. Competitive sport is strong and ranges from lacrosse and tennis to riding and golf. Sixth Form students are encouraged to devise their own extra-curricular education schedule.

Prior's Field School was founded in 1902 by Julia Huxley, the School being a listed building set in 25 acres outside Godalming. Access from Heathrow and Gatwick Airports and A3, M3, M4 and M25 is easy, as it is from London Waterloo by rail.

Prior's Field School Trust is a charitable trust which is proud to offer an education combining the best from tradition with innovation. The young people who leave our Sixth Form are poised to embrace the adult world.

Rannoch School

(Founded 1959)

Rannoch, By Pitlochry, Perthshire PH17 2QQ

Tel: 01882 632332 Fax: 01882 632443
e-mail: Headmaster@rannoch-school.demon.co.uk
Internet: http://www.rannoch-school.demon.co.uk

Head: Dr John D Halliday BA, PhD

Date of appointment: 1997

Member of: SHMIS, GBA, Round Square Conference

Co-educational Boarding & Day

Religious affiliation: Inter-denominational

Age range of pupils: 10 – 18

Boarders from 10

No. of students enrolled as at 1.9.98: 210

Boys: 130 Girls: 80 VIth Form: 88

Average size of class: 12 to 20

Teacher/Pupil ratio: 1:10

Curriculum: All usual subjects to GCSE Standard Grade, Scottish Higher and A level. Special subjects - Computer Studies, Economics and Craft and Design.

Entry requirements: Entry at all ages by interview and school report. There are various entrance scholarships at 10+, 13+ and on entry to the Sixth Form.

Range of fees per annum as at 1.9.98:

Day: £6105

Boarding: £9702 – £11,655

Rannoch is unique. So is each child. Set in an environment of unsurpassed beauty on the magnificent loch from which the school takes its name Rannoch provides a world-class education in the heart of the Highlands of Scotland. The needs and talents of every individual boy or girl are assessed, nurtured and challenged both inside and outside the classroom to foster self-confidence, self-reliance, a zest for life and a responsibility towards others.

Rannoch School Ltd is registered in Scotland as an Educational Charity.

Ratcliffe College

(Founded 1847)

Fosse Way, Ratcliffe on the Wreake,
Leicester, LE7 4SG

Tel: 01509 817000 Fax: 01509 817004

Headmaster/President: Mr T A Kilbride BA

Date of appointment: Sept 96

Member of: HMC

Co-educational Boarding & Day

Religious affiliation: Roman Catholic

Age range of pupils: 9 – 18

Boarders from 11

No. of students enrolled as at 1.9.98: 530

VIth Form: 150

Average size of class: 20

Teacher/Pupil ratio: 1:12

Curriculum: Full range of subjects including Computer Studies, Art, Drama, Music leading to GCSE. Then A levels in Science and Arts including Economics, Drama and Media Studies.

Entry requirements: Entry at 9-12 is by interview and entrance examination. Registration for tests and interview in January prior to entry. At 13 by school examination or Common Entrance, interview and assessments. Sixth Form entry based on GCSE results and interview.

Range of fees per annum as at 1.9.98:

Day: £6888

Weekly Boarding: £10,329

Boarding: £10,329

Junior School: Day: £5478

Weekly Boarding: £10,329

Boarding: £8214

Ratcliffe College, founded in 1847, set in its own grounds of 100 acres in rural Leicestershire, on the A46, is a fully co-educational day and boarding Catholic school. There is a family atmosphere with an emphasis on both academic and cultural activities. The East Midlands airport is 15 miles away.

EXCITING NEW DEVELOPMENTS AT RATCLIFFE COLLEGE.

Ratcliffe College is already one of the largest Catholic co-educational day and boarding schools in the United Kingdom, with a long tradition of offering an excellent academic education in a Christian, caring community. The opening of a Nursery School in September 1998, along with a new Year 5 class for 9 year-olds, is part of the development plan for Ratcliffe College to provide a continuous education on one site for children aged 3 to 18+. In 1999 Year 1and Year 4 classes will open, folowed in the year 2000 by Year 2 and Year 3 classes.

Ratcliffe is a Charitable Trust Catholic School, whose principal aim is to provide an education for Catholic young people and to offer this to sympathetic people of Christian and non Christian denominations.

Rathdown School

Founded 1919 (Hillcourt School) 1973 (renamed Rathdown on amalgamation with two other schools)

Glenageary, Co Dublin

Tel: 00 3531 285 3133 Fax: 00 3531 284 0738

Headmistress: Miss Stella G Mew MA, HDipEd(Hons), DipBibStud

Date of appointment: 1972

Member of: ISA

Girls Boarding & Day

Religious affiliation: Protestant

Age range of pupils: 3 – 18

Boarders from 12 years

No. of students enrolled as at 1.9.98: 510

Girls: 510 VIth Form: 92

Average size of class: 20

Teacher/Pupil ratio: 1:10

Curriculum: Wide range of Academic subjects for Irish Department of Education and Science Junior and Leaving Certificate courses. Entry to British, Irish and overseas Universities including Oxbridge. Excellent results.

Entry requirements: Applications accepted on receipt of Entry form, Registration Fee of IR£50, Birth Certificate and latest School Report.

Range of fees per annum as at 1.9.98:

Day: IR£945-IR£1815 Boarding: Tuition Fee + IR£3600 Sixth Form: Day IR£1815, Boarders IR£5415

The 17 acre landscaped site offers excellent sports facilities and is close to the sea, mountains and city of Dublin. Train and bus close by.

Rishworth School

(Founded 1724)

Rishworth, Halifax, West Yorkshire HX6 4QA

Tel: 01422 822217 Fax: 01422 820911
Internet: www.rishworth-school.co.uk

Head: Mr R A Baker MA

Date of appointment: 1998

Member of: SHMIS and GBA

Co-educational Day & Boarding School with separate Preparatory School and Nursery

Religious affiliation: Church of England

Age range of pupils: 4 – 18

Boarders from 11. Nursery from age 3.

No. of students enrolled as at 1.9.98: 485

Boys: 255 Girls: 230

Curriculum: Full range of subjects leading to preparation for GCSE at all levels, A level, university entrance, and vocational courses.

Entry requirements: Entry at 11 by Entrance Exam. Entry at other times subject to interview and satisfactory reports from previous school. Generous scholarships and bursaries available.

Range of fees per annum as at 1.9.98:

Day: £2790 – £5460

Boarding: £9720 – £10,560

School lunches: Day pupils £85; Infants £70. 10% discount for Forces parents; discounts for younger brothers and sisters.

Rishworth School stands in 130 acres of a beautiful Pennine valley, six miles south-west of Halifax and close to the M62.

This establishment is a registered charity and exists solely to provide educational facilities to the community.

Sherborne School International College

(Founded: Sherborne School - 1550, International College - 1977)

Newell Grange, Newell, Sherborne, Dorset DT9 4EZ

Tel: 01935 814743 Fax: 01935 816863

Principal: Dr Christopher Greenfield MA, MEd

Date of appointment: 1997

Co-educational Boarding

Religious affiliation: Multi-denominational

Age range of pupils: 10 – 16

No. of students enrolled as at 1.9.98: 120

Average size of class: 7

Teacher/Pupil ratio: 1:4

Curriculum: The International College of Sherborne School provides a 'bridge' which enables pupils educated in other countries to prepare themselves thoroughly and carefully for success in top UK schools. Our aim is to ensure that when our pupils go on to other schools they have a good command of spoken and written English, and a sound foundation in other subjects. With this preparation they are able to thrive, rather than merely survive, when they join in the larger classes of native English speaking children.

Subject specialities and academic track record: We specialise in preparing boys and girls from overseas for entrance to good independent boarding schools. Some pupils are native English speakers, but most are learning English. Excellent success rate at Common Entrance and GCSE examinations.

Entry requirements: Previous school report requested. No entry examination.

Range of fees per annum as at 1.9.98:

Boarding: £17,250

Lab fees, textbooks and essential materials are included.

Examinations offered including boards: Common Entrance examination at 13+, GCSE (All Boards), University of Cambridge Examinations in English.

Destination/career prospects of leavers: Our pupils gain admission to the best of UK Schools, *eg* Winchester, Sherborne, Westminster, Harrow, and achieve high levels of success there as a result of the sound foundation acquired in the College.

Academic & leisure facilities: Classes are small -

average seven pupils. Every pupil receives careful personal attention, in and out of lessons, and lives and studies in the happy family atmosphere of a small school which believes in helping every pupil to make the most of his or her potential. Standards of good manners and discipline are high. In 1991 we moved into new buildings with first-class living accommodation and excellent classroom and laboratory facilities. A new classroom block is being completed this year.

Our aim in the International College is to provide a happy and hard-working atmosphere in which children from overseas can prepare themselves, academically and socially for the more robust conditions which they will find.

Sherborne School is a Registered Charity which exists to provide a complete and well-balanced education for children.

Information about day schools can be found in
Which School ?
also published by John Catt Educational Ltd

Shrewsbury School

(Founded 1552)

The Schools, Shrewsbury, Shropshire SY3 7BA

Tel: 01743 344537 Fax: 01743 340048
e-mail: hm_office@shrewsbury.demon.co.uk

Shrewsbury School sets out to achieve its aims within the traditional structure of house communities and with a boys-only entry. It offers a combination of different elements – established educational virtues and new ideas, a distinctive geographical position looking North and South and a unique site combining town and country.

Head: Mr F E Maidment MA

Date of appointment: 1988

Member of: HMC

Boys Boarding & Day

Religious affiliation: Church of England

Age range of pupils: 13 – 18

Boarders from 13 years

No. of students enrolled as at 1.9.98: 700

Boys: 700 VIth Form: 302

Average size of class: GCSE: 18; A level: 8

Teacher/Pupil ratio: 1:8.6

Curriculum: The School aims at the highest academic standards appropriate to the ability of each individual boy. About 95% of boys stay on for A levels.

Entry requirements: 13+: Common Entrance, Scholarship or school's own entrance test. 16+: Sixth Form Scholarship examination or interview plus minimum of six B grades at GCSE.

Range of fees per annum as at 1.9.98:

Day: £10,080

Boarding: £14,325

Shrewsbury School stands in 105 acres of ground on a high bluff, looking across the River Severn to the ancient town of Shrewsbury.

Shrewsbury School is a registered charity in the field of secondary education.

Sidcot School

(Founded 1699; re-founded 1808)

Winscombe, North Somerset BS25 1PD

Tel: 01934 843102 Fax: 01934 844181

e-mail: sidcotad@aol.com

Head: Angus Slesser MA

Date of appointment: 1997

Member of: SHMIS, GBA, ECIS

Co-educational Boarding & Day

Religious affiliation: Quaker

Age range of pupils: 9 – 18

Boarders from 9

No. of students enrolled as at 1.9.98: 396

Boys: 243 Girls: 153 VIth Form: 117

Average size of class: 16

Teacher/Pupil ratio: 1:10

Curriculum: A broad academic and social programme leading to GCSEs and A levels and GNVQ (Intermediate and Advanced Levels). Special emphasis on Music, Drama and Personal Education.

Entry requirements: Own tests or Common Entrance Examination, plus interview.

Range of fees per annum as at 1.9.98:

Day: £4800 – £6450

Boarding: £11,175

Excellent educational and sporting facilities. Set in more than 100 acres of Mendip countryside. Very wide range of extra-curricular activities. New Library, Sports Centre, Stables, Science Block and Refectory.

Sidcot is a Quaker Charitable foundation, welcoming pupils of all denominations.

St Bede's School

The Dicker, Hailsham, East Sussex BN27 3QH

Tel: 01323 843252 Fax: 01323 442628
e-mail: school.office@stbedes.e-sussex.sch.uk Internet: www.stbedes.e-sussex.sch.uk

Head: Mr R A Perrin MA

Member of: SHMIS and GBA

Co-educational Boarding & Day

Religious affiliation: Inter-denominational

Age range of pupils: 12½ – 18

No. of students enrolled as at 1.9.98: 532

Boys: 350 Girls: 182 VIth Form: 203

Average size of class: 14 (Senior) 8 (Sixth Form)

Teacher/Pupil ratio: 1:7.5

Range of fees per annum as at 1.9.98:

Day: £7875

Boarding: £13,050

The School enjoys a very strong reputation in Art, Music and Drama in addition to its academic and sporting success. Located in the Sussex countryside, the School offers excellent facilities which include a new indoor sports centre with squash courts, fitness studio and competition sized swimming pool, riding stables and practice golf course. There are excellent rail and road links to London, Gatwick and Heathrow airports and Ashford International station.

St Bede's is a boarding school whose whole programme is designed to serve the needs of its boarding students. There are five comfortable boarding houses staffed by resident Housemistresses, Housemasters, tutors and Matrons who look after the welfare and travel arrangements of their students.

There are over 30 subjects taught at both GCSE and A level. AS levels are offered in a wide range of subjects in addition to selected Advanced GNVQ courses. The curriculum is exceptionally wide and flexible and there is great scope for students to follow carefully tailored individual programmes of work. Entry is by Scholarship Examination, Common Entrance or by interview with the Headmaster.

An exceptionally wide club activities programme operates which offers over 100 activities each week ranging from numerous outdoor pursuits and sports to activities within the fields of art, music, drama, journalism, science, agriculture, technology and social sciences.

Younger students wishing to start at St Bede's may join St Bede's Preparatory School Eastbourne which is an excellent preparation for life at The Dicker.

St Bede's is a charitable trust which exists to educate young children.

St Bees School

(Founded 1583)

St Bees, Cumbria CA27 0DS

Tel: 01946 822263 Fax: 01946 823657

e-mail: mailbox@st-bees-school.co.uk

Headmistress: Mrs J D Pickering BSc

Date of appointment: January 1998

Member of: HMC

Co-educational Boarding & Day

Religious affiliation: Church of England

Age range of pupils: 11 – 18

Boarders from 11

No. of students enrolled as at 1.9.98: 298

Boys: 173 Girls: 125 VIth Form: 89

Average size of class: 15

Teacher/Pupil ratio: 1:10

Curriculum: A wide variety of subjects leading to GCSE, A level and Oxbridge Entrance Examinations.

Entry requirements: St Bees Entrance Scholarship and Assisted Places Examinations at 11+; Common Entrance. Sixth Form Entry - minimum requirement of five GCSE passes at grade C or higher.

Range of fees per annum as at 1.9.98:

Day: £6939 – £8556

Weekly Boarding: £7830 – £11,070

Boarding: £9096 – £12,435

The School stands in 150 acres of the attractive valley of St Bees, half a mile from a sandy beach and on the western edge of the Lake District. Recent developments include a £1 million Business Centre with extensive facilities for IT, Modern Languages and Business Studies and an International Centre.

The St Bees School Charity Trust exists to provide high quality education for boys and girls.

St Catherine's School

(Founded 1885)

Bramley, Guildford, Surrey GU5 0DF

Tel: 01483 893363 Fax: 01483 893003

Head: Mrs C M Oulton MA(Oxon)

Date of appointment: September 1994

Member of: GSA, BSA and IAPS

Girls Day & Boarding

Religious affiliation: Church of England

Age range of pupils: 4 – 18

Boarders from 9

No. of students enrolled as at 1.9.98: 693

VIth Form: 102

Average size of class: Lower School 20, Sixth Form 6

Teacher/Pupil ratio: 1:9

Curriculum: 21 subjects are offered at GCSE, 19 at A level. There is also a wide choice of extra-curricular activities, clubs and societies.

Entry requirements: Own entrance examination at all age groups. Scholarships available at 11 and 16, including Art Sport and Music scholarships.

Range of fees per annum as at 1.9.98:

Day: £3615 – £7230

Boarding: £10,680 – £11,985

A Happy School for Bright Girls

St Catherine's is set in extensive grounds in the lovely Surrey village of Bramley, within easy reach of London and the home counties. Both Gatwick and Heathrow are easily accessible, and travel arrangements are made for overseas boarders.

The School provides a secure environment for boarders from the age of nine upwards. The number of boarders is limited so that we can provide the best possible care for both weekly and full boarders. They flourish in the friendly and supportive atmosphere, and benefit from the added stimulus of a lively population of day girls. Places at the school are keenly sought after. Each year a number of day girls choose to move into boarding, frequently because they have already boarded whilst their parents have been away, and greatly enjoyed the experience.

Boarders benefit from the discipline that boarding gives to academic study and from taking part in the wide range of activities that successful schools like St Catherine's make available. Sport is very strong, with St Catherine's girls regularly competing at County level in lacrosse and netball, in regional competitive and international tours. In 1997 the lacrosse and netball team toured Australia. Music, the arts, and drama thrive, and there is a 'Culture Vultures' club which organises regular visits to theatre, the opera and exhibitions. Boarders are the mainstay of the Chamber choir, and many sing in Chapel choir and choral performances.

The School has an outstanding academic record, and most girls go on to university. Boarders are given individual attention, helping them achieve their full potential, and the scope to enlarge their horizons and aim for the very best in life.

The Corporation of Cranleigh and Bramley Schools is a registered charity, which exists to provide high quality education for girls in accordance with the principles of the Church of England.

St Christopher School

(Founded 1915)

Barrington Road, Letchworth, Hertfordshire SG6 3JZ

Tel: 01462 679301 Fax: 01462 481578
e-mail: stchris.admin@rmplc.co.uk
Internet: http://www.rmplc.co.uk/eduweb/sites/stchris

Headmaster: Mr Colin Reid MA

Date of appointment: 1981

Member of: SHMIS, GBA

Co-educational Day & Boarding

Religious affiliation: Non-denominational

Age range of pupils: Boys 3 – 18 Girls 3 – 18

Boarders from 7

No. of students enrolled as at 1.9.98: 536

Boys: 337 Girls: 199 VIth Form: 102

Average size of class: 16

Teacher/Pupil ratio: 1:7

Curriculum: The core areas of the National Curriculum are covered with all pupils continuing with Physics, Chemistry and Biology to Double Certificate Level at the GCSE. Foreign languages have a strongly practical emphasis with all pupils paying at least two visits to our exchange schools in France and/or Germany in years II, III and IV. The creative arts and technology are particularly encouraged and the facilities are available and staffed at weekends. Internationalist and green values are encouraged.

Entry requirements: Entry for boarders is usually at age 11 with some joining at 9 and others at 13. Decisions are made in the light of interview, school reports and informal tests usually conducted on the day of interview. We look for an ability to respond to the spirit and opportunities of St Christopher. Direct entrants to the Sixth Form have to show the ability to follow a 3 A/AS level programme. The School provides for children of average to outstanding ability aiming to help everyone achieve their full potential.

Range of fees per annum as at 1.9.98:

Day: £1779 – £7122

Boarding: £10,065 – £12,564

The average amount required to cover educational extras is £30 a term plus any public exam fees.

Examinations offered including boards: GCSE, (MEG, NEG, SEG), GCE A and A/S Levels (O & C, JMB, AEB London) in 18 subjects. GNVQ Advanced Business Studies.

Destination and career prospects of leavers: Almost all leavers go on to a course in further or higher education, ranging from Universities (regularly including Oxbridge) to courses in engineering, business, the applied and performing arts and vocations such as nursing and social work.

Academic & leisure facilities: The School has all the usual specialist rooms and science laboratories with particularly fine Theatre, Music, Arts and Technology Centres added in recent years. As one of the pilot schools of Education 2000 it has pioneered major developments in information technology and two computer networks link the library and all the teaching areas. We complement academic study with learning through experience. There is a strong emphasis on Outdoor Pursuits (with all pupils learning to canoe, sail and rock climb) on service to the community and on self government through which pupils learn both how to put forward their own ideas and listen to those of others.

Values: The School is an unusually tolerant community, recognising and caring for all as individuals. There is no compulsory worship so people of different religions and of none feel equally at home. There is a significant period of silence in every assembly. The diet is vegetarian.

Longterm aims: St Christopher has long been noted for its success in developing lifelong self confidence. The School is informal (there is no uniform and all children and adults are called by their first names); at the same time it is purposeful and challenging of mind, body and spirit. We aim for our young people to develop an effective competence, a social conscience, moral courage, a sense of initiative, the capacity for friendship and a true zest for life.

St Christopher School is a charity providing education for 2 ½ to 18 year olds, with boarders from age 7.

For further information about independent and non-maintained special schools, why not consult
Which School ? for Special Needs,
also published by John Catt Educational Ltd

St Edmund's College

(Founded 1568)

Old Hall Green, Near Ware, Hertfordshire SG11 1DS

Tel: 01920 821504 Fax: 01920 823011
e-mail: registrar@secware.demon.co.uk
Internet: http://www.secware.demon.co.uk

Head: Mr D J J McEwen MA(Oxon), FRSA

Member of: HMC

Co-educational Day & Boarding

Religious affiliation: Roman Catholic, all welcome

Age range of pupils: 3 – 18

Boarders from 7

No. of students enrolled as at 1.9.98: 520

Boys: 310 Girls: 210 VIth Form: 130

Range of fees per annum as at 1.9.98:

Day: £3960 – £7185

Weekly Boarding: £8745 – £10,695

Boarding: £9315 – £11,535

The College is in 400 acres of private parkland, only 50 minutes from central London or Cambridge by road. Nearest railway station Ware is only 30 minutes from London's Liverpool Street Station.

Computer rooms, science laboratories, art and technology workshops and multi-sports hall. Dedicated Sixth Form Centre. GNVQ courses in Business, and Art and Design alongside traditional range of A levels. In 1998 92% of our A level candidates took up university places. Full boarder, day pupils or weekly boarders accepted. High level of pastoral care. Wide range of extra-curricular sports and activities. Indoor heated swimming pool on campus.

St Edmund's College, a registered charity, exists to provide a Catholic education for children.

St Edward's, Oxford

(Founded 1863)

Woodstock Road, Oxford, Oxfordshire OX2 7NN

Tel: 01865 319200 Fax: 01865 319202
e-mail: registrar.stedwards@rmplc.co.uk
Internet: www.stedward.oxon.sch.uk

Head: David Christie BA, BSc(Econ)

Date of appointment: September 1998

Co-educational Boarding & Day

Age range of pupils: 13 – 18

Boarders from 13

No. of students enrolled as at 1.9.98: 568

Boys: 468 Girls: 100

Curriculum: The first year is a foundation year, in which pupils take the full range of subjects, including Art and Design and a choice of Greek, German or Spanish. In the two years to GCSE, 10 subjects are studied. There is a wide range of choices within a framework of a balance of Arts, Sciences and Languages.

A good range of A level subjects is available including Politics, Economics, Design, Spanish and German. Over 90% of pupils go on to Higher Education.

Entry requirements: For boys and girls at 13+ by Common Entrance, the Scholarship examination, or our own Assessment Day (for pupils from maintained schools). Up to 15 scholarships and exhibitions are available, including awards for Music and Art and for all-round ability. Assisted places are available for 13+ and Lower Sixth entrants.

Entry for boys and girls into the Sixth Form is by examination and interview in November. Up to six Scholarships and Exhibitions are available. Sixth Form entrants may also enter for the Music Scholarship.

Range of fees per annum as at 1.9.98:

Day: £9600

Boarding: £13,425

St Edward's aims to bring out the best in each of its pupils, offering high academic standards combined with a friendly, caring atmosphere and strong traditions in music, drama, art and sport.

There are seven boys and two girls boarding houses. Each house has a resident Housemaster/Housemistress assisted by several tutors and a House Nurse.

Resident new facilities include the Design Centre, a Mathematics building (with its own computer network), a new IT Centre and an Astroturf all-weather pitch.

St Edward's School, which is a charity, exists to provide an excellent all round education for its pupils.

St Margaret's School

(Founded 1749)

Merry Hill Road, Bushey, Hertfordshire WD2 1DT

Tel: 0181 950 1548 Fax: 0181 950 1677

e-mail: smbushey@aol.com

Headmistress: Miss M de Villiers BA

Date of appointment: 1992

Member of: GBGSA, GSA, BSA

Girls Boarding & Day

Religious affiliation: Anglican

Age range of pupils: 4 – 18

Boarders from 11

No. of students enrolled as at 1.9.98: 480

Girls: 480

Average size of class: 20

Teacher/Pupil ratio: 1:9

Curriculum: All subjects for GCSE and A level examinations and for entrance to University.

Entry requirements: Entry is by assessment and interview at 4+ and by the School's own Entrance Examination and interview at 11+ and 13+. Sixth Form places are conditional on GCSE results and report.

Range of fees per annum as at 1.9.98:

Day: £3975 – £6405

Boarding: £9405 – £10,695

Scholarships: Scholarships and Concessions for Sisters, Services and daughters of living and deceased clergy.

The School enjoys a rural aspect although within easy reach of Central London with good access to the M1 and M25, major airports and railheads. A School Coach service is provided for Day pupils living in the surrounding area.

The School exists to provide high quality education for girls. Charity registration no: 1056228.

St Mary's Hall

(Founded 1836)

Eastern Road, Brighton, East Sussex BN2 5JF

Tel: 01273 606061 Fax: 01273 620782

Headmistress: Mrs S M Meek MA

Member of: GSA, BSA

Girls Day & Boarding with Boys in the Junior Department

Religious affiliation: Church of England

Age range of pupils: Boys 3 – 8 Girls 3 – 18

Boarders from 8 years

No. of students enrolled as at 1.9.98: 403

Boys: 7 Girls: 369 VIth Form: 40

Entry requirements: Own examinations, interview and school reports.

Range of fees per annum as at 1.9.98:

Day: £4089 – £6675

Boarding: £7875 – £10,215

Nursery: from £445

Scholarships: Music (including Organ), Academic, VIth form, own Assisted Places, Clergy and Forces Bursaries.

History and Academic Strengths:

St Mary's Hall was established in 1836 by a Church of England Clergyman, Henry Venn Elliott. It remains true to its Christian foundation, but welcomes pupils of all religions into its community. Girls are accepted from 3 to 18 years, and boys from 3 to 8 years. Boarding is offered from the age of eight. The main building is still in use, but modern buildings are also to be found on the attractive campus, close to the centre of Brighton, and within sight of the sea.

The school is divided into a Nursery and Pre-Prep (Gloucester House, opened by the Duchess of Gloucester in 1989), a Prep School (Elliott House, named after the founder of the school) and the senior school. The VIth form occupy a modern building, (Venn House, opened in1981), which serves as Senior Boarding house and a study centre.

The philosophy of the school is 'To Educate for Confidence'. **Our aim is to develop the personal qualities necessary to make a positive contribution**

to a changing and unpredictable world.

This requires each individual in the community to be ready for life-long learning, to be adaptable, to have the courage to face challenges, to acquire transferable skills, to be able to work independently and as part of a team, to show self-discipline, commitment, flexibility and openness to change.

To achieve this the school will:

encourage a culture of learning and a respect for **knowledge and achievement;**

focus upon the individual and each pupil's **academic and personal development** in preparation for higher education, the world of work and personal responsibilty;

promote the shared and lasting values of **love, knowledge, integrity and truth** within a caring multi-cultural community which fosters understanding, tolerance and consideration of others in accordance with the School's Christian foundation and ethos.

It is always difficult to summarise a dynamic organisation in a few words, but St Mary's Hall prides itself on the individual care and attention given to each pupil, and on its full range of extra-curricular activities.

In terms of examination results, the school enables pupils to maximise their potential, but the overall aim is to develop each individual to the point where they can face adult life with confidence, as well-rounded personalities. Examination results for summer 1998 were pleasing, with an overall A level pass rate of 93.3%. 30% of the A level passes were grades A or B, and of the 17 subjects offered at A level, 14 had 100% pass rates. At GCSE 90% of all grades were C or above - the national average this year was 54.7%. 37% of all grades were A or A*, and 12 subjects had 100% pass rates.

It is a happy school, as noted in inspection reports, and the realtionships between staff and pupils are both relaxed and respectful. Special features include an indoor swimming pool, a full range of science laboratories, modern IT and CDT workrooms, and exceptional Art and Music facilities.

Visits, conducted by a senior pupil, can be arranged at mutually convenient times. Please telephone 01273 60 60 61 for an appointment.

St Mary's Hall exists to provide quality education for children.

St Mary's School Ascot

(Founded 1885)

St Mary's Road, Ascot, Berkshire SL5 9JF

Tel: 01344 623721 Fax: 01344 873281

e-mail: admissions@st-marys-ascot.co.uk

Principal: Mrs Mary Breen BSc, MSc

Date of appointment: January 1999

Member of: GSA, GBSA

Girls Boarding & Day

Religious affiliation: Roman Catholic

Age range of pupils: 11 – 18

Boarders from 11 years

No. of students enrolled as at 1.9.98: 354

VIth Form: 108

Average size of class: 18

Teacher/Pupil ratio: 2:7

Curriculum: All usual subjects to GCSE and A level with Careers advice integral to the curriculum.

99% go on to Higher Education, with 83% A+B grades at A level (1998) and 98% ABC grades at GCSE.

Entry requirements: Entry at 11+, 13+ as a result of School's own assessment and interview. Entry at 16+ subject to GCSE results and interview.

Range of fees per annum as at 1.9.98:

Day: £8730

Boarding: £13,440

St Mary's Ascot is set in 45 acres of Berkshire close to the M4, the M3 and the M25, ten miles from Heathrow Airport. Entry is selective and the majority of pupils stay on to Sixth Form. The school offers termly and not weekly boarding with a wide variety of weekend activities.

St Mary's School Ascot, a registered charity, exists to provide high quality education for Roman Catholic girls.

St Mary's School

(Founded 1873)
Calne, Wiltshire SN11 0DF
Tel: 01249 857200 Fax: 01249 857207

Headmistress: Mrs C J Shaw BA(London)

Date of appointment: 1996

Member of: GSA

Girls Boarding & Day

Religious affiliation: Church of England

Age range of pupils: Girls 11 – 18

Boarders from 11

No. of students enrolled as at 1.9.98: 388

VIth Form: 88

Average size of class: 16

Teacher/Pupil ratio: 1:8

Curriculum: Girls are prepared for GCSE and A level and University entrance.

Entry requirements: Common Entrance at 11+ and 12+.

Range of fees per annum as at 1.9.98:

Day: £8370

Boarding: £13,620

St Mary's School, which is set in attractive grounds of 25 acres on the edge of Calne, is an independent boarding and day school for 300 girls, most of whom go on to Universities or Colleges of Higher Education.

St Mary's has within its grounds its own Co-educational Day Preparatory School for boys and girls aged 4-11 years.

St Margaret's School (Calne 01249 857220) provides a happy environment in which boys and girls learn the value of hard work and how to accept discipline and responsibility.

For a prospectus please telephone either school's secretary.

The School has charity status (No A309482) and provides high quality education for children.

St Mary's Westbrook

Ravenlea Road, Folkestone, Kent CT20 2JU

Tel: 01303 851222 Fax: 01303 249901
e-mail: hm@marybrook.demon.co.uk
Internet: marybrook.demon.co.uk

Head: Christopher FitzGerald BA, CertEd, ACP, FRSA

Co-educational Day & Boarding

Age range of pupils: 2 – 16

Boarders from 7 years

No. of students enrolled as at 1.9.98: 222

Boys: 115 Girls: 107

Curriculum: National Curriculum plus Kent test; Common Entrance and GCSE. EAL for those for whom English is not their first language. Broad curriculum.

Entry requirements: Entry by interview and/or test. Scholarships for academics, sport, music, all-rounder.

Range of fees per annum as at 1.9.98:

Day: £3720 – £6615

Boarding: £7095 – £8865

A local international boarding and day school. Ten minutes from the Channel Tunnel. Excellent facilities and easily accessible from London and mainland Europe.

St Mary's Westbrook is a registered charity which exists to provide high quality education for children.

St Swithun's School

(Founded 1884)

Alresford Road, Winchester, Hampshire SO21 1HA

Tel: 01962 835700 Fax: 01962 835779

Headmistress: Dr H L Harvey BSc, PhD(London)

Date of appointment: 1995

Member of: GBGSA, GSA, BSA

Girls Boarding & Day

Religious affiliation: Church of England

Age range of pupils: Girls 11 – 18

Boarders from 11

No. of students enrolled as at 1.9.98: 580

Girls: 580 VIth Form: 117

Average size of class: 18-20

Curriculum: The School offers a flexible and broadly based academic education which enables girls to develop their individual potential. Nineteen subjects are offered at GCSE. Girls choose nine of which at least four are selected on an individual basis. Sixth Formers are offered a free choice from twenty-three subjects at A level plus A level General Studies.

Entry requirements: Common Entrance or testing and interview.

Range of fees per annum as at 1.9.98:

Day: £7740

Boarding: £12,795

Examinations offered including boards: GCSE: MEG, SEG, EdExcel, LEAG, NEAB; A Level: UCLES, NEAB, AEB, EdExcel, OCSEB; Music: Guildhall and Associated Board; Speech & Drama: Guildhall and Poetry Society.

The School occupies a fine site of 45 acres on the Downs to the east of Winchester, a mile from the centre of the town.

St Swithun's School Winchester is a registered charity (No. 307335) which exists to provide education to girls aged 11-18 years.

Stamford High School

(Founded 1876)

St Martin's, Stamford, Lincolnshire PE9 2LJ

Tel: 01780 484200 Fax: 01780 484201

e-mail: headss@shs.lincs.sch.uk

Excellent academic standards: GCSE: pass rate A*-C 98.21%; A Level: pass rate 55.36% A, B grades. High standards in Performing Arts, Music, Duke of Edinburgh Award and sport.

Principal: Dr P R Mason BSc, PhD, FRSA

Date of appointment: 1 September 1997

Member of: GSA

Girls Day & Boarding

Age range of pupils: 2 – 18

Boarders from 8

No. of students enrolled as at 1.9.98: 933

Boys: 62 Girls: 871 VIth Form: 184

Average size of class: 16-19

Teacher/Pupil ratio: 1:11.7

Curriculum: Full range of GCSE and A level subjects. Impressive university entrance, including Oxbridge.

Entry requirements: Own entrance examination.

Range of fees per annum as at 1.9.98:

Day: £3828 – £4848

Boarding: £8424 – £8508

The School is an integral part of this medieval market town of outstanding beauty. Excellent road and rail links. First class facilities. Boys' School (same foundation) close by. Continuity of education available at the Stamford Endowed Schools (Stamford High School and Stamford School) for Girls and Boys from 2-18 years.

The Stamford Endowed Schools exist to provide quality education for boys and girls.

Stamford School

(Founded 1532)

St Paul's Street, Stamford, Lincolnshire PE9 2BS

Tel: 01780 750300 Fax: 01780 750336

e-mail: headss@stamfordschool.lincs.sch.uk

Excellent academic standards: GCSE: pass rate A*-C 93.50%; A level: pass rate 58.14% A, B grades. High standards in Drama, Music, Duke of Edinburgh Award and sport. Large voluntary CCF.

Head: Dr P R Mason BSc, PhD, FRSA

Date of appointment: 1 September 1997

Member of: HMC, IAPS

Boys Day & Boarding

Religious affiliation: Church of England

Age range of pupils: 8 – 18

Boarders from 8

Co-educational Nursery: 2-4

Pre-Preparatory at Sister School: 4-8

No. of students enrolled as at 1.9.98: 863

Boys: 855 VIth Form: 195

Average size of class: 16-19

Teacher/Pupil ratio: 1:11.3

Curriculum: Full range of GCSE and A level subjects. Impressive university entrance, including Oxbridge.

Entry requirements: Own entrance examination.

Range of fees per annum as at 1.9.98:

Day: £3828 – £4848

Boarding: £8424 – £11,148

The School is an integral part of this medieval market town of outstanding beauty. Excellent road and rail links. First class facilities. Girls' School (same Foundation) close by. Continuity of education available at the Stamford Endowed Schools (Stamford School and Stamford High School) for Boys and Girls from 2-18 years.

The Stamford Endowed Schools exist to provide quality education for boys and girls.

Stanbridge Earls School

(Founded 1952)

Stanbridge Lane, Romsey, Hampshire SO51 0ZS

Tel: 01794 516777 Fax: 01794 511201

Head: Mr H Moxon MA, DipEd

Date of appointment: 1984

Member of: SHMIS, BSA, GBA, Corporate member British Dyslexia Association, CReSTeD

Co-educational Boarding & Day

Religious affiliation: Interdenominational

Age range of pupils: 11 – 18

Boarders from 11

No. of students enrolled as at 1.9.98: 182

Boys: 147 Girls: 35 VIth Form: 40

Average size of class: 10

Teacher/Pupil ratio: 1:6

Curriculum: All the traditional subjects are offered up to GCSE level but there is a great variety of alternatives designed to develop the strengths and interests of every pupil, such as Drama, Craft, Design and Technology, Motor Vehicle Studies, Photography. 13 subjects are available at A level, and GNVQ in Leisure and Tourism, Intermediate and Advanced Level. Many pupils are dyslexic but everyone takes GCSE and most achieve at least five C grades. A number of leavers go to University, Polytechnics, and other centres of Higher Education.

Entry requirements: By interview, School report and where appropriate educational psychologists' report.

Range of fees per annum as at 1.9.98:

Day: £9150 – £10,050

Boarding: £12,300 – £13,500

Examinations offered including boards: GCSE - SEG, MEG and NEA; A - London and AEB; GNVQ Leisure & Tourism, RSA.

Destination and career prospects of leavers: University, Polytechnics and other centres of further education or the Services, Banking, Engineering and Farming *etc.*

Academic & leisure facilities: The School has excellent facilities for all academic subjects. Accelerated learning centre for those with specific word learning difficulties (Dyslexia), 14 experienced specialist teachers. Maths Skills Centre for those with Dyscalcula, five specialist staff. Nearly all special needs lessons are one-to-one. There is a wide choice of games and the School has a large sports hall, indoor swimming pool, squash courts, floodlit tennis courts, vehicle engineering workshops and playing fields. Sailing is done from Lymington.

Stanbridge Earls is on the edge of the New Forest. It has 48 acres of beautiful wooded grounds which contain a chain of small lakes.

Stanbridge Earls is an educational charitable trust providing an education for boys and girls.

Don't forget to read the articles which appear at the front of this book.
They may save you a lot of time and trouble

The Edinburgh Academy

(Founded 1824)

42 Henderson Row, Edinburgh, EH3 5BL

Tel: 0131 556 4603 Fax: 0131 556 9353

Head: Rector J V Light MA

Date of appointment: 1994

Member of: HMC, IAPS

Boys Day & Boarding

Religious affiliation: Inter-denominational

Age range of pupils: Boys 11 – 18 Girls 16 – 18

Boarders from 8+ years

No. of students enrolled as at 1.9.98: 460

Boys: 460 VIth Form: 157

Average size of class: Max. 24

Teacher/Pupil ratio: 1:13

Curriculum: The Academy combines the strengths of Scottish education, to Higher, and English specialisation to A level and beyond. Eight to ten GCSE subjects ensure a broad general education on which career plans can be securely founded. Well run boarding houses in a City day school have special advantages for pupils and parents.

Entry requirements: Entry is by Head's report, entrance test or examination and interview.

Range of fees per annum as at 1.9.98:

Day: £5013 – £5703

Boarding: £11,469 – £12,159

Examinations offered including boards: GCSE (MEG), Highers (SQA), A levels (OCR), STEP, Oxford Entrance.

Over 80% of our pupils proceed to degree courses, mostly at Universities throughout UK.

The average amount required by a pupil in the Upper School to cover educational extras is £60 to £100 for books termly, and £80-£150 for examination fees (GCSE, Higher and A levels).

We have recent Oxford and Cambridge places in Classics, English, History, Mathematics, Modern Languages, Science and Engineering.

The Edinburgh Academy is a registered charity and exists to provide high quality education for boys and girls.

The International School of Choueifat UK

(Founded 1886, UK School Foundation 1983)

Ashwicke Hall, Marshfield, Wiltshire SN14 8AG

Tel: 01225 891841 Fax: 01225 891011
e-mail: iscuk@sabis.net
Internet: http://www..iscuk-sabis.net

Director: Salah Ayche BSc, MSc

Date of appointment: 1994

Co-educational Boarding

Age range of pupils: 10 – 18+

No. of students enrolled as at 1.9.98:

Boys: 76 Girls: 14 VIth Form: 44

Teacher/Pupil ratio: 1:5

Curriculum: The International School of Choueifat offers courses leading to IGCSE and A levels (London, Cambridge, SEG & AEB Boards), SAT I and II and Advanced Placement. It also offers intensive courses to students with academic problems or students wishing to transfer from their national curriculum to the English or American system.

Subject specialities and academic track record: The School stresses Mathematics, Sciences and bilingualism. Its primary academic objective is to prepare students for university, and it has placed students in some of the most prestigious universities of the western world.

Entry requirements: Grade and report from previous school, interview and placement exam.

Range of fees per annum as at 1.9.98:

Boarding: £9400 – £10,300

Average amount required by pupil to cover educational extras is £350 per annum.

Academic & leisure facilities:

The academic/leisure/sports facilities include, besides the standard facilities, science laboratories and a computer room, music rooms and a sports complex that includes a heated swimming pool, a squash court and a cafeteria. The combination of the estate and the modern sports complex allows extensive facilities for recreational and physical education. The School grounds also provide settings and subjects for students of art and nature. Those who enjoy music, folk dancing, photography or simply rambling will find their tastes amply catered for.

Situated in 150 acres of woodlands in the heart of Wiltshire, the School is within convenient reach of Heathrow Airport. It is one of a group of 18 schools established in the Middle East, Europe, the USA and Asia. Ease of movement between branches is ensured by a common educational system and philosophy.

The King's School, Canterbury

(Founded 597)

Canterbury, Kent CT1 2ES

Tel: 01227 595501 Fax: 01227 595595
e-mail: headmaster@kings-school.co.uk
Internet: www.kings-school.co.uk

Head: Rev Canon Keith Wilkinson BA, MA, FRSA

Date of appointment: 1996

Member of: HMC

Co-educational Boarding & Day

Religious affiliation: Church of England

Age range of pupils: 13 – 18

Boarders from 13

No. of students enrolled as at 1.9.98: 754

Boys: 424 Girls: 330 VIth Form: 346

Average size of class: 16 to GCSE; 10 in Sixth Form

Teacher/Pupil ratio: 1:9

Curriculum: All pupils study a broad range of subjects in the first year. In the second and third years, for GCSE, they choose 10 subjects. English, Maths, Science and French are compulsory. Pupils also choose four subjects from a further thirteen subjects (including at least one chosen creative subject) without timetabling restrictions. Pupils may offer the three separate sciences instead of double-award science. In the Sixth Form all do at least three A level subjects, and are also expected to take a subsidiary subject (perhaps AS level or GCSE) and to take part in a modular general studies programme.

Entry requirements: At 13 pupils take CE or an entrance scholarship exam; it is also possible to enter at 16. At 16 the method of entry is by test (taken at King's in the preceding November) and interview. Scholarships may be awarded on the basis of this entrance test.

Range of fees per annum as at 1.9.98:

Day: £6945 – £10,335

Boarding: £9885 – £14,955

Pre-prep: £3960

Examinations offered including boards: GCSE and A level; several different Boards are used.

Subject specialities and academic track record: In league tables based on pupils' performance (ie points score per pupil) the School comes in the top 30 with the highest ranking of any co-educational boarding school.

Destination/career prospects of leavers: More than 99% go on to degree courses (20% to Oxbridge).

Academic & leisure facilities: Classrooms are either purpose-built or converted from the monastic buildings. The School has a new recreation centre which includes a full-size heated swimming pool, six squash courts and a fitness suite, and the extensive playing fields include two Astroturf surfaces.

Religious activities: Each Sunday there is a service in

the Cathedral, daily communion is held in school chapels. There are daily assemblies and regular House prayers.

Scholarships: Up to 20 academic scholarships and about a dozen music scholarships may be awarded each year, their value ranging from 20% to 50% of fees. Additional (means-tested) help may be available. There are also Art scholarships whose value is about 10% of fees.

The King's School is an ancient foundation whose roots go back to the sixth century and the founder of English Christianity, St Augustine. Almost all the school buildings are in the superb setting of the Cathedral Precincts or the nearby St Augustine's Abbey. The Senior School, which became fully co-educational in 1990, is organised around 13 Houses which are divided between the Cathedral Precincts and St Augustine's Abbey. The Junior School is situated some two and a half miles away at Sturry, in a 16th Century manor house set in 80 acres.

The music in the school is of outstanding quality and vigour. Drama is also very strong. Each year the school presents its own festival of music and drama (King's Week) which is attended by thousands. Cultural recreations and hobbies are encouraged through some 25 societies managed (with advice) by the boys and girls themselves, and through a programme of 'Activities' which occupies one afternoon each week. There is a flourishing CCF contingent and considerable emphasis on outdoor pursuits and a fine record in the Duke of Edinburgh's Award Scheme. Lectures and recitals by distinguished visitors take place each term.

The King's School, a registered charity, exists to provide education for boys and girls aged 5 to 18 inclusive.

The King's School Ely

(Established before 970 AD)

Ely, Cambridgeshire CB7 4DB

Tel: 01353 660700 Fax: 01353 662187

The King's School Ely is welcoming, enthusiastic and well ordered. It develops children to be confident, well adjusted, considerate and prepared for their future life, whether their interests lie in academic or other activity. Sport, music, art, drama and outdoor pursuits are all strong. The delightful setting beside Ely's majestic Cathedral makes real the school's 1000-year history.

Head: Mr R H Youdale MA(Cantab)

Date of appointment: 1991

Member of: GSA, HMC, IAPS, CSA

Co-educational Day & Boarding

Religious affiliation: Church of England

Age range of pupils: 2 – 18

Boarders from 8

No. of students enrolled as at 1.9.98: 878

Boys: 489 Girls: 389 VIth Form: 126

Average size of class: 20

Teacher/Pupil ratio: 1:7.5

Curriculum: A full range to GCSE and A level, including Design & Technology, Sports Studies, Classics, Business Studies, Music, Psychology and Spanish; and many available at AS level.

Entry requirements: For entry at 11+: passing the school's own one-day assessment. For the Senior School: the 13+ Entrance Examination or, for 16+, five passes at GCSE.

Range of fees per annum as at 1.9.98:

Day: £4068 – £9108

Weekly Boarding: £9294 – £12,948

Boarding: £9549 – £13,263

Magnificent medieval buildings (and purpose-built new ones) beside the great Cathedral. Small and peaceful, Ely is only one hour from London by rail and easily reached from M11 and A14.

The King's School Ely exists to educate young people.

The Red Maids' School

(Founded 1634)

Westbury-on-Trym, Bristol BS9 3AW

Tel: 0117 962 2641 Fax: 0117 962 1687

Headmistress: Miss Susan Hampton JP, BSc

Date of appointment: 1987

Member of: GSA and GBGSA

Girls Boarding & Day

Religious affiliation: Non-denominational. Boarders attend a Church of England service or Roman Catholic Mass on Sundays.

Age range of pupils: Girls 11 – 18

Boarders from 11

No. of students enrolled as at 1.9.98: 500

Girls: 500 VIth Form: 140

Average size of class: 20 to 25

Teacher/Pupil ratio: 1:11

Curriculum: Religious Education, English, History, Geography, Spanish, French, German, Italian, Latin, Civilisation, Russian, Economics, Business Studies, Mathematics, Physics, Chemistry, Biology, Technology, Home Economics, Textiles, Art, Music, Drama, Information Technology and Physical Education.

Entry requirements: Entrance examination held in January to select girls for admission the following September. Papers taken in English, Mathematics and Verbal Reasoning. Also direct entry to Sixth Form.

Range of fees per annum as at 1.9.98:

Day: £4260

Boarding: £8520

Since its founding in 1634 the School has grown and developed to become a highly successful school for girls with a strong academic bias.

The Red Maids' School is a registered charity and has existed since 1634 to provide an education for girls.

Information about day schools can be found in
Which School ?
also published by John Catt Educational Ltd

The Royal Masonic School for Girls

(Founded 1788)

Rickmansworth Park, Rickmansworth, Hertfordshire WD3 4HF

Tel: 01923 773168 Fax: 01923 896729
e-mail: enquiries@royalmasonic.herts.sch.uk Internet: www.royalmasonic.herts.sch.uk

Headmistress: Mrs I M Andrews MA(Oxon)

Date of appointment: 1992

Member of: GSA

Girls Day & Boarding

Religious affiliation: Church of England

Age range of pupils: 4 – 18

Boarders from 7

No. of students enrolled as at 1.9.98: 720

Girls: 720 VIth Form: 120

Average size of class: 18

Teacher/Pupil ratio: 1:12

Curriculum: A broad and balanced education leads to a wide range of GCSE options in addition to the core curriculum of Mathematics, English, Integrated Science, French and PE. 19 different Advanced levels, as well as one or two year vocational courses, are available for Sixth Form girls.

Subject specialities: Flexible combinations of A levels in Sciences, Humanities, Languages and Social Sciences. GNVQ courses in Business Studies and Health & Social Care provide an alternative to A levels. Information Technology and Word Processing is available to all girls. Excellent Music and Drama.

Entry requirements: School Entrance Exam and interview.

Range of fees per annum as at 1.9.98:

Day: £3093 – £6009

Boarding: £6078 – £9876

No additional charges for field work courses or examination fees.

Examinations offered including boards: A variety of GCSE boards, and A levels Boards. Associated Board Examinations in Music, Speech & Drama. RSA and Cambridge IT Certificates.

Destination/career prospects of leavers: Most girls go on to Higher Education in Universities and Polytechnics. Others embark directly on business careers, enter service and leisure industries or caring professions.

The Royal Masonic School Charitable Trust exists for the advancement of education.

The Royal School, Hampstead

(Founded 1855)

65 Rosslyn Hill, Hampstead, London NW3 5UD

Tel: 0171 794 7707 Fax: 0171 431 6741

Headmistress: Mrs C A Sibson BA(Oxon)

Date of appointment: 1992

Girls Day & Boarding

Religious affiliation: All religions welcome

Age range of pupils: 4 – 18

Boarders from 7

No. of students enrolled as at 1.9.98: 200

Girls: 200 VIth Form: 15

Average size of class: 18

Teacher/Pupil ratio: 1:10

Curriculum: Balanced curriculum, including two languages and three sciences leading to GCSE and A levels. Wide range of sports offered, together with music and drama.

Entry requirements: Entry by interview, tests and previous school reports. Scholarships available at 11 and for Sixth Form.

Range of fees per annum as at 1.9.98:

Day: £3855 – £4587

Weekly Boarding: £6300 – £8262

Boarding: £8100 – £10,062

The School stands in pleasant spacious surroundings with excellent access to all major termini and to London's cultural, educational and recreational facilities.

The Royal School, Hampstead, exists as a charitable trust to provide a sound education for servicemens' daughters and other girls.

Authoritative articles covering many aspects of boarding are at the front of this book

---

The Royal Wolverhampton School

(Founded 1850)

Penn Road, Wolverhampton, West Midlands WV3 0EG

Tel: 01902 341230 Fax: 01902 344496
e-mail: head-rws@btinternet.com

The Royal Wolverhampton School offers continuity of education for boys and girls from nursery up to university entrance. Behind its impressive Victorian facade lies a school with thoroughly modern facilities. Noted for its friendly atmosphere, small classes and excellent pastoral care, the School aims to produce confident and well-rounded individuals.

Headmistress: Mrs B A Evans BSc, HNC

Date of appointment: 1995

Co-educational Day & Boarding

Age range of pupils: 2 – 18

Boarders from 7 years.

No. of students enrolled as at 1.9.98: 673

Boys: 290 Girls: 183 VIth Form: 100

Average size of class: 15

Teacher/Pupil ratio: 1:13

Curriculum: Our School provides a broad-based curriculum, designed to highlight the strengths of each pupil. Senior School offers a choice of tweny subjects at GCSE and A/AS level. In Junior School, National Curriculum tests are taken at the end of key stages 1 and 2 and excellent results are achieved.

Subject specialities and academic track record: Music and Sport play a major role. Pupils have an opportunity to play over twenty different instruments and can participate in fifteen sporting activities.

Entry requirements: Entry to Junior School by informal test and to Senior School by own entrance examination. Academic, Music and Sport Scholarships. Bursary for service families.

Range of fees per annum as at 1.9.98:

Day: £2820 – £5880

Boarding: £9525 – £11,625

Examinations offered including boards: Most pupils take nine GCSEs, comprising 6 compulsory subjects and three options. At A level, students take three or four examinations in addition to General Studies.

Destination/career prospects of leavers: Great care is taken to advise students on universities and careers. At least 95% of Sixth Formers continue their education at university.

Academic & leisure facilities: Our modern facilities include a 25m indoor Swimming Pool, 3 Information Technology suites, an Art Craft and Design centre, boarding houses and 6 Science Laboratories.

Our 26½ acre site is conveniently situated in a residential area of Wolverhampton, which provides easy access to the Midlands' motorway network.

The Royal Wolverhampton School is a registered charity which exists solely to provide an education for children

Truro High School for Girls

(Founded 1880)

Falmouth Road, Truro, Cornwall TR1 2HU
Tel: 01872 272830 Fax: 01872 279393
e-mail: thsl@rmplc.co.uk

Head: Mr J Graham-Brown BA(Hons), MPhil

Date of appointment: September 1992

Member of: GSA, GBSA

Girls Day & Boarding

Religious affiliation: Church of England

Age range of pupils: Boys 3 – 5 Girls 3 – 18

Boarders from 9

No. of students enrolled as at 1.9.98: 487

VIth Form: 89

Average size of class: Junior 15, Senior 20

Teacher/Pupil ratio: 1:10

Curriculum: Wide academic curriculum to GCSE and A level.

Entry requirements: Own entrance test for junior and main school, five academic GCSEs and school reference for Sixth Form.

Range of fees per annum as at 1.9.98:

Day: £3330 – £5025

Boarding: £9285

Separate fees for nursery class

Ex. Direct-grant. The School is on high ground overlooking Truro, near areas of outstanding beauty and interest, but a short walk from the city centre.

Truro High School for Girls Charitable Trust exists to give education to children.

Tudor Hall School

(Founded 1850)

Wykham Park, Banbury, Oxfordshire OX16 9UR
Tel: 01295 263434 Fax: 01295 253264

Headmistress: Miss N Godfrey BA

Date of appointment: 1984

Member of: GSA

Girls Boarding

Religious affiliation: Church of England

Age range of pupils: 11 – 18

Boarders from 11

No. of students enrolled as at 1.9.98: 265

Girls: 265 VIth Form: 79

Average size of class: 16

Teacher/Pupil ratio: 1:8

Curriculum: English, Maths, History, Geography, Religious Education, three Sciences, Computing, Latin, French, German, Spanish, Italian, Art; Cookery, Russian and Japanese are also available. Needlework, Music, Art History, Economics and Theatre Studies to A level and general subjects. Greek, CDT, Politics.

Entry requirements: 11+, 12+, 13+ Common Entrance. Sixth Form selection day plus five GCSEs including English Language, with B grades in subjects to be taken at A level.

Range of fees per annum as at 1.9.98:

Boarding: £11,955

Tudor Hall is a country house on the outskirts of Banbury situated near Junction 11 of the M40 between Oxford and Stratford, London and Birmingham. There are modern facilities for music, sports, art, CDT, languages, information technology and home economics. There are a wide range of activities and senior girls take part in social service.

Tudor Hall School is a registered charity providing good quality education for girls aged 11-18 years.

Warwick School

(Founded 914)

Myton Road, Warwick, Warwickshire CV34 6PP

Tel: 01926 776400 Fax: 01926 401259

e-mail: enquiries@warwick.warwks.sch.uk

Head: Dr P J Cheshire BSc, PhD

Date of appointment: September 1988

Member of: HMC and GBA

Boys Day & Boarding

Religious affiliation: Christian

Age range of pupils: 7 – 18

No. of students enrolled as at 1.9.98: 1014

VIth Form: 200

Average size of class: 20

Teacher/Pupil ratio: 1:11

Curriculum: A broad curriculum to GCSE of English, Mathematics, Science, French, DT, Art, Music or Drama, IT, History and/or Geography; a further language. Either four A levels or three A levels and two AS levels, to include General Studies A level in the Sixth Form.

Entry requirements: Entrance examinations in English and Mathematics at 7+, 8+, 9+, 10+, 11+ and 12+, examinations based on Common Entrance syllabus at 13+. Five GCSE exams at A*, A or B for Sixth Form.

Subject specialities and academic track record: On average 94% gain A, B or C gardes in GCSE; 92% pass rate at A level; 14 places p.a. at Oxbridge.

Destination and career prospects of leavers: Mainly University and Professions - Engineering, Medicine, Law, Accountancy and Business.

Range of fees per annum as at 1.9.98:

Day: £4830 – £5466

Weekly Boarding: £10,263 – £10,899

Boarding: £11,031 – £11,667

No additional fees are needed for educational extras.

Academic & leisure facilities: Each academic department has its own premises and resource area. Extensive investment in Academic and Boarding facilities in the last ten years. There are seventy five societies in the School; many opportunities for drama and music. Recent developments include new building for ICT and Library together with an imaginative visionary Performing Arts Theatre. Extensive playing fields - most sports played.

Fifty acre site on outskirts of Warwick - two miles from Leamington Railway Station and about two miles from M40.

Warwick Schools Charity exists to provide high quality education.

Wispers School

(1947)

High Lane, Haslemere, Surrey GU27 1AD

Tel: 01428 643646 Fax: 01428 641120
e-mail: head@wispers.prestel.co.uk
Internet: www.homeusers.prestel.co.uk/wispers

Wispers School is an independent boarding, weekly and day school for 100 girls aged between 11 and 18. The School is administered by a Board of Governors and is registered as an Educational Charitable Trust, formed for the purpose of excellence in education.

Head: Henry Beltran BA(Hons), PGCE
Date of appointment: 1.9.79
Girls Boarding & Day
Age range of pupils: Girls 11 – 18
No. of students enrolled as at 1.9.98: 100

Range of fees per annum as at 1.9.98:
Day: £6990
Boarding: £10,860
Why choose Wispers?
Wispers School is the only small independent school

for girls aged 11 to 18 in and around Haslemere, Surrey. This means that we know every girl and her parents extremely well.

Our GCSE and A level timetables are tailor made to suit each girl's requirements. Our pupils obtain sound results. We expect our bright pupils to excel. Our less gifted pupils often do extremely well. Public examination results for 1998 were GCSE 77% pass rate A to C and A and AS level 85% pass rate grades A to E. Our size allows more girls to represent the school in sports, public speaking, school productions, concerts, charity and general activities.

We welcome girls from abroad and from counties all across the United Kingdom. Special arrangements are made for overseas boarders to ensure safe transfers from home to school. Many of our pupils live in Surrey and many in London are weekly boarders going home on weekends.

We are a few miles from Guildford, conveniently equidistant from Heathrow and Gatwick airports, and also within easy reach of Chichester, Portsmouth and London.

Wispers has always been a small school and we have maintained our unique identity in times of change and school mergers. Our school's security lies in its rich assets, it has wonderful facilities and is set in 26 acres of outstanding natural beauty.

A partnership with parents

We provide a caring, responsible and forward looking approach to education in partnership with you. We welcome discussion about your daughter and we will keep in touch with you every step of the way.

The school puts on an equal footing with academic sucess and university entrance, moral awareness and a wide ecumenical experience of Christian witness. In particular we expect all our pupils to willingly accept their school and local community responsibilities and to develop adult life skills needed for employment and life long learning in the 21st century.

With the guidance offered by our specialist staff and the support you provide, our pupils distinguish themselves with academic success and by being decent, trustworthy people.

"It was particularly pleasant to note that the older boarders are encouraged, and appear to take pleasure in acting as role models to the younger pupils. This approach appears to have successfully fostered a sense of responsibilty and younger boarders spoken to appeared confident in approaching the older girls if they were experiencing any problems" Inspection Report (The Children Act) November 1998.

Their readiness to serve others is widely known and respected. The girls develop lifelong loyalties to their friends and school. The proof of this loyalty and of the school's success is that so many of them continue to keep in touch with us, often helping current pupils with work experience, and decide to send their own daughters to Wispers.

We are particularly interested in encouraging specialised vocal potential through our voice/choral scholarships. Successful applicants study singing under our Director of Music who is Head of Junior Voice at the Royal Academy of Music, London. Several former pupils have entered both the Royal Academy of Music and the Royal Northern College of Music, Manchester. Further details can be gained from the admissions secretary.

We look forward to welcoming you at Wispers.

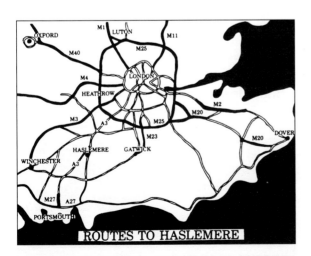

ROUTES TO HASLEMERE

Wychwood School

(Founded 1897)

74 Banbury Road, Oxford, Oxfordshire OX2 6JR
Tel: 01865 557976 Fax: 01865 556806

Headmistress: Mrs S Wingfield Digby BA(Hons) Oxon, PGCE(London)

Date of appointment: 1997

Member of: GSA, GBGSA, ISIS, SHA

Girls Boarding & Day

Religious affiliation: Non denominational

Age range of pupils: 11 – 18

Boarders from 11

No. of students enrolled as at 1.9.98: 170

Girls: 170 VIth Form: 30

Average size of class: 22

Teacher/Pupil ratio: 1:8

Curriculum: All traditional subjects taught to GCSE, A level and Oxbridge.

There are strong traditions in music, art, the sciences and languages; computer studies available to everyone.

Entry requirements: Wychwood Entrance Test at 10+ and interview. Minimum of six GCSE levels (C grades and above) for entry to VIth Form. Interviews at other entry points.

Range of fees per annum as at 1.9.98:

Day: £5070

Boarding: £8040

Wychwood is a charitable trust set up for educational purposes and situated near the centre of Oxford, makes maximum use of all the cultural and sporting facilities of a university city. Co-operative government by staff and girls exists.

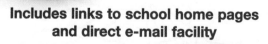

Directory of
Pre-Preparatory, Preparatory and
Senior Independent Boarding Schools

Bedfordshire

Bedford

BEDFORD HIGH SCHOOL
Bromham Road, Bedford, Bedfordshire MK40 2BS
Tel: 01234 360221
Head: Mrs B E Stanley BA
Type: Girls Day & Boarding 7 –18
No of pupils: G926 VIth240
Fees: FB £8601–£10,170 WB £8601–£10,170
DAY £3831 –£5400

BEDFORD MODERN SCHOOL
Manton Lane, Bedford, Bedfordshire MK41 7NT
Tel: 01234 364331
Head: S Smith MA
Type: Boys Day & Boarding 12 –18
No of pupils: B1103 VIth278
Fees: FB £7560–£9189
DAY £3210 –£4839

BEDFORD PREPARATORY SCHOOL
De Parys Avenue, Bedford, Bedfordshire MK40 2TU
Tel: 01234 352007/352740
Head: Mr C Godwin BSc, MA
Type: Boys Boarding & Day 7 –13
No of pupils: 412 B412
Fees: FB £8235–£9765 WB £7875–£9405
DAY £4965 –£6495

BEDFORD SCHOOL
De Parys Avenue, Bedford, Bedfordshire MK40 2TU
Tel: 01234 353493
Head: Dr I P Evans MA, PhD, CChem, FRSC
Type: Boys Day & Boarding 13 –18
No of pupils: 803 B803 VIth298
Fees: FB £14,130WB £13,005 DAY £8010

Berkshire

Ascot

★HEATHFIELD SCHOOL
London Road, Ascot, Berkshire SL5 8BQ
Tel: 01344 882955
Head: Mrs J M Benammar BA, MèsL
Type: Girls Boarding 11 –18
No of pupils: 215 G215 VIth54
Fees: FB £14,625

HURST LODGE
Bagshot Road, Ascot, Berkshire SL5 9JU
Tel: 01344 622154
Head: Mrs A Smit
Type: Girls Day & Boarding B2–7 G2–18
No of pupils: B40 G170 VIth10
Fees: FB £11,550
DAY £2100 –£6825

LICENSED VICTUALLERS' SCHOOL
London Road, Ascot, Berkshire SL5 8DR
Tel: 01344 882770
Head: I A Mullins BEd(Hons), MSc, MBIM
Type: Co-educational Boarding & Day 5 –18
No of pupils: 701 B356 G345 VIth120
Fees: FB £8468–£11,130 WB £8468–£11,130
DAY £3375 –£6810

★PAPPLEWICK
Windsor Road, Ascot, Berkshire SL5 7LH
Tel: 01344 621488
Head: Mr D R Llewellyn BA, DipEd
Type: Boys Boarding & Day 7 –13
No of pupils: 186
Fees: FB £10,920 DAY £8388

ST GEORGE'S SCHOOL
Ascot, Berkshire SL5 7DZ
Tel: 01344 620273
Principle: Mrs A M Griggs BA, TCert
Type: Girls Boarding & Day 11 –18
No of pupils: G214 VIth75
Fees: FB £11,625 DAY £6825

★ST MARY'S SCHOOL, ASCOT
St Mary's Road, Ascot, Berkshire SL5 9JF
Tel: 01344 623721
Principal: Mrs Mary Breen
Type: Girls Boarding & Day 11 –18
No of pupils: 354 VIth108
Fees: FB £13,440 DAY £8730

SUNNINGDALE SCHOOL
Sunningdale, Ascot, Berkshire SL5 9PY
Tel: 01344 620159
Head: A J N Dawson DipIAPS & T M E Dawson DipIAPS
Type: Boys Boarding 8 –13
No of pupils: 105 B105
Fees: FB £8800

Bracknell

LAMBROOK HAILEYBURY SCHOOL
Winkfield Row, Bracknell, Berkshire RG42 6LU
Tel: 01344 882717
Head: Mr B J Hare MA
Type: Co-educational Boarding & Day 4 –13
No of pupils: B255 G30
Fees: FB £2300–£3100 DAY £1175 –£2220

Crowthorne

WELLINGTON COLLEGE
Crowthorne, Berkshire RG45 7PU
Tel: 01344 771588
Head: C J Driver BA, BEd, MPhil
Type: Boys Boarding & Day B13–18 G16–18
No of pupils: 809 B752 G57 VIth364
Fees: FB £13,350 DAY £9735

Newbury

CHEAM HAWTREYS
Headley, Newbury, Berkshire RG19 8LD
Tel: 01635 268381
Head: Mr M R Johnson BEd
Type: Co-educational Day & Boarding 3 –13
No of pupils: 218 B141 G77
Fees: FB £10,725 DAY £4320 –£7905

HORRIS HILL
Newtown, Newbury, Berkshire RG20 9DJ
Tel: 01635 40594
Head: N J Chapman BA
Type: Boys Boarding & Day 7 –13
No of pupils: 115 B115
Fees: FB £10,920 DAY £7650

MARLSTON HOUSE PREPARATORY SCHOOL
Hermitage, Newbury, Berkshire RG18 9UL
Tel: 01635 200293
Head: N P W Park MA(Oxon)
Type: Girls Day 3 –13
No of pupils: 70 G70
Fees: DAY £3650

Reading

BRADFIELD COLLEGE
Bradfield, Reading, Berkshire RG7 6AR
Tel: 0118 974 4203
Head: Mr P B Smith MA
Type: Boys Boarding B13–18 G16–18
No of pupils: B500 G120
Fees: FB £4275 DAY £3206

DOUAI SCHOOL
Upper Woolhampton, Reading, Berkshire RG7 5TH
Tel: 0118 971 5200
Head: Dr Peter M McLaughlin BA(Hons), PhD
Type: Co-educational Boarding & Day 10 –18
No of pupils: B143 G48 VIth54
Fees: FB £9240–£11,520 DAY £6060 –£7440

ELSTREE SCHOOL
Woolhampton, Reading, Berkshire RG7 5TD
Tel: 0118 971 3302
Head: Mr S M Hill MA(Cantab)
Type: Co-educational Day & Boarding B3–13 G3–8
No of pupils: 250 B235 G15
Fees: FB £10,500 DAY £4425 –£7500

LEIGHTON PARK SCHOOL
Shinfield Road, Reading, Berkshire RG2 7DH
Tel: 0118 987 2065
Head: J H Dunston MA, AIL, FRSA
Type: Co-educational Boarding & Day 11 –18
No of pupils: 367 B235 G132 VIth131
Fees: FB £10,890–£12,807 DAY £8082 –£9612

*PANGBOURNE COLLEGE
Pangbourne, Reading, Berkshire RG8 8LA
Tel: 01189 842101
Head: Mr Anthony Hudson MA(Oxon), DipEd(London)
Type: Co-educational Boarding & Day 11 –18
No of pupils: 354 VIth110
Fees: FB £9240–£13,197 DAY £6705 –£10,485

QUEEN ANNE'S SCHOOL
6 Henley Road, Caversham, Reading, Berkshire RG4 6DX
Tel: 0118 947 1582
Head: Mrs Deborah Forbes MA(Oxon)
Type: Girls Boarding & Day 11 –18
No of pupils: G320 VIth80
Fees: FB £12,465 DAY £8160

ST ANDREW'S SCHOOL
Buckhold, Pangbourne, Reading, Berkshire RG8 8QA
Tel: 0118 974 4276
Head: Mr J M Snow BA, CertEd
Type: Co-educational Day & Boarding 3 –13
No of pupils: B158 G102
Fees: WB £8700–£8820 DAY £3900 –£6930

THE ORATORY PREPARATORY SCHOOL
Great Oaks, Goring Heath, Reading, Berkshire RG8 7SF
Tel: 0118 984 4511
Head: D L Sexon BA, PGCE
Type: Co-educational Day & Boarding 3 –13
No of pupils: 340 B260 G80
Fees: FB £8970 DAY £1795 –£6475

THE ORATORY SCHOOL
Woodcote, Reading, Berkshire RG8 OPJ
Tel: 01491 680207
Head: Mr S W Barrow BA
Type: Boys Boarding & Day 11 –18
No of pupils: B384 VIth133
Fees: FB £10,557–£13,560 DAY £7686 –£9480

Sandhurst

EAGLE HOUSE
Sandhurst, Berkshire GU47 8PH
Tel: 01344 772134
Head: Mr S J Carder MA(Oxon), MBA(Educ)
Type: Co-educational Day & Boarding 3 –13
No of pupils: B201 G32
Fees: FB £10,335 DAY £4320 –£7260

Sonning-on-Thames

READING BLUE COAT SCHOOL
Holme Park, Sonning Lane, Sonning-on-Thames,
Berkshire RG4 6SU
Tel: 0118 944 1005
Head: S James W McArthur BSc, MA, FcollP
Type: Boys Day & Boarding B11–18 G16–18
No of pupils: B550 G50 Vlth190
Fees: FB £10,554 WB £10,221 DAY £5790

Thatcham

★DOWNE HOUSE SCHOOL
Cold Ash, Thatcham, Berkshire RG18 9JJ
Tel: 01635 200286
Head: Mrs E McKendrick BA(Liverpool)
Type: Girls Boarding & Day 11 –18
No of pupils: 554 G554 Vlth166
Fees: FB £14,175 DAY £10,275

Windsor

ETON COLLEGE
Windsor, Berkshire SL4 6DW
Tel: 01753 671000
Head: John E Lewis MA
Type: Boys Boarding 13 –18
No of pupils: B1286 Vlth515
Fees: FB £13,947

ST GEORGE'S SCHOOL
Windsor Castle, Windsor, Berkshire SL4 1QF
Tel: 01753 865553
Head: Rev Roger P Marsh, BD, MA, ACK, CertEd
Type: Boys Boarding & Day 3 –13
No of pupils: B132 G44
Fees: FB £9495–£9690 DAY £1410 –£7215

ST JOHN'S BEAUMONT
Windsor, Berkshire SL4 2JN
Tel: 01784 432428
Head: D St J Gogarty MA, PGCE
Type: Boys Boarding & Day 4 –13
No of pupils: B250
Fees: FB £10,767 WB £9096 DAY £3762 –£6612

Wokingham

BEARWOOD COLLEGE
Bearwood, Wokingham, Berkshire RG41 5BG
Tel: 0118 978 6915
Head: Mr S G G Aiano MA(Cantab)
Type: Co-educational Boarding & Day 11 –18
No of pupils: 228
Fees: FB £10,590–£11,700 DAY £6204 –£6825

LUCKLEY-OAKFIELD SCHOOL
Luckley Road, Wokingham, Berkshire RG40 3EU
Tel: 0118 978 4175
Head: Mr R C Blake MA(Oxon), MPhil(Soton)
Type: Girls Day & Boarding 11 –18
No of pupils: G272 Vlth72
Fees: FB £10,092 WB £9315 DAY £5805

LUDGROVE
Wokingham, Berkshire RG40 3AB
Tel: 0118 978 9881
Head: G W P Barber MA & C N J Marston MA
Type: Boys Boarding 8 –13
No of pupils: B197
Fees: FB £9150

Bristol

Bristol

BADMINTON JUNIOR SCHOOL
Westbury-on-Trym, Bristol BS9 3BA
Tel: 0117 905 5222
Head: Mrs A Lloyd CertEd(Oxford), LGSM
Type: Girls Boarding & Day 4 –11
No of pupils: G84
Fees: FB £9375 DAY £3525 –£4950

CLIFTON COLLEGE
32 College Road, Bristol BS8 3JH
Tel: 0117 973 9187
Head: A H Monro MA(Cantab)
Type: Co-educational Boarding & Day 13 –18
No of pupils: 680 B490 G190 VIth280
Fees: FB £13,245 DAY £9035

CLIFTON COLLEGE PREPARATORY SCHOOL
The Avenue, Clifton, Bristol BS8 3HE
Tel: 0117 973 7264
Head: Dr R J Acheson MA, PhD
Type: Co-educational Boarding & Day 3 –13
No of pupils: 378 B261 G117
Fees: FB £8910–£9225 DAY £2370 –£6315

CLIFTON HIGH SCHOOL
College Road, Clifton, Bristol BS8 3JD
Tel: 0117 973 0201
Head: Mrs M C Culligan BA(Hons)
Type: Co-educational Day & Boarding B3–11 G3–18
No of pupils: 736 B101 G635 VIth91
Fees: FB £8070 DAY £1275 –£4710

COLSTON'S COLLEGIATE SCHOOL
Stapleton, Bristol BS16 1BJ
Tel: 0117 965 5207
Head: D G Crawford BA, DLC
Type: Co-educational Boarding & Day 3 –18
No of pupils: 638 B464 G174 VIth63
Fees: FB £9615–£11,460 WB £9315–£11,010
DAY £3570 –£6210

QUEEN ELIZABETH'S HOSPITAL
Berkeley Place, Clifton, Bristol BS8 1JX
Tel: 0117 929 1856
Head: Dr Richard Gliddon BSc, PhD, FIBiol
Type: Boys Day & Boarding 11 –18
No of pupils: B530 VIth130
Fees: FB £8385 DAY £4560

THE DOWNS SCHOOL
Wraxall, Bristol BS48 1PF
Tel: 01275 852008
Head: Mr J K Macpherson BEd, JP
Type: Co-educational Boarding & Day 3 –13
No of pupils: B210 G70
Fees: FB £8430 DAY £1935 –£5775

★THE RED MAIDS' SCHOOL
Westbury-on-Trym, Bristol BS9 3AW
Tel: 0117 962 2641
Head: Miss Susan Hampton JP, BSc
Type: Girls Boarding & Day 11 –18
No of pupils: 500 G500 VIth140
Fees: FB £8520 DAY £4260

TOCKINGTON MANOR SCHOOL
Tockington, Bristol BS32 4NY
Tel: 01454 613229
Head: Mr R G Tovey CertEd
Type: Co-educational Day & Boarding 2 –14
No of pupils: B130 G90
Fees: FB £8595–£9555 DAY £3240 –£6330

WESTWING SCHOOL
Kyneton House, Thornbury, Bristol BS12 2JZ
Tel: 01454 412311
Head: Mrs D Kershaw BA(Hons), PGCE, MEd
Type: Co-educational Boarding & Day 3 –18
No of pupils: B23 G60 VIth5
Fees: FB £8550–£9339 DAY £2361 –£4608

Buckinghamshire

Aylesbury

ASHFOLD SCHOOL
Dorton, Aylesbury, Buckinghamshire HP18 9NG
Tel: 01844 238237
Head: Mr M O M Chitty
Type: Co-educational Boarding & Day 3 –14
No of pupils: B120 G50
Fees: FB £7965 WB £7965 DAY £1935 –£6060

Buckingham

STOWE SCHOOL
Buckingham, Buckinghamshire MK18 5EH
Tel: 01280 813164
Head: Jeremy G L Nichols MA
Type: Boys Boarding & Day B13–18 G16–18
No of pupils: B256 G104 VIth301
Fees: FB £14,175 DAY £9950

Farnham Royal

CALDICOTT
Crown Lane, Farnham Royal, Buckinghamshire SL2 3SL
Tel: 01753 644457
Head: Mr S J G Doggart BA(Cantab)
Type: Boys Boarding & Day 7 –13
No of pupils: 257 B257
Fees: FB £10,200 DAY £7650

High Wycombe

GODSTOWE PREPARATORY SCHOOL
Shrubbery Road, High Wycombe, Buckinghamshire
HP13 6PR
Tel: 01494 529273
Head: Mrs Frances J Henson BA(Hons), PGCE
Type: Girls Boarding & Day B3–8 G3–13
No of pupils: B25 G426
Fees: FB £10,110 DAY £1725 –£5850

*PIPERS CORNER SCHOOL
Great Kingshill, High Wycombe, Buckinghamshire
HP15 6LP
Tel: 01494 718255
Head: Mrs V M Stattersfield MA(Oxon), PGCE
Type: Girls Boarding & Day 4 –18
No of pupils: 350 G350 VIth60
Fees: FB £9147–£11,010 WB £9018–£10,860
DAY £3000 –£6588

WYCOMBE ABBEY SCHOOL
High Wycombe, Buckinghamshire HP11 1PE
Tel: 01494 520381
Head: Mrs P Davies BSc, MEd
Type: Girls Boarding & Day 11 –18
No of pupils: 522 G522 VIth84
Fees: FB £14,250 DAY £10,689

Milton Keynes

GYOSEI INTERNATIONAL SCHOOL UK
Japonica Lane, V10 Brickhill Street, Willen Park, Milton
Keynes, Buckinghamshire MK15 9JX
Tel: 01908 690100
Head: Mr W Takada
Type: Co-educational Boarding & Day 12 –18
No of pupils: B93 G44
Fees: FB £13,050 DAY £7300

SWANBOURNE HOUSE SCHOOL
Swanbourne, Milton Keynes, Buckinghamshire MK17 0HZ
Tel: 01296 720264
Head: S D Goodhart BEd & Mrs J S Goodhart BEd
Type: Co-educational Boarding & Day 2 –13
No of pupils: 400 B220 G180
Fees: FB £9300 DAY £4230 –£7320

THORNTON COLLEGE
Convent of Jesus & Mary, Thornton, Milton Keynes,
Buckinghamshire MK17 0HJ
Tel: 01280 812610
Head: Miss Agnes Williams
Type: Girls Day & Boarding B2–7 G2–16
No of pupils: 245 B32 G213
Fees: FB £7620–£8750 DAY £3730 –£5410

Cambridgeshire

Cambridge

KING'S COLLEGE SCHOOL
West Road, Cambridge CB3 9DN
Tel: 01223 365814
Head: Mr Nicholas Robinson BA, PGCE
Type: Co-educational Day & Boarding 4 –13
No of pupils: B186 G105
Fees: FB £9576 DAY £3078 –£6180

ST JOHN'S COLLEGE SCHOOL
73 Grange Road, Cambridge CB3 9AB
Tel: 01223 353532
Head: Mr K L Jones MA(Cantab)
Type: Co-educational Day & Boarding 4 –13
No of pupils: B260 G185
Fees: FB £9240 DAY £3528 –£5850

ST MARY'S SCHOOL
Bateman Street, Cambridge CB2 1LY
Tel: 01223 353253
Head: Mrs Gina Piotrowska
Type: Girls Day & Boarding 11 –18
No of pupils: G522 Vlth107
Fees: WB £8745 DAY £4890

THE LEYS SCHOOL
Cambridge CB2 2AD
Tel: 01223 508904
Head: Rev Dr John C A Barrett MA, FRSA
Type: Co-educational Boarding & Day 11 –18
No of pupils: B265 G175 Vlth190
Fees: FB £9480–£13,290 DAY £5670 –£9690

Ely

★THE KING'S SCHOOL ELY
Ely, Cambridgeshire CB7 4DB
Tel: 01353 660700
Head: Mr R H Youdale MA(Cantab)
Type: Co-educational Day & Boarding 2 –18
No of pupils: 878 B489 G389 Vlth126
Fees: FB £9549–£13,263 WB £9294–£12,948
DAY £4068 –£9108

Huntingdon

KIMBOLTON SCHOOL
Kimbolton, Huntingdon, Cambridgeshire PE18 0EA
Tel: 01480 860505
Head: R V Peel BSc, FRSA
Type: Co-educational Day & Boarding 7 –18
No of pupils: B413 G353 Vlth152
Fees: FB £9969 DAY £2703 –£5859

Peterborough

OUNDLE SCHOOL
Oundle, Peterborough, Cambridgeshire PE8 4EN
Tel: 01832 273536
Head: D B McMurray MA
Type: Co-educational Boarding 11 –18
No of pupils: B362 G165 Vlth357
Fees: FB £10,635–£13,920

PETERBOROUGH HIGH SCHOOL
Westwood House, Thorpe Road, Peterborough,
Cambridgeshire PE3 6JF
Tel: 01733 343357
Head: Mrs A J V Storey BA
Type: Girls Day & Boarding B4–8 G4–18
No of pupils: B12 G278
Fees: FB £7380–£7863 DAY £3270 –£3915

Channel Islands

Guernsey

ELIZABETH COLLEGE
Guernsey, Channel Islands GY1 2PY
Tel: 01481 726544
Head: Mr D E Toze
Type: Boys Day & Boarding B4–18 G16–18
No of pupils: B556 VIth151
Fees: FB £2730–£6930 DAY £2730 –£6930

Cheshire

Alderley Edge

THE RYLEYS SCHOOL
Ryleys Lane, Alderley Edge, Cheshire SK9 7UY
Tel: 01625 583241
Head: P G Barrett BA, CertEd
Type: Boys Day 3 –13
No of pupils: B256
Fees: DAY £3480 –£4365

Cheadle

RAMILLIES HALL SCHOOL
Cheadle Hulme, Cheadle, Cheshire SK8 7AJ
Tel: 0161 485 3804
Head: Miss D M Patterson BA, PGCE & Mrs A L Poole
Type: Co-educational Day & Boarding 0 –13
No of pupils: B86 G58
Fees: FB £6930–£7890 WB £6480–£7260
DAY £3105 –£4050

Chester

HAMMOND SCHOOL
Hoole Bank, Mannings Lane, Chester CH2 2PB
Tel: 01244 328542
Head: Mrs P Dangerfield BA(Hons)
Type: Co-educational Day & Boarding 11 –19
No of pupils: B13 G143 VIth30
Fees: FB £12,165 DAY £4350 –£8580

Crewe

TERRA NOVA SCHOOL
Jodrell Bank, Holmes Chapel, Crewe, Cheshire CW4 8BT
Tel: 01477 571251
Head: Mr T R Lewis BSc, CertEd
Type: Co-educational Day & Boarding 3 –13
No of pupils: B147 G82
Fees: FB £2–£2875 DAY £600 –£2330

Wilmslow

POWNALL HALL SCHOOL
Carrwood Road, Wilmslow, Cheshire SK9 5DW
Tel: 01625 523141
Head: Mr J J Meadmore RD, BSc, CertEd
Type: Boys Day 2 –11
No of pupils: B190 G10
Fees: DAY £2600 –£4890

Cornwall

Bude

ST PETROC'S SCHOOL
Ocean View Road, Bude, Cornwall EX23 8NJ
Tel: 01288 352876
Head: Mr R N Baird BA, PGCE
Type: Co-educational Boarding & Day 3 –13
No of pupils: B56 G52
Fees: FB £7560 WB £6840 DAY £2760 –£4560

Launceston

ST JOSEPH'S SCHOOL
15 St Stephen's Hill, Launceston, Cornwall PL15 8HN
Tel: 01566 772988
Head: Peter S Larkman LVO, MA, CertEd
Type: Girls Day & Boarding B3–11 G3–16
No of pupils: 176 B27 G149
Fees: FB £9540 WB £7155 DAY £3000 –£4620

Penzance

THE BOLITHO SCHOOL
Polwithen, Penzance, Cornwall TR18 4JR
Tel: 01736 363271
Head: Mr N P Johnson MA, dpBA
Type: Co-educational Day & Boarding 4 –18
No of pupils: B71 G94 VIth4
Fees: FB £7950–£9750 DAY £2775 –£5100

Truro

POLWHELE HOUSE SCHOOL
Newquay Road, Truro, Cornwall TR4 9AE
Tel: 01872 273011
Head: Mr & Mrs R I White CertEd, BA
Type: Co-educational Day & Boarding 3 –13
No of pupils: B92 G79
Fees: FB £8640–£9504 DAY £1236 –£5304

THE DUCHY GRAMMAR SCHOOL
Tregeye, Truro, Cornwall TR3 6JH
Tel: 01872 862289
Head: Mr M L Fuller MSc, BSc, CertEd
Type: Co-educational Day & Boarding 3 –18
No of pupils: B79 G43 VIth9
Fees: FB £7908–£10,371 WB £7008–£9471
DAY £2373 –£5721

TRELISKE SCHOOL
Highertown, Truro, Cornwall TR1 3QN
Tel: 01872 272616
Head: Mr Russell Hollins BA, BEd, CertEd
Type: Co-educational Day & Boarding 3 –11
No of pupils: B116 G81
Fees: FB £7107–£8730 WB £7107–£8730
DAY £675 –£4851

★TRURO HIGH SCHOOL FOR GIRLS
Falmouth Road, Truro, Cornwall TR1 2HU
Tel: 01872 272830
Head: Mr J Graham-Brown BA(Hons), MPhil
Type: Girls Day & Boarding B3–5 G3–18
No of pupils: 487 VIth89
Fees: FB £9285 DAY £3330 –£5025

TRURO SCHOOL
Trennick Lane, Truro, Cornwall TR1 1TH
Tel: 01872 272763
Head: Mr G A G Dodd MA
Type: Co-educational Day & Boarding 11 –18
No of pupils: B500 G270 VIth255
Fees: FB £10,065 DAY £5304

Cumbria

Carlisle

AUSTIN FRIARS SCHOOL
Etterby Scaur, Carlisle, Cumbria CA3 9PB
Tel: 01228 528042
Head: Rev D Middleton OSA, BA, STL
Type: Co-educational Boarding & Day 11 –18
No of pupils: 304 B184 G120 VIth69
Fees: FB £8787–£9345 DAY £5145 –£5215

★LIME HOUSE SCHOOL
Holm Hill, Dalston, Carlisle, Cumbria CA5 7BX
Tel: 01228 710225
Principal: Mr N A Rice BA, CertEd
Type: Co-educational Boarding & Day 5 –18
No of pupils: 185 VIth30
Fees: FB £3000–£8850 DAY £4350

Kendal

HOLME PARK PREPARATORY SCHOOL
Hill Top, New Hutton, Kendal, Cumbria LA8 0AH
Tel: 01539 721245
Head: N J V Curry BA, CertEd
Type: Co-educational Day & Boarding 4 –13
No of pupils: B50 G16
Fees: FB £5640 DAY £4440

Seascale

HARECROFT HALL SCHOOL
Gosforth, Seascale, Cumbria CA20 1HS
Tel: 01946 725220/25678
Head: Mr D G Hoddy BSc(Hons), PGCE
Type: Co-educational Day & Boarding 2 –16
No of pupils: 134
Fees: FB £7770–£8520 WB £7410–£8175
DAY £3855 –£5415

Sedbergh

SEDBERGH SCHOOL
Sedbergh, Cumbria LA10 5HG
Tel: 01539 620535
Head: Mr C H Hirst MA
Type: Boys Boarding & Day 8 –18
No of pupils: B350 VIth130
Fees: FB £9135–£13,900 DAY £6180 –£10,290

St Bees

★ST BEES SCHOOL
St Bees, Cumbria CA27 0DS
Tel: 01946 822263
Head: Mrs J D Pickering BSc
Type: Co-educational Boarding & Day 11 –18
No of pupils: 298 B173 G125 VIth89
Fees: FB £9096–£12,435 WB £7830–£11,070
DAY £6939 –£8556

Windermere

ST ANNE'S
Browhead, Windermere, Cumbria LA23 1NW
Tel: 01539 446164
Head: R D Hunter MA(Cantab)
Type: Girls Day & Boarding 11 –18
No of pupils: G166 VIth74
Fees: FB £9540 DAY £5700 –£6330

ST ANNE'S SCHOOL (JUNIOR DEPT)
Elleray, Windermere, Cumbria LA23 1AP
Tel: 01539 443308
Head: Mrs S Burkett-Cooper BEd
Type: Co-educational Boarding & Day 1 –11
No of pupils: B46 G110
Fees: FB £7350 DAY £1200

Derbyshire

Bakewell

S ANSELM'S SCHOOL

Stanedge Road, Bakewell, Derbyshire DE45 1DP
Tel: 01629 812734
Head: R J Foster BEd
Type: Co-educational Boarding & Day 3 –13
No of pupils: B94 G75
Fees: FB £9600 DAY £6495 –£7335

Chesterfield

BARLBOROUGH HALL SCHOOL

Barlborough, Chesterfield, Derbyshire S43 4TJ
Tel: 01246 810511
Head: Mrs Wanda E Parkinson BEd
Type: Co-educational Day & Boarding 3 –11
No of pupils: 118 B58 G60
Fees: DAY £2868 –£5160

Derby

OCKBROOK SCHOOL

The Settlement, Ockbrook, Derby, Derbyshire DE7 3RJ
Tel: 01332 673532
Head: Ms Denise P Bolland BA, MSc, MIMgt
Type: Girls Day & Boarding B3–11 G3–18
No of pupils: 460 B70 G390
Fees: FB £7392 DAY £3978

REPTON PREPARATORY SCHOOL

Foremarke Hall, Milton, Derby, Derbyshire DE65 6EJ
Tel: 01283 703269
Head: Mr R C Theobald BA
Type: Co-educational Day & Boarding 3 –13
No of pupils: B242 G108
Fees: FB £8850 DAY £4050 –£6630

Matlock

ST ELPHIN'S SCHOOL

Darley Dale, Matlock, Derbyshire DE4 2HA
Tel: 01629 732687
Head: Mrs Valerie Fisher BA(Theo), PGCE
Type: Girls Day & Boarding B2–7 G2–18
No of pupils: G190 VIth45
Fees: FB £9198–£10,545 DAY £2451 –£6141

STANCLIFFE HALL

Darley Dale, Matlock, Derbyshire DE4 2HJ
Tel: 01629 732310
Head: Mr D K Geddes MA
Type: Co-educational Day & Boarding 3 –13
No of pupils: B105 G45
Fees: FB £8850 DAY £3645 –£6870

Near Sheffield

*MOUNT ST MARY'S COLLEGE

Spinkhill, Near Sheffield, Derbyshire S21 3YL
Tel: 01246 433388
Head: Mr P G MacDonald MA(Oxon)
Type: Co-educational Boarding & Day 11 –19
No of pupils: 430 B253 G177 VIth122
Fees: FB £10,200 DAY £6150

Repton

REPTON SCHOOL

The Hall, Repton, Derbyshire DE65 6FH
Tel: 01283 559220
Head: G E Jones MA
Type: Co-educational Boarding & Day 13 –18
No of pupils: 556 B391 G165 VIth250
Fees: FB £12,720 DAY £9555

Devon

Barnstaple

ST MICHAEL'S SCHOOL
Tawstock Court, Barnstaple, Devon EX31 3HY
Tel: 01271 343242
Head: Mr J W Pratt GRSM(Hons), CertEd
Type: Co-educational Day & Boarding 0 –13
No of pupils: B113 G70
Fees: FB £8550–£8820 DAY £2790 –£5625

WEST BUCKLAND PREPARATORY SCHOOL
Barnstaple, Devon EX32 0SX
Tel: 01598 760281
Head: G D Benfield BEd, MIMgt
Type: Co-educational Day & Boarding 3 –11
No of pupils: B62 G57
Fees: FB £3295 DAY £865 –£1865

WEST BUCKLAND SCHOOL
Barnstaple, Devon EX32 0SX
Tel: 01598 760281
Head: J Vick MA(Cantab)
Type: Co-educational Day & Boarding 11 –18
No of pupils: B362 G224 VIth119
Fees: FB £3295 DAY £865 –£1865

Beaworthy

SHEBBEAR COLLEGE
Shebbear, Beaworthy, Devon EX21 5HJ
Tel: 01409 281228
Head: Mr L D Clark BSc, BA
Type: Co-educational Boarding & Day 3 –18
No of pupils: B178 G129 VIth60
Fees: FB £7260–£10,905 WB £6750 DAY £1830 –£5850

Bideford

EDGEHILL COLLEGE
Northdown Road, Bideford, Devon EX39 3LY
Tel: 01237 471701
Head: Mrs E M Burton BSc, AKC
Type: Co-educational Boarding & Day 3 –18
No of pupils: B123 G323 VIth83
Fees: FB £10,740 WB £7725–£10,650 DAY £2850 –£5880

GRENVILLE COLLEGE
Belvoir Road, Bideford, Devon EX39 3JR
Tel: 01237 472212
Head: Dr M C V Cane PhD, BSc, MRSC
Type: Co-educational Boarding & Day G22 –18
No of pupils: B157 G96 VIth76
Fees: FB £8190–£10,551 WB £7710–£10,404
DAY £2538 –£5175

GRENVILLE COLLEGE JUNIOR (STELLA MARIS)
The Strand, Bideford, Devon EX39 2PW
Tel: 01237 472208
Head: T H Andrew
Type: Girls Day & Boarding B3–11 G3–18
No of pupils: B79 G313
Fees: FB £5160–£6270 WB £5160–£5670
DAY £2370 –£2940

GRENVILLE COLLEGE JUNIOR SCHOOL
(Stella Maris), Moreton House, Abbotsham Road, Bideford,
Devon EX39 3QN
Tel: 01237 472208
Head: Mrs L Maggs-Wellings BEd
Type: Co-educational Boarding & Day 2 –11
No of pupils: B59 G38
Fees: FB £2170–£2894 DAY £768 –£1416

Chulmleigh

OSHO KO HSUAN SCHOOL
Chawleigh, Chulmleigh, Devon EX18 7EX
Tel: 01769 580896
Head: R A Jones
Type: Co-educational Boarding 7 –16
No of pupils: 56 B25 G31
Fees: FB £5775

Exeter

BRAMDEAN GRAMMAR SCHOOL
Richmond Lodge, Homefield Road, Heavitree, Exeter,
Devon EX1 2QR
Tel: 01392 273387
Head: D A Connett
Type: Boys Day & Boarding B11–17 G16–17
No of pupils: B180
Fees: WB £4092 DAY £627

BRAMDEAN PREP & GRAMMAR SCHOOL
Richmond Lodge, Homefield Road, Heavitree, Exeter,
Devon EX1 2QR
Tel: 01392 273387
Head: D Stoneman
Type: Boys Day & Boarding 7 –11
No of pupils: B140 G6
Fees: WB £4092 DAY £627

EXETER CATHEDRAL SCHOOL
The Chantry, Palace Gate, Exeter, Devon EX1 1HX
Tel: 01392 255298
Head: Clive Dickinson BA
Type: Co-educational Day & Boarding 3 –13
No of pupils: 160 B96 G64
Fees: FB £7440–£7875 DAY £2730 –£4815

EXETER SCHOOL
Victoria Park Road, Exeter, Devon EX2 4NS
Tel: 01392 258712
Head: Mr N W Gamble BA, MEd
Type: Co-educational Boarding & Day 7 –18
No of pupils: B709 G58 VIth228
Fees: FB £4410 DAY £4929

Exmouth

ST PETER'S SCHOOL
Harefield, Lympstone, Exmouth, Devon EX8 5AU
Tel: 01395 272148
Head: Mr C N C Abram CertEd
Type: Co-educational Day & Boarding 3 –13
No of pupils: B140 G72
Fees: WB £7380 DAY £3135 –£5175

Honiton

MANOR HOUSE SCHOOL
Springfield House, Honiton, Devon EX14 8TL
Tel: 01404 42026
Head: Mr S J Bage BA(Hons), PGCE
Type: Co-educational Day 3 –11
No of pupils: 100 B55 G45
Fees: DAY £900 –£3060

Newton Abbot

STOVER SCHOOL FOR GIRLS
Newton Abbot, Devon TQ12 6QG
Tel: 01626 354505
Head: Mr P E Bujak BA, MA, CertEd, ARHists
Type: Girls Day & Boarding 3 –18
No of pupils: G268 VIth52
Fees: FB £9885 DAY £5085

WOLBOROUGH HILL SCHOOL
South Road, Newton Abbot, Devon TQ12 1HH
Tel: 01626 354078
Head: Mr R P Merriman BSc(Hons), FCollP
Type: Co-educational Day & Boarding 4 –13
No of pupils: B127 G60
Fees: WB £7200 DAY £3375 –£4935

Plymouth

*PLYMOUTH COLLEGE
Ford Park, Plymouth, Devon PL4 6RN
Tel: 01752 203300
Head: Mr A J Morsley BSc, ARCS, AFIMA, FRSA
Type: Co-educational Boarding & Day 11 –18
No of pupils: 605 VIth179
Fees: FB £10,977 DAY £5721

ST DUNSTAN'S ABBEY SCHOOL
The Millfields, Plymouth, Devon PL1 3JL
Tel: 01752 201350
Head: Mrs Barbara Brown
Type: Girls Day & Boarding 3 –18
No of pupils: G340 VIth30
Fees: FB £6936–£9246 WB £5898–£8208
DAY £2730 –£5190

Sidmouth

ST JOHN'S SCHOOL
Broadway, Sidmouth, Devon EX10 8RG
Tel: 01395 513984
Head: Mr Neil R Pockett BA, DLC, CertEd
Type: Co-educational Day & Boarding 2 –13
No of pupils: B140 G100
Fees: FB £7185 DAY £1206 –£4260

Tavistock

KELLY COLLEGE
Tavistock, Devon PL19 0HZ
Tel: 01822 612010
Head: M Turner MA
Type: Co-educational Day & Boarding 3 –18
No of pupils: 470 B250 G220 VIth120
Fees: FB £11,175–£13,095 WB £11,175–£13,095
DAY £2955 –£8220

MOUNT HOUSE PREPARATORY SCHOOL
Tavistock, Devon PL19 9JL
Tel: 01822 612244
Head: Mr C D Price BA
Type: Co-educational Day & Boarding 3 –13
No of pupils: B150 G50
Fees: FB £9231 DAY £1902 –£6789

Teignmouth

TRINITY SCHOOL
Buckeridge Road, Teignmouth, Devon TQ14 8LY
Tel: 01626 774138
Head: Mr C J Ashby BSc(Hons), PGCE
Type: Co-educational Day & Boarding 3 –19
No of pupils: B170 G161 VIth28
Fees: FB £9480 DAY £4083

Tiverton

BLUNDELL'S SCHOOL
Tiverton, Devon EX16 4DN
Tel: 01884 252543
Head: Mr J Leigh MA(Cantab)
Type: Co-educational Boarding & Day 11 –18
No of pupils: 454 B308 G146 VIth149
Fees: FB £8475–£12,750 DAY £4500 –£7785

ST AUBYN'S SCHOOL
Howden Court, Tiverton, Devon EX16 5PB
Tel: 01884 252393
Head: Mr Brian J McDowell CertEd
Type: Co-educational Day & Boarding 0 –11
No of pupils: B168 G128
Fees: FB £6936–£8046 DAY £624 –£5100

Torquay

STOODLEY KNOWLE SCHOOL
Ansteys Cove Road, Torquay, Devon TQ1 2JB
Tel: 01803 293160
Head: Sister Perpetua
Type: Girls Day & Boarding 2 –18
No of pupils: G207 VIth15
Fees: WB £4485–£5073 DAY £2763 –£3594

Dorset

Blandford Forum

BRYANSTON SCHOOL
Blandford Forum, Dorset DT11 0PX
Tel: 01258 452411
Head: Mr T D Wheare MA
Type: Co-educational Day & Boarding 13 –18
No of pupils: B366 G275 VIth274
Fees: FB £14,982 DAY £10,338

CLAYESMORE PREPARATORY SCHOOL
Iwerne Minster, Blandford Forum, Dorset DT11 8PH
Tel: 01747 811707
Head: Mr M G Cooke BEd(Hons), FCollP, FGMS
Type: Co-educational Boarding & Day 2 –13
No of pupils: 286 B178 G108
Fees: FB £9576 DAY £3108 –£6834

CLAYESMORE SCHOOL
Iwerne Minster, Blandford Forum, Dorset DT11 8LL
Tel: 01747 811217
Head: Mr D J Beeby MA(Cantab)
Type: Co-educational Boarding & Day 13 –18
No of pupils: 307 B189 G118 VIth98
Fees: FB £12,726 DAY £8913

HANFORD SCHOOL
Childe Okeford, Blandford Forum, Dorset DT11 8HL
Tel: 01258 860219
Heads: Miss S B Canning MA,
Mr & Mrs R A McKenzie Johnston MA
Type: Girls Boarding 7 –13
No of pupils: G115
Fees: FB £9000

KNIGHTON HOUSE
Durweston, Blandford Forum, Dorset DT11 0PY
Tel: 01258 452065
Head: T Mooney MA(TCD), HdipEd
Type: Girls Boarding & Day B4–7 G4–13
No of pupils: B22 G126
Fees: FB £9585 DAY £2610 –£7035

MILTON ABBEY SCHOOL
Blandford Forum, Dorset DT11 0BZ
Tel: 01258 880484
Head: W V Hughes-D'Aeth BA
Type: Boys Boarding & Day 13 –18
No of pupils: 200 B200 VIth70
Fees: FB £13,500 DAY £9450

Bournemouth

WENTWORTH COLLEGE
College Road, Bournemouth, Dorset BH5 2DY
Tel: 01202 423266
Head: Miss Sandra D Coe BA(Hons), PGCE, FRGS
Type: Girls Boarding & Day 11 –18
No of pupils: G240 Vlth56
Fees: FB £10–£10,140 DAY £6360

Christchurch

HOMEFIELD SCHOOL (PREP & SENIOR DEPTS)
Salisbury Road, Winkton, Christchurch, Dorset BH23 7AR
Tel: 01202 476644
Head: Mr A C Partridge DipEd, ACP, FRSA
Type: Co-educational Boarding & Day 3 –16
No of pupils: B150 G150
Fees: FB £10,425 DAY £2775 –£4320

Lyme Regis

ALL HALLOWS COLLEGE
Rousdon, Lyme Regis, Dorset DT7 3RA
Tel: 01297 626110
Head: K R Moore MA, FGS, CGeol
Type: Co-educational Boarding & Day 11 –18
No of pupils: B115 G50 Vlth54
Fees: FB £10,650 WB £10,650 DAY £4185 –£5625

Shaftesbury

PORT REGIS
Motcombe Park, Shaftesbury, Dorset SP7 9QA
Tel: 01747 852566
Head: P A E Dix BA(Hons)(Natal), MA(Cantab)
Type: Co-educational Boarding & Day 2 –13
No of pupils: 398 B227 G171
Fees: FB £11,985 DAY £3120 –£8985

ST MARY'S SCHOOL
Shaftesbury, Dorset SP7 9LP
Tel: 01747 854005
Head: Sister M Campion Livesey IBVM, MA(Cantab)
Type: Girls Boarding & Day 9 –18
No of pupils: G313 Vlth84
Fees: FB £10,050–£10,590 DAY £6525 –£6870

Sherborne

SHERBORNE PREPARATORY SCHOOL
Acreman Street, Sherborne, Dorset DT9 3NY
Tel: 01935 812097
Head: Mr P S Tait MA(Massey)
Type: Co-educational Day & Boarding 2 –13
No of pupils: 161 B108 G53
Fees: FB £7965–£8667 DAY £1404 –£5778

SHERBORNE SCHOOL
Abbey Road, Sherborne, Dorset DT9 3AP
Tel: 01935 812249
Head: Mr P H Lapping MA(Oxon)
Type: Boys Boarding & Day 13 –18
No of pupils: B570 Vlth260
Fees: FB £13,770 DAY £10,350

SHERBORNE SCHOOL FOR GIRLS
Sherborne, Dorset DT9 3QN
Tel: 01935 812245
Head: Miss J M Taylor BSc, DipEd
Type: Girls Boarding & Day 11 –18
No of pupils: 429 G272 Vlth157
Fees: FB £12,960 DAY £9060

*SHERBORNE SCHOOL INTERNATIONAL COLLEGE
Newell Grange, Newell, Sherborne, Dorset DT9 4EZ
Tel: 01935 814743
Principal: Dr Christopher Greenfield MA, MEd
Type: Boys Boarding 10 –16
No of pupils: 120
Fees: FB £17,250

ST ANTONY'S-LEWESTON PREPARATORY SCHOOL
Sherborne, Dorset DT9 6EN
Tel: 01963 210790
Head: Mrs L M Walker CertEd, RTC, DipAdv, MEd, DipRSA(SpLD)
Type: Co-educational Boarding & Day 3 –11
No of pupils: B45 G75
Fees: FB £8000 DAY £3900 –£4500

ST ANTONY'S-LEWESTON SCHOOL
Leweston, Sherborne, Dorset DT9 6EN
Tel: 01963 210691
Head: Miss Brenda A King BA, BD
Type: Girls Day & Boarding 11 –18
No of pupils: 270 G270 Vlth70
Fees: FB £12,402 DAY £8172

Swanage

THE OLD MALTHOUSE
Langton Matravers, Swanage, Dorset BH19 3HB
Tel: 01929 422302
Head: J H L Phillips BEd(Hons)
Type: Boys Day & Boarding B4–13 G4–7
No of pupils: B94 G10
Fees: FB £9495 DAY £3645 –£7200

Weymouth

THORNLOW JUNIOR SCHOOL
Connaught Road, Weymouth, Dorset DT4 0SA
Tel: 01305 785703
Head: Mr R A Fowke, BEd(Hons)
Type: Co-educational Day & Boarding 3 –13
No of pupils: B30 G26
Fees: FB £8085 WB £7485 DAY £2385 –£2685

THORNLOW SCHOOL
101 Buxton Road, Weymouth, Dorset DT4 9PR
Tel: 01305 782977
Head: D H Crocker CertEd
Type: Co-educational Day & Boarding 11 –16
No of pupils: B113 G70
Fees: FB £7290–8520 DAY £2340 –£3810

Wimborne

CANFORD SCHOOL
Canford Heath, Wimborne, Dorset BH21 3AD
Tel: 01202 841254
Head: J D Lever MA
Type: Co-educational Boarding & Day 13 –18
No of pupils: B242 G21 VIth242
Fees: FB £12,380 DAY £9285

DUMPTON SCHOOL
Deans Grove House, Wimborne, Dorset BH21 7AF
Tel: 01202 883818
Head: A G M Watson MA, DipEd
Type: Co-educational Day & Boarding 3 –13
No of pupils: B186 G44
Fees: FB £8385 DAY £1350 –£6480

County Durham

Barnard Castle

BARNARD CASTLE SCHOOL
Barnard Castle, County Durham DL12 8UN
Tel: 01833 690222
Head: M D Featherstone MA
Type: Co-educational Boarding & Day 4 –18
No of pupils: B494 G150 VIth169
Fees: FB £7194 DAY £2425 –£5556

Darlington

POLAM HALL
Grange Road, Darlington, County Durham DL1 5PA
Tel: 01325 463383
Head: Mrs H C Hamilton BSc
Type: Girls Day & Boarding 4 –18
No of pupils: G480 VIth80
Fees: FB £8316–£10,290 WB £8241–£10,215
DAY £2322 –£5034

POLAM HALL JUNIOR SCHOOL
Grange Road, Darlington, County Durham DL1 5PA
Tel: 01325 350697
Head: Mrs D M Blackburn CertEd
Type: Co-educational Day

Durham

BOW SCHOOL
South Road, Durham, County Durham DH1 3LS
Tel: 0191 384 8233
Head: J P Wansey BA
Type: Boys Day & Boarding 3 –13
No of pupils: 166 B166
Fees: FB £8328 DAY £2628 –£5328

DURHAM SCHOOL
Durham, County Durham DH1 4SZ
Tel: 0191 384 7977
Head: Mr N G Kern MA, MSc, MIBiol
Type: Boys Day & Boarding 11 –18
No of pupils: 313 B278 G35 VIth137
Fees: FB £10,521–£12,360 DAY £5589 –£8091

THE CHORISTER SCHOOL
off South Bailey, Durham, County Durham DH1 3EL
Tel: 0191 384 2935
Head: Mr C S S Drew MA
Type: Co-educational Day & Boarding 4 –13
No of pupils: B155 G30
Fees: FB £7557 DAY £3636 –£5163

Essex

Brentwood

BRENTWOOD SCHOOL
Ingrave Road, Brentwood, Essex CM15 8AS
Tel: 01277 212271
Head: J A B Kelsall MA
Type: Co-educational Day & Boarding 3 –18
No of pupils: 1488 B1001 G487 VIth341
Fees: FB £11,991 DAY £5238 –£6891

Chelmsford

*NEW HALL PREPARATORY SCHOOL
Chelmsford, Essex CM3 3HT
Tel: 01245 467588
Head: Mr Gerard Hudson BSc(Hons), PGCE, CertRE
Type: Co-educational Day & Boarding 4 –11
No of pupils: B85 G170
Fees: FB £7860 WB £7740 DAY £3900

*NEW HALL SCHOOL
Chelmsford, Essex CM3 3HT
Tel: 01245 467588
Head: Sr Anne Marie CRSS, MA(Cantab)
Type: Girls Boarding & Day B4 –11 G4 –18
No of pupils: 637 B85 G552 VIth115
Fees: FB £12,240 WB £11,865 DAY £3900 –£7950

Chigwell

CHIGWELL SCHOOL
High Road, Chigwell, Essex IG7 6QF
Tel: 0181 501 5702
Head: Mr D F Gibbs BA
Type: Co-educational Boarding & Day 7 –19
No of pupils: B635 G80 VIth155
Fees: FB £6993–£11,019 DAY £4713 –£7248

Colchester

HOLMWOOD HOUSE
Lexden, Colchester, Essex CO3 5ST
Tel: 01206 574305
Head: Mr H S Thackrah BEd(Hons)
Type: Co-educational Day & Boarding 4 –13
No of pupils: B232 G128
Fees: FB £8910–£9975 DAY £4335 –£7710

Great Dunmow

FELSTED PREPARATORY SCHOOL
Felsted, Great Dunmow, Essex CM6 3JL
Tel: 01371 820252
Head: Mr M P Pomphrey BSc
Type: Co-educational Boarding & Day 4 –13
No of pupils: B172 G147
Fees: FB £10,170 DAY £3045 –£7440

FELSTED SCHOOL
Felsted, Great Dunmow, Essex CM6 3LL
Tel: 01371 820258
Head: S C Roberts MA
Type: Co-educational Boarding & Day 13 –18
No of pupils: 395 B268 G127 VIth169
Fees: FB £11,277–£14,301 DAY £10,458

Halstead

GOSFIELD SCHOOL
Cut Hedge Park, Halstead Road, Gosfield, Halstead,
Essex CO9 1PF
Tel: 01787 474040
Head: Mr John Shaw MA, MABE
Type: Co-educational Day & Boarding 2 –18
No of pupils: B108 G62 VIth17
Fees: FB £8700–£11,265 DAY £3225 –£6030

Saffron Walden

FRIENDS' SCHOOL
Mount Pleasant Road, Saffron Walden, Essex CB11 3EB
Tel: 01799 525351
Head: Mrs Jane Laing BA
Type: Co-educational Day & Boarding 3 –18
No of pupils: B185 G180 VIth35
Fees: FB £7632–£11,700 DAY £4122 –£7020

Gloucestershire

Cheltenham

CHELTENHAM COLLEGE
Bath Road, Cheltenham, Gloucestershire GL53 7LD
Tel: 01242 513540
Head: Mr P Chamberlain MSc
Type: Boys Day & Boarding B13–18 G16–18
No of pupils: 546 B455 G91 VIth318
Fees: FB £13,200 DAY £9975

CHELTENHAM COLLEGE JUNIOR SCHOOL
Thirlestaine Road, Cheltenham, Gloucestershire GL53 7AB
Tel: 01242 522697
Head: Mr N I Archdale BEd, MEd
Type: Co-educational Boarding & Day 3 –13
No of pupils: 400 B270 G130
Fees: FB £7485–£9300 DAY £2295 –£7200

★DEAN CLOSE JUNIOR SCHOOL
Lansdown Road, Cheltenham, Gloucestershire GL51 6QS
Tel: 01242 512217
Head: Mr Stephen W Baird BA
Type: Co-educational Day & Boarding 3 –13
No of pupils: 303 B167 G136
Fees: FB £10,245 DAY £6975

★DEAN CLOSE SCHOOL
Cheltenham, Gloucestershire GL51 6HE
Tel: 01242 522640
Head: Rev Timothy M Hastie-Smith MA
Type: Co-educational Boarding & Day 12 –18
No of pupils: 432 B249 G183 VIth180
Fees: FB £14,055 DAY £9810

THE CHELTENHAM LADIES' COLLEGE
Bayshill Road, Cheltenham, Gloucestershire GL50 3EP
Tel: 01242 520691
Head: Mrs A V Tuck MA, PGCE, MIL
Type: Girls Boarding & Day 11 –18
No of pupils: G856 VIth305
Fees: FB £14,340–£15,720 DAY £9105 –£10,080

Cirencester

HATHEROP CASTLE PREPARATORY SCHOOL
Hatherop, Cirencester, Gloucestershire GL7 3NB
Tel: 01285 750206
Head: P Easterbrook BEd
Type: Co-educational Boarding & Day 2 –13
No of pupils: B119 G121
Fees: FB £7950 DAY £3060 –£5160

RENDCOMB COLLEGE
Rendcombe, Cirencester, Gloucestershire GL7 7HA
Tel: 01285 831213
Head: J N Tolputt MA
Type: Co-educational Boarding & Day 11 –18
No of pupils: B153 G87 VIth82
Fees: FB £8400–£10,800 DAY £6450 –£8550

Gloucester

THE KING'S SCHOOL
Pitt Street, Gloucester GL1 2BG
Tel: 01452 521251
Head: Mr P R Lacy MA, PGCE, FRSA
Type: Co-educational Day & Boarding 3 –18
No of pupils: B275 G192 VIth76
Fees: FB £11,700–£12,850 DAY £6750 –£7800

WYNSTONES SCHOOL
Whaddon Green, Gloucester GL4 0UF
Tel: 01452 522475
Head: Chairman of the College of Teachers
Type: Co-educational Day & Boarding 4 –18
No of pupils: B153 G159
Fees: FB £6339–£6510 DAY £2535 –£3576

Moreton-in-Marsh

KITEBROOK HOUSE
Moreton-in-Marsh, Gloucestershire GL56 0RP
Tel: 01608 674350
Head: Mrs A McDermott NFF
Type: Girls Boarding & Day B4–8 G4–13
No of pupils: B44 G136
Fees: WB £7500 DAY £1590 –£4470

Nailsworth

ACORN SCHOOL
Church Street, Nailsworth, Gloucestershire GL6 0BP
Tel: 01453 836508
Head: G E B Whiting
Type: Co-educational Day & Boarding 3 –19
No of pupils: 68 B34 G34
Fees: DAY £700 –£1200

Stonehouse

WYCLIFFE COLLEGE
Stonehouse, Gloucestershire GL10 2JQ
Tel: 01453 822432
Head: Dr R A Collins MA, MPhil, DPhil
Type: Co-educational Boarding & Day 13 –18
No of pupils: B225 G192 VIth174
Fees: FB £13,245–£14,805 DAY £9315 –£9660

Stroud

BEAUDESERT PARK
Minchinhampton, Stroud, Gloucestershire GL6 9AF
Tel: 01453 832072
Head: Mr J P R Womersley BA, PGCE
Type: Co-educational Boarding & Day 4 –13
No of pupils: B190 G148
Fees: FB £3369 DAY £1240 –£2480

Tetbury

WESTONBIRT SCHOOL
Westonbirt, Tetbury, Gloucestershire GL8 8QG
Tel: 01666 880333
Head: Mrs G Hylson-Smith BA, DipCEG
Type: Girls Boarding & Day 11 –18
No of pupils: G220 VIth70
Fees: FB £12,828 DAY £8430

Tewkesbury

*BREDON SCHOOL
Pull Court, Bushley, Tewkesbury, Gloucestershire GL20 6AH
Tel: 01684 293156
Head: Mr Colin E Wheeler BEd, MIMgt
Type: Co-educational Boarding & Day 3 –18
No of pupils: 253
Fees: FB £9000–£13,500 WB £8820–£13,320
DAY £2940 –£8550

BREDON SCHOOL - JUNIOR SCHOOL
Pull Court, Bushley, Tewkesbury, Gloucestershire GL20 6AH
Tel: 01684 293156
Head: Mr Colin E Wheeler BEd, MIMgt
Type: Co-educational Boarding & Day 3 –11
No of pupils: B38 G17
Fees: FB £9000–£13,500 WB £8820–£13,320
DAY £2940 –£8550

Wotton-under-Edge

ROSE HILL SCHOOL
Alderley, Wotton-under-Edge, Gloucestershire GL12 7QT
Tel: 01453 843196
Head: R G C Lyne-Pirkis, BA, CertEd, MBIM
Type: Co-educational Boarding & Day 2 –13
No of pupils: B109 G101
Fees: FB £2180–£2705 DAY £1010 –£2075

Hampshire

Andover

FARLEIGH SCHOOL
Red Rice, Andover, Hampshire SP11 7PW
Tel: 01264 710766
Head: J E Murphy BSc, PGCE
Type: Co-educational Day & Boarding 3 –13
No of pupils: B268 G108
Fees: FB £9399 DAY £1758 –£6675

ROOKWOOD SCHOOL
Weyhill Road, Andover, Hampshire SP10 3AL
Tel: 01264 352855
Head: Mrs S Hindle BA(Hons), FCollP
Type: Co-educational Day & Boarding 3 –16
No of pupils: B128 G241
Fees: FB £7710–£10,155 WB £7155–£9600
DAY £630 –£5400

ST BENEDICT'S CONVENT SCHOOL
Penton Lodge, Andover, Hampshire SP11 0RD
Tel: 01264 772291
Head: Mrs J Taylor
Type: Co-educational Boarding & Day B2–11 G2–16
Fees: FB £5610–£6840 DAY £1500 –£2985

Basingstoke

NORTH FORELAND LODGE
Sherfield-on-Loddon, Nr Basingstoke,
Hampshire RG27 0HT
Tel: 01256 884800
Head: Miss S R Cameron BA
Type: Girls Boarding & Day 11 –18
No of pupils: 170 G170 VIth45
Fees: FB £13,650 DAY £8700

Bramdean

BROCKWOOD PARK SCHOOL
Bramdean, Hampshire SO24 0LQ
Tel: 01962 771744
Heads: Dr Foster & L Peters
Type: Co-educational Boarding 14 –19
No of pupils: B30 G30
Fees: FB £8500

Fareham

BOUNDARY OAK SCHOOL
Roche Court, Fareham, Hampshire PO17 5BL
Tel: 01329 280955
Head: R B Bliss CertEd
Type: Co-educational Day & Boarding 3 –13
No of pupils: B160 G55
Fees: FB £6630–£8325 WB £6630–£8325
DAY £1650 –£5625

WEST HILL PARK PREPARATORY SCHOOL
Titchfield, Fareham, Hampshire PO14 4BS
Tel: 01329 842356
Head: E P K Hudson CertEd
Type: Co-educational Boarding & Day 3 –13
No of pupils: B202 G98
Fees: FB £2900 DAY £360 –£2180

Fordingbridge

FORRES SANDLE MANOR
Fordingbridge, Hampshire SP6 1NS
Tel: 01425 653181
Head: Mr R P J Moore BA, PGCE
Type: Co-educational Boarding & Day 3 –13
No of pupils: 233 B132 G101
Fees: FB £10,014 WB £10,014 DAY £2160 –£7320

Hook

LORD WANDSWORTH COLLEGE
Long Sutton, Hook, Hampshire RG29 1TB
Tel: 01256 862482
Head: Mr Ian Power MA
Type: Boys Day & Boarding 11 –18
No of pupils: 475 B419 G56 VIth144
Fees: FB £10,212–£10,764 DAY £7968 –£9045

Liphook

HIGHFIELD SCHOOL
Liphook, Hampshire GU30 7LQ
Tel: 01428 722228
Head: N O Ramage MA
Type: Co-educational Boarding & Day 7 –13
No of pupils: B105 G76
Fees: FB £8325 –£9450 DAY £6300 –£7350

Lymington

HORDLE WALHAMPTON SCHOOL
Walhampton, Lymington, Hampshire SO41 5ZG
Tel: 01590 672013
Head: R H C Phillips BA(Hons), CertEd, LGSM
Type: Co-educational Boarding & Day 2 –13
No of pupils: 282 B157 G125
Fees: FB £9480 DAY £2730 –£7230

New Milton

BALLARD COLLEGE
Fernhill Lane, New Milton, Hampshire BH25 5JL
Tel: 01425 611090
Head: Mr Paul Stockdale
Type: Co-educational Boarding & Day 11 –18
No of pupils: 100 VIth20
Fees: FB £8850 WB £8295 DAY £5655

BALLARD LAKE PREPARATORY SCHOOL
Fernhill Lane, New Milton,
Hampshire BH25 5JL
Tel: 01425 611153
Head: Miss Gill Morris
Type: Co-educational Boarding & Day 2 –13
No of pupils: 230
Fees: FB £8205 WB £7395 DAY £3105 –£5550

DURLSTON COURT
Becton Lane, Barton-on-Sea, New Milton, Hampshire
BH25 7AQ
Tel: 01425 610010
Head: Mr E G Liston BSc, CertEd
Type: Co-educational Day & Boarding 3 –13
No of pupils: B138 G103
Fees: FB £9285 DAY £1950 –£6585

Petersfield

BEDALES JUNIOR SCHOOL (DUNHURST)
Alton Road, Steep, Petersfield, Hampshire GU31 2DP
Tel: 01730 300100
Head: Mr Michael Piercy BA
Type: Co-educational Boarding & Day 8 –13
No of pupils: 146 B65 G81
Fees: FB £10,347–£10,389 DAY £7281 –£7440

BEDALES SCHOOL
Church Road, Steep, Petersfield, Hampshire GU32 2DG
Tel: 01730 300100
Head: Alison Willcocks MA, BMus
Type: Co-educational Boarding & Day 13 –18
No of pupils: 400 B200 G200 VIth160
Fees: FB £13,647 DAY £10,236

Ringwood

MOYLES COURT SCHOOL
Moyles Court, Ringwood, Hampshire BH24 3NF
Tel: 01425 472856/473197
Head: Mr Dean
Type: Co-educational Day & Boarding 3 –16
No of pupils: B83 G63
Fees: FB £6690–£7740 DAY £3285 –£4650

Romsey

EMBLEY PARK SCHOOL
Embley Park, Romsey, Hampshire SO51 6ZE
Tel: 01794 512206
Head: David Chapman BA(Dunelm), FCollP
Type: Co-educational Boarding & Day 3 –18
No of pupils: 420 B260 G160 VIth70
Fees: FB £5350–£10,695 WB £5350–£10,695
DAY £3260 –£6510

*STANBRIDGE EARLS SCHOOL
Stanbridge Lane, Romsey, Hampshire SO51 0ZS
Tel: 01794 516777
Head: Mr H Moxon MA, DipEd
Type: Co-educational Boarding & Day 11–18
No of pupils: 182 B147 G35 VIth40
Fees: FB £12,300–£13,500 DAY £9150–£10,050

Southsea

ST JOHN'S COLLEGE
Grove Road South, Southsea, Hampshire PO5 3QW
Tel: 01705 815118
Head: Mr G Morgan
Type: Co-educational Day & Boarding 4–18
No of pupils: B555 G55 VIth90
Fees: FB £7140–£8100 DAY £2820–£4050

Wickham

*ROOKESBURY PARK SCHOOL
Wickham, Hampshire PO17 6HT
Tel: 01329 833108
Head: Mrs S M Cook BA(Hons), PGCE
Type: Girls Day & Boarding B3–7 G3–13
No of pupils: 135
Fees: FB £7425–£8730 DAY £1740–£5985

Winchester

*ST SWITHUN'S SCHOOL
Alresford Road, Winchester, Hampshire SO21 1HA
Tel: 01962 835700
Head: Dr H L Harvey BSc, PhD(London)
Type: Girls Boarding & Day 11–18
No of pupils: 580 G580 VIth117
Fees: FB £12,795 DAY £7740

THE PILGRIMS' SCHOOL
3 The Close, Winchester, Hampshire SO23 9LT
Tel: 01962 854189
Head: Dr Brian Rees BA, BD, DipMin, PhD
Type: Boys Boarding & Day 7–13
No of pupils: 200 B200
Fees: FB £9495 DAY £7095

TWYFORD SCHOOL
Twyford, Winchester, Hampshire SO21 1NW
Tel: 01962 712269
Head: Mr P F Fawkes CertEd, MBA(Ed)
Type: Co-educational Day & Boarding 3–13
No of pupils: B208 G92
Fees: FB £10,320 DAY £2100–£7575

WINCHESTER COLLEGE
College Street, Winchester, Hampshire SO23 9NA
Tel: 01962 621100
Head: J P Sabben-Clare MA
Type: Boys Boarding & Day 13–18
No of pupils: 680 B680 VIth280
Fees: FB £15,345 DAY £7671–£11,709

Herefordshire

Bromyard

*ST RICHARD'S SCHOOL
Bredenbury Court, Bromyard, Herefordshire HR7 4TD
Tel: 01885 482491
Head: Mr R E H Coghlan MA(Cantab)
Type: Co-educational Boarding & Day 4–13
No of pupils: 138 B73 G65
Fees: FB £7500–£8025 DAY £1980–£5475

Hereford

HEREFORD CATHEDRAL JUNIOR SCHOOL
28 Castle Street, Hereford HR1 2NW
Tel: 01432 363511
Head: Mr T R Lowe BA, CertEd, FCollP
Type: Co-educational Day & Boarding 3–11
No of pupils: B178 G102
Fees: FB £6090–£7290 DAY £2733–£4008

THE HEREFORD CATHEDRAL SCHOOL
Old Deanery, Cathedral Close Hereford, HR1 2NG
Tel: 01432 363522
Head: Dr H C Tomlinson BA, FRHistS, FRSA
Type: Co-educational Day & Boarding 3–18
No of pupils: 630 B325 G305 VIth175
Fees: FB £7980 DAY £4530

Hertfordshire

Aldenham Village

EDGE GROVE SCHOOL
Aldenham Village, Hertfordshire WD2 8BL
Tel: 01923 855724
Head: Mr John R Baugh BEd
Type: Boys Boarding & Day B3–13 G3–7
No of pupils: B233 G39
Fees: FB £9300 DAY £2130 –£6750

Berkhamsted

BERKHAMSTED COLLEGIATE SCHOOL
131 High Street, Berkhamsted, Hertfordshire HP4 2DJ
Tel: 01442 877522
Head: Dr P Chadwick MA, PhD, FRSA
Type: Boys Day & Boarding 11 –18
No of pupils: B700 G325 VIth290
Fees: FB £10,971–£12,381 DAY £6534 –£7683

Bishops Stortford

BISHOP'S STORTFORD COLLEGE
Maze Green Road, Bishops Stortford,
Hertfordshire CM23 2QZ
Tel: 01279 838575
Head: S G G Benson
Type: Boys Boarding & Day B13–18 G16–18
No of pupils: B318 G30
Fees: FB £10,020 DAY £7230

BISHOP'S STORTFORD COLLEGE JUNIOR SCHOOL
Maze Green Road, Bishops Stortford,
Hertfordshire CM23 2PH
Tel: 01279 653616
Head: D J Defoe BSc, CChem, MRSC
Type: Co-educational Day & Boarding 4 –13
No of pupils: B252 G38
Fees: FB £7200–£7860 WB £7200–£7860
DAY £3600 –£5970

Bushey

★ST MARGARET'S SCHOOL
Merry Hill Road, Bushey, Hertfordshire WD2 1DT
Tel: 0181 950 1548
Head: Miss M de Villiers BA
Type: Girls Boarding & Day 4 –18
No of pupils: 480 G480
Fees: FB £9405–£10,695 DAY £3975 –£6405

THE PURCELL SCHOOL, LONDON
Aldenham Road, Bushey, Hertfordshire WD2 3TS
Tel: 01923 331100
Head: Mr K J Bain MA, FRSA
Type: Co-educational Day & Boarding 7 –18
No of pupils: B60 G126 VIth101
Fees: FB £13,536–£15,348 DAY £7428 –£9060

Elstree

ALDENHAM SCHOOL
Elstree, Hertfordshire WD6 3AJ
Tel: 01923 858122
Head: S R Borthwick BSc, CPhys, MInstP
Type: Boys Boarding & Day B11–18 G16–18
No of pupils: B375 VIth120
Fees: FB £8316–£11,910 DAY £5196 –£8175

Harpenden

ALDWICKBURY SCHOOL
Wheathampstead Road, Harpenden, Hertfordshire AL5 1AE
Tel: 01582 713022
Head: P H Jeffery BA
Type: Boys Day & Boarding B4–13 G4–7
No of pupils: B295 G20
Fees: WB £6195–£6540 DAY £4290 –£4965

Hatfield

QUEENSWOOD SCHOOL
Shepherd's Way, Brookmans Park, Hatfield,
Hertfordshire AL9 6NS
Tel: 01707 652262
Head: Ms Clarissa Farr BA(Hons), MA, PGCE
Type: Girls Boarding & Day 11 –18
No of pupils: G405 VIth137
Fees: FB £12,330–£13,425 DAY £7620 –£8310

Hemel Hempstead

★ABBOT'S HILL JUNIOR SCHOOL ST NICHOLAS HOUSE
Bunkers Lane, Hemel Hempstead, Hertfordshire HP3 8RP
Tel: 01442 211156
Head: Mrs B Vaughan CertEd(Reading)
Type: Co-educational Boarding & Day B3–7 G3–11
No of pupils: 280 B130 G150
Fees: FB £11,820 WB £11,745 DAY £3810 –£4710

★ABBOT'S HILL SCHOOL
Bunkers Lane, Hemel Hempstead, Hertfordshire HP3 8RP
Tel: 01442 240333
Head: Mrs K Lewis MA(Cantab), BSc(Open), PGCE, FRSA,
MIMgt
Type: Girls Boarding & Day 11 –16
No of pupils: 165 G165
Fees: FB £11,820 WB £11,745 DAY £7050

LOCKERS PARK SCHOOL
Lockers Park Lane, Hemel Hempstead,
Hertfordshire HP1 1TL
Tel: 01442 251712
Head: Mr D R Lees-Jones ARCM, GRSM
Type: Boys Boarding & Day 7 –13
No of pupils: B125
Fees: FB £9570 DAY £5880 –£6960

WESTBROOK HAY SCHOOL
London Road, Hemel Hempstead, Hertfordshire HP1 2RF
Tel: 01442 256143
Head: Keith Young BEd(Hons)Exeter
Type: Co-educational Day & Boarding 2 –13
No of pupils: 210 B150 G60
Fees: WB £8100 DAY £3300 –£6600

Hertford

HAILEYBURY
Haileybury, Hertford SG13 7NU
Tel: 01992 463353
Head: S A Westley MA
Type: Boys Boarding & Day 11 –18
No of pupils: 591 B506 G85
Fees: FB £13,338 DAY £6405 –£9672

HEATH MOUNT SCHOOL
Woodhall Park, Watton-at-Stone, Hertford SG14 3NG
Tel: 01920 830230
Head: Rev H J Matthews MA, BSc, PGCE
Type: Co-educational Boarding & Day 3 –13
No of pupils: 354 B229 G125
Fees: FB £7635–£8835 DAY £1875 –£6585

Hitchin

THE PRINCESS HELENA COLLEGE
Temple Dinsley, Preston, Hitchin, Hertfordshire SG4 7RT
Tel: 01462 432100
Head: Mrs Anne-Marie Hodgkiss BScEcon(London), PGCE
Type: Girls Boarding & Day 11 –18
No of pupils: 144 G144
Fees: FB £9270–11,610 DAY £6270 –£7920

Letchworth

⋆ST CHRISTOPHER SCHOOL
Barrington Road, Letchworth, Hertfordshire SG6 3JZ
Tel: 01462 679301
Head: Mr Colin Reid MA
Type: Co-educational Day & Boarding B3–18 G3–18
No of pupils: 536 B337 G199 VIth102
Fees: FB £10,065–£12,564 DAY £1779 –£7122

ST FRANCIS' COLLEGE
The Broadway, Letchworth, Hertfordshire SG6 3PJ
Tel: 01462 670511
Head: Miss M Hegarty BA, HDipEd, DHS
Type: Girls Day & Boarding B3–7 G3–18
No of pupils: B13 G282 VIth52
Fees: FB £9375–£10,965 WB £8745–£10,305
DAY £2820 –£5625

Near Ware

⋆ST EDMUND'S COLLEGE
Old Hall Green, Near Ware, Hertfordshire SG11 1DS
Tel: 01920 821504
Head: Mr D J J McEwen MA(Oxon), FRSA
Type: Co-educational Day & Boarding 3 –18
No of pupils: 520 B310 G210 VIth130
Fees: FB £9315–£11,535 WB £8745–£10,695
DAY £3960 –£7185

Rickmansworth

⋆THE ROYAL MASONIC SCHOOL FOR GIRLS
Rickmansworth Park, Rickmansworth,
Hertfordshire WD3 4HF
Tel: 01923 773168
Head: Mrs I M Andrews MA(Oxon)
Type: Girls Day & Boarding 4 –18
No of pupils: 720 G720 VIth120
Fees: FB £6078–£9876 DAY £3093 –£6009

St Albans

BEECHWOOD PARK
Markyate, St Albans, Hertfordshire AL3 8AW
Tel: 01582 840333
Head: D S Macpherson MA
Type: Boys Day & Boarding 4 –13
No of pupils: 407 B295 G112
Fees: FB £8895 DAY £4515 –£6180

Tring

THE ARTS EDUCATIONAL SCHOOL
Tring Park, Tring, Hertfordshire HP23 5LX
Tel: 01442 824255
Head: Mrs J D Billing GGSM(London), CertEd, FRSA
Type: Co-educational Boarding & Day 8 –18
No of pupils: 231
Fees: FB £9540–£13,410 DAY £5502 –£7812

Watford

STANBOROUGH SCHOOL
Stanborough Park, Garston, Watford, Hertfordshire
WD2 6JT
Tel: 01923 673268
Head: Dr A Luxton PhD
Type: Co-educational Day & Boarding 3 –18
No of pupils: 215
Fees: FB £7215–£8220 WB £6195–£7200
DAY £2280 –£3375

Welwyn

SHERRARDSWOOD SCHOOL
Lockleys, Welwyn, Hertfordshire AL6 0BJ
Tel: 01438 714282
Head: Martin Lloyd MA
Type: Co-educational Day & Boarding 4 –18
No of pupils: B159 G138 VIth20
Fees: FB £6804–£8385 DAY £2706 –£4437

Isle of Man

Castletown

KING WILLIAM'S COLLEGE
Castletown, Isle of Man IM9 1TP
Tel: 01624 822551
Head: Mr K Fulton-Peebles MA
Type: Co-educational Day & Boarding 11 –18
No of pupils: B165 G135 VIth80
Fees: FB £10,200–£12,630 DAY £6660 –£9090

THE BUCHAN SCHOOL
West Hill, Castletown, Isle of Man IM9 1RD
Tel: 01624 822526
Head: Mr P H Moody MA(Cantab)
Type: Co-educational Day & Boarding 3 –11
No of pupils: B116 G98
Fees: FB £9060–£9855 DAY £4005 –£6135

Isle of Wight

Ryde

RYDE SCHOOL WITH UPPER CHINE
Queens Road, Ryde, Isle of Wight PO33 3BE
Tel: 01983 562229
Head: Dr N J England MA, DPhil
Type: Co-educational Day & Boarding 3 –18
No of pupils: B371 G294 VIth114
Fees: FB £8550–£9690 WB £8550–£9690
DAY £1950 –£4740

Kent

Ashford

*ASHFORD SCHOOL
East Hill, Ashford, Kent TN24 8PB
Tel: 01233 625171/2
Head: Mrs J Burnett BEd(Durham), MA(Bristol)
Type: Girls Day & Boarding 3 –18
No of pupils: 525 G525 VIth111
Fees: FB £10,674–£12,897 DAY £1167 –£8541

FRIARS SCHOOL
Great Chart, Ashford, Kent TN23 3DJ
Tel: 01233 620493
Head: P M Ashley CertEd, BA
Type: Co-educational Boarding & Day 3 –13
No of pupils: 225 B150 G75
Fees: WB £8490 DAY £1920 –£6090

Broadstairs

WELLESLEY HOUSE
114 Ramsgate Road, Broadstairs, Kent CT10 2DG
Tel: 01843 862991
Head: R R Steel BSc
Type: Co-educational Boarding & Day 7 –13
No of pupils: B94 G55
Fees: FB £9600 WB £9300 DAY £7200

Bromley

BASTON SCHOOL
Baston Road, Hayes, Bromley, Kent BR2 7AB
Tel: 0181 462 1010
Head: Charles R C Wimble MA(Cantab), PGTC
Type: Girls Day & Boarding 2 –18
No of pupils: 177 G177 VIth22
Fees: FB £10,350 WB £10,200 DAY £1125 –£5250

Canterbury

KENT COLLEGE
Whitstable Road, Canterbury, Kent CT2 9DT
Tel: 01227 763231
Head: E B Halse BSc Wales
Type: Co-educational Day & Boarding 3 –18
No of pupils: B307 G218 VIth160
Fees: FB £8481–£10,770 DAY £6048

KING'S JUNIOR SCHOOL
Milner Court, Sturry, Canterbury, Kent CT2 0AY
Tel: 01227 714000
Head: Mr R G Barton MA
Type: Co-educational Boarding & Day 4 –13
No of pupils: B186 G115
Fees: FB £9885 DAY £3960 –£6945

ST EDMUND'S JUNIOR SCHOOL
St Thomas Hill, Canterbury, Kent CT2 8HU
Tel: 01227 454575
Head: R G Bacon BA(Hons)(Durham)
Type: Co-educational Day & Boarding 3 –13
No of pupils: 217 B140 G95
Fees: FB £8100 DAY £2985 –£5655

ST EDMUND'S SCHOOL
St Thomas' Hill, Canterbury, Kent CT2 8HU
Tel: 01227 454575
Head: Mr A N Ridley MA(Oxon)
Type: Co-educational Day & Boarding 3 –18
No of pupils: B310 G186 VIth102
Fees: FB £9576–£13,923 DAY £4851 –£8988

*THE KING'S SCHOOL, CANTERBURY
Canterbury, Kent CT1 2ES
Tel: 01227 595501
Head: Rev Canon Keith Wilkinson BA, MA, FRSA
Type: Co-educational Boarding & Day 13 –18
No of pupils: 754 B424 G330 VIth346
Fees: FB £9885–£14,955 DAY £6945 –£10,335

VERNON HOLME
(Kent College Infant & Junior Sch), Harbledown, Canterbury,
Kent CT2 9AQ
Tel: 01227 762436
Head: Mr T J Smith BA
Type: Co-educational Day & Boarding 3 –11
No of pupils: B119 G99
Fees: FB £8994 DAY £3105 –£6216

Chislehurst

*FARRINGTONS & STRATFORD HOUSE
Perry Street, Chislehurst, Kent BR7 6LR
Tel: 0181 467 0256
Head: Mrs Catherine James MA
Type: Girls Day & Boarding 11 –18
No of pupils: 285 VIth60
Fees: FB £11,880 WB £11,490 DAY £6030

***FARRINGTONS & STRATFORD HOUSE
JUNIOR SCHOOL**
Perry Street, Chislehurst, Kent BR7 6LR
Tel: 0181 467 0256/0395
Head: Mrs Catherine James MA
Type: Girls Boarding & Day 2 –11
No of pupils: 212
Fees: FB £10,770 WB £10,320 DAY £4230

Cranbrook

*BEDGEBURY SCHOOL
Bedgebury Park, Goudhurst, Cranbrook, Kent TN17 2SH
Tel: 01580 211221/211954
Head: Mrs L J Griffin BA, BPhil
Type: Girls Boarding & Day B3–7 G3–18
No of pupils: 360 B9 G360 VIth81
Fees: FB £8286–£12,570 DAY £1830 –£7806

BENENDEN SCHOOL
Cranbrook, Kent TN17 4AA
Tel: 01580 240592
Head: Mrs G duCharme MA
Type: Girls Boarding 11 –18
No of pupils: 440 G440 VIth140
Fees: FB £13,260

BETHANY SCHOOL
Goudhurst, Cranbrook, Kent TN17 1LB
Tel: 01580 211273
Head: Mr N D B Dorey MA (Oxon)
Type: Co-educational Boarding & Day 11 –18
No of pupils: B230 G55 VIth85
Fees: FB £11,136–£11,742 WB £11,136–£11,742
DAY £7125 –£7228

★DULWICH PREPARATORY SCHOOL
Coursehorn, Cranbrook, Kent TN17 3NP
Tel: 01580 712179
Head: Mr M C Wagstaffe BA(Hons), PGCE
Type: Co-educational Day & Boarding 3 –13
No of pupils: 536 B288 G248
Fees: FB £9660–£9900 DAY £2250 –£6510

Deal

NORTHBOURNE PARK SCHOOL
Betteshanger, Deal, Kent CT14 0NW
Tel: 01304 611215/218
Head: Mr F Roche BEd(Hons), MA
Type: Co-educational Day & Boarding 3 –13
No of pupils: B124 G104
Fees: FB £8445–£10,380 DAY £4185 –£6705

Dover

DOVER COLLEGE
Effingham Crescent, Dover, Kent CT17 9RH
Tel: 01304 205969
Head: Mr Howard W Blackett MA
Type: Co-educational Boarding & Day 11 –18
No of pupils: 260 B149 G111 VIth86
Fees: FB £10,155–£11,997 WB £8955–£10,122
DAY £4455 –£7122

★DUKE OF YORK'S ROYAL MILITARY SCHOOL
Guston, Dover, Kent CT15 5EQ
Tel: 01304 245024
Head: Col G H Wilson BA, DipEd, MEd, FRSA
Type: Co-educational Boarding 11 –18
No of pupils: 500 VIth110
Fees: FB £855

Folkestone

★ST MARY'S WESTBROOK
Ravenlea Road, Folkestone, Kent CT20 2JU
Tel: 01303 851222
Head: Christopher FitzGerald BA, CertEd, ACP, FRSA
Type: Co-educational Day & Boarding 2 –16
No of pupils: 222 B115 G107
Fees: FB £7095–£8865 DAY £3720 –£6615

Gravesend

COBHAM HALL SCHOOL
Cobham, Gravesend, Kent DA12 3BL
Tel: 01474 823371
Head: Mrs Rosalind McCarthy BA
Type: Girls Boarding & Day 11 –19
No of pupils: 260 G200 VIth60
Fees: FB £12,750 DAY £7140 –£8665

Hawkhurst

MARLBOROUGH HOUSE SCHOOL
High Street, Hawkhurst, Kent TN18 4PY
Tel: 01580 753555
Head: Mr David N Hopkins MA(Oxon), PGCE
Type: Co-educational Day & Boarding 3 –13
No of pupils: B156 G104
Fees: FB £9570 WB £9570 DAY £1995 –£7350

ST RONAN'S
Hawkhurst, Kent TN18 5DJ
Tel: 01580 752271
Head: Mr E Yeats-Brown MA
Type: Co-educational Boarding & Day 2 –13
No of pupils: B100 G26
Fees: FB £2995 WB £2995 DAY £122 –£2205

Maidstone

SUTTON VALENCE SCHOOL
Sutton Valence, Maidstone, Kent ME17 3HN
Tel: 01622 842281
Head: Mr N A Sampson MA
Type: Co-educational Day & Boarding 3 –18
No of pupils: 693 B396 G297 VIth112
Fees: FB £9900–£13,140 DAY £3570 –£8400

Ramsgate

ST LAWRENCE COLLEGE IN THANET
Ramsgate, Kent CT11 7AE
Tel: 01843 587666
Head: Mark Slater, MA
Type: Co-educational Boarding & Day 4 –18
No of pupils: B321 G204 VIth132
Fees: FB £8880–£11,835 DAY £5820 –£7905

THE JUNIOR SCHOOL, ST LAWRENCE COLLEGE
College Road, Ramsgate, Kent CT11 7AF
Tel: 01843 591788
Head: Rev D D R Blackwall BSc
Type: Co-educational Day & Boarding 4 –13
No of pupils: B85 G64
Fees: FB £8880 DAY £2070 –£5820

Rochester

KING'S PREPARATORY SCHOOL
King Edward Road, Rochester, Kent ME1 1UB
Tel: 01634 843657
Head: Mr C J Nickless BA
Type: Co-educational Day & Boarding 3 –13
No of pupils: 349
Fees: FB £10,245–£11,115 DAY £5850 –£6720

KING'S SCHOOL, ROCHESTER
Satis House, Boley Hill, Rochester, Kent ME1 1TE
Tel: 01634 843913
Head: Dr I R Walker BA, PhD, LTh, ABIA, FCollP, FRSA
Type: Co-educational Day & Boarding 8 –18
No of pupils: B440 G130 Vlth125
Fees: FB £10,245–£14,025 DAY £5850 –£8085

Sevenoaks

THE NEW BEACON
Brittains Lane, Sevenoaks, Kent TN13 2PB
Tel: 01732 452131
Head: Mr R Constantine MA(Cantab)
Type: Boys Day & Boarding 5 –13
No of pupils: B415
Fees: WB £7815 DAY £2895 –£5115

WALTHAMSTOW HALL
Sevenoaks, Kent TN13 3UL
Tel: 01732 451334
Head: Mrs J S Lang MA(Oxford)
Type: Girls Day & Boarding 3 –18
No of pupils: G455 Vlth90
Fees: FB £13,500 DAY £600 –£7290

Tonbridge

TONBRIDGE SCHOOL
Tonbridge, Kent TN9 1JP
Tel: 01732 365555
Head: J M Hammond MA
Type: Boys Boarding & Day 13 –18
No of pupils: 702 B702 Vlth286
Fees: FB £14,400 DAY £10,170

Tunbridge Wells

BEECHWOOD SACRED HEART
12 Pembury Road, Tunbridge Wells, Kent TN2 3QD
Tel: 01892 532747
Head: Susana M Price-Cabrera BSc, PhD, FedTC, PGDPC
Type: Girls Day & Boarding B2–11 G2–18
No of pupils: B32 G192 Vlth50
Fees: FB £8700–£11,700 WB £8700–£11,700
DAY £1350 –£7020

HOLMEWOOD HOUSE
Langton Green, Tunbridge Wells, Kent TN3 0EB
Tel: 01892 860000
Head: Mr A S R Corbett MA
Type: Co-educational Day & Boarding 3 –13
Fees: FB £12,225 DAY £2595 –£8220

KENT COLLEGE JUNIOR SCHOOL
Aultmore House, Old Church Road, Pembury, Tunbridge
Wells, Kent TN2 4AX
Tel: 01892 820204
Head: Mrs Diana Dunham CertEd
Type: Girls Day & Boarding 3 –11
No of pupils: G186
Fees: FB £10,035 WB £8835 DAY £3525 –£5295

KENT COLLEGE, PEMBURY
Pembury, Tunbridge Wells, Kent TN2 4AX
Tel: 01892 822006
Head: Miss B J Crompton BSc, CPhys, MInstP
Type: Girls Boarding & Day 3 –18
No of pupils: 437 G437 Vlth57
Fees: FB £10,035–£13,635 WB £8835–£12,720
DAY £5295 –£7995

Westgate-on-Sea

URSULINE COLLEGE
225 Canterbury Road, Westgate-on-Sea, Kent CT8 8LX
Tel: 01843 834431
Head: Sr Alice Montgomery OSU, MEd
Type: Co-educational Boarding & Day 4 –18
No of pupils: B128 G189 Vlth120
Fees: FB £10,248–£11,793 DAY £1590 –£5979

Lancashire

Carnforth

CASTERTON SCHOOL
Kirby Lonsdale, Carnforth, Lancashire LA6 2SG
Tel: 01524 279200
Head: Mr A F Thomas MA(Cantab)
Type: Girls Day & Boarding 8 –18
No of pupils: G351 VIth78
Fees: FB £8607–£10,755 DAY £5940 –£6840

Clitheroe

MOORLAND SCHOOL
Ribblesdale Avenue, Clitheroe, Lancashire BB7 2JA
Tel: 01200 423833
Head: Mrs M Ashcroft MIMgt, FRSA
Type: Co-educational Boarding & Day 2 –16
No of pupils: B70 G75
Fees: FB £8250–£8670 WB £8160–£8580
DAY £2370 –£3912

STONYHURST COLLEGE
Stonyhurst, Clitheroe, Lancashire BB7 9PZ
Tel: 01254 826345
Head: Mr A J F Aylward MA(Oxon), PGCE
Type: Co-educational Boarding & Day B13–18 G16–18
No of pupils: B370 G30 VIth190
Fees: FB £12,540–£21,540 DAY £7800

Fleetwood

ROSSALL PREPARATORY SCHOOL
Fleetwood, Lancashire FY7 8JW
Tel: 01253 774222
Head: Mr David Mitchell Bed
Type: Co-educational Day & Boarding 2 –11
No of pupils: B148 G134
Fees: FB £8190–£12,090 DAY £4725

Lancaster

BENTHAM GRAMMAR SCHOOL
Bentham, Lancaster, Lancashire LA2 7DB
Tel: 01524 261275
Head: Mr T Halliwell BSc, MA
Type: Co-educational Boarding & Day 3 –18
No of pupils: 268 B146 G122 VIth50
Fees: FB £8160–£9690 WB £8160–£9690
DAY £2850 –£4830

Preston

*KIRKHAM GRAMMAR SCHOOL
Ribby Road, Kirkham, Preston, Lancashire PR4 2BH
Tel: 01772 671079
Head: B Stacey MA, DipEd(Oxon), FRSA
Type: Co-educational Day & Boarding 4 –18
No of pupils: 867 B439 G428 VIth179
Fees: FB £8463 DAY £3255 –£4335

Stonyhurst

ST MARY'S HALL
Stonyhurst, Lancashire BB7 9PU
Tel: 01254 826242
Head: Mr R F O'Brien BA(London), FTII, PGCE
Type: Co-educational Boarding & Day 7 –13
No of pupils: B192 G36
Fees: FB £8985 WB £8310 DAY £4365 –£6315

Leicestershire

Coalville

GRACE DIEU MANOR SCHOOL
Grace Dieu, Coalville, Leicestershire LE67 5UG
Tel: 01530 222276
Head: Mr T Kilbride BA
Type: Co-educational Day 3–13
No of pupils: B242 G107
Fees: DAY £3267 –£5295

Leicester

*RATCLIFFE COLLEGE
Fosse Way, Ratcliffe on the Wreake, Leicester LE7 4SG
Tel: 01509 817000
Head: Mr T A Kilbride BA
Type: Co-educational Boarding & Day 9–18
No of pupils: 530 VIth150
Fees: FB £10,329 WB £10,329 DAY £6888

Loughborough

*LOUGHBOROUGH GRAMMAR SCHOOL
6 Burton Walks, Loughborough, Leicestershire LE11 2DU
Tel: 01509 233233
Head: P B Fisher MA
Type: Boys Day & Boarding 10–18
No of pupils: 970 B970 VIth280
Fees: FB £9369 WB £8235 DAY £5148

Market Harborough

NEVILL HOLT SCHOOL
Market Harborough, Leicestershire LE16 8EG
Tel: 01858 565234
Head: Mr I P Mackenzie BA
Type: Co-educational Day & Boarding 4–13
No of pupils: B80 G40
Fees: FB £8430 DAY £2910 –£6360

Lincolnshire

Bourne

WITHAM HALL
Whitham-on-the-Hill, Bourne, Lincolnshire PE10 0JJ
Tel: 01778 590222
Head: D Telfer BA, CertEd & Mrs S Telfer CertEd
Type: Co-educational Day & Boarding 4–14
No of pupils: B100 G58
Fees: FB £8010 WB £8010 DAY £3420 –£5970

Lincoln

LINCOLN MINSTER PREPARATORY SCHOOL
Eastgate, Lincoln, Lincolnshire LN2 1QG
Tel: 01522 523769
Head: Mr C Rickart
Type: Co-educational Day & Boarding 2–13
No of pupils: B112 G66
Fees: FB £8016–£9267 DAY £3591 –£4878

LINCOLN MINSTER SCHOOL
Hillside, Lindum Terrace, Lincoln, Lincolnshire LN2 5PR
Tel: 01522 543764
Head: Mrs M Bradley BEd, MEd
Type: Girls Day & Boarding 11–18
No of pupils: B75 G167 VIth40
Fees: FB £8016–£9267 DAY £3591 –£4878

Stamford

*STAMFORD HIGH SCHOOL
St Martin's, Stamford, Lincolnshire PE9 2LJ
Tel: 01780 484200
Head: Dr P R Mason BSc, PhD, FRSA
Type: Girls Day & Boarding B2–8 G2–18
No of pupils: 933 B62 G871 VIth184
Fees: FB £8424–£11,148 DAY £3828 –£4848

STAMFORD HIGH SCHOOL JUNIOR SCHOOL
Kettering Road, Stamford, Lincolnshire PE9 2LR
Tel: 01780 484400
Head: Miss E M Craig CertEd(Cambridge)
Type: Co-educational Boarding & Day 2–11
No of pupils: B50 G180
Fees: FB £9000 DAY £3850

*STAMFORD SCHOOL
St Paul's Street, Stamford, Lincolnshire PE9 2BS
Tel: 01780 750300
Head: Dr P R Mason BSc, PhD, FRSA
Type: Boys Day & Boarding 8–18
No of pupils: 863 B863 VIth195
Fees: FB £8424–£11,148 DAY £3828 –£4848

STAMFORD SCHOOL JUNIOR SCHOOL
St Paul's Street, Stamford, Lincolnshire PE9 2BS
Tel: 01780 750306
Head: D R Moss-Bowpitt JP, BEd(Exeter)
Type: Boys Day & Boarding 8 –13
No of pupils: B347
Fees: FB £8139 –£9048 DAY £3615 –£4524

Woodhall Spa

ST HUGH'S SCHOOL
Cromwell Avenue, Woodhall Spa, Lincolnshire LN10 6TQ
Tel: 01526 352169
Head: P M Wells BEd(Hons)
Type: Co-educational Boarding & Day 4 –13
No of pupils: 155
Fees: FB £7800 WB £7800 DAY £3120 –£5769

N E Lincolnshire

Grimsby

ST JAMES' SCHOOL
22 Bargate, Grimsby, N E Lincolnshire DN34 4SY
Tel: 01472 362093/4
Head: D J Berisford BA, CertEd
Type: Co-educational Boarding & Day 3 –18
No of pupils: 251 B149 G102 VIth26
Fees: FB £6867 –£8916 WB £6426 –£8475
DAY £2325 –£5325

London

London

★DULWICH COLLEGE
London SE21 7LD
Tel: 0181 693 3601
Head: G G Able MA, MA
Type: Boys Day & Boarding 7 –18
No of pupils: 1396 B1396 VIth391
Fees: FB £13,410 –£13,965 DAY £6705 –£7080

★DULWICH COLLEGE PREPARATORY SCHOOL
42 Alleyn Park, Dulwich, London SE21 7AA
Tel: 0181 670 3217
Head: Mr George Marsh MA(Oxon), CertEd
Type: Boys Boarding & Day B3 –13 G3 –5
No of pupils: 802 B785 G17
Fees: WB £9213 –£9966 DAY £6108 –£6861

ELTHAM COLLEGE
Grove Park Road, Mottingham, London SE9 4QF
Tel: 0181 857 1455
Head: Mr D M Green MA, FRSA
Type: Boys Day & Boarding B7 –18 G16 –18
No of pupils: 774 B734 G40 VIth189
Fees: FB £12,625 –£13,225 DAY £5300 –£6400

FOREST BOYS SCHOOL
College Place, Snaresbrook, London E17 3PY
Tel: 0181 520 1744
Head: Mr A G Boggis MA(Oxon)
Type: Co-educational Boarding & Day B11 –18 G16 –18
No of pupils: B740 VIth248
Fees: FB £10,284 DAY £6552

FOREST PREP SCHOOL
Snaresbrook, London E17 3PY
Tel: 0181 520 1744
Head: R T Cryer MEd
Type: Boys Day & Boarding B7 –13 G7 –11
No of pupils: B350 G50
Fees: FB £6366 –£9087 WB £6051 –£9087
DAY £3960 –£5790

MILL HILL SCHOOL
The Ridgeway, Mill Hill Village, London NW7 1QS
Tel: 0181 959 1176
Head: William R Winfield MA
Type: Co-educational Boarding & Day 13 –18
No of pupils: B460 G65 VIth200
Fees: FB £4216 –£4466 DAY £2735 –£2985

★ST PAUL'S CATHEDRAL SCHOOL
2 New Change, London EC4M 9AD
Tel: 0171 248 5156
Head: Mr Stephen S Sides BEd(Oxon), CertEd
Type: Boys Boarding & Day B4 –13 G4 –7
No of pupils: 142
Fees: FB £3360 DAY £5100 –£5580

ST PAUL'S PREPARATORY SCHOOL
Colet Court, Lonsdale Road, London, London SW13 9JT
Tel: 0181 748 3461
Head: Mr G J Thompson BA, CertEd, MEd, CBiol, MIBiol, FLS, FCP, FRSA
Type: Boys Day & Boarding 7 –13
No of pupils: B437
Fees: FB £12,045 DAY £7245

*THE ROYAL SCHOOL, HAMPSTEAD
65 Rosslyn Hill, Hampstead, London, London NW3 5UD
Tel: 0171 794 7707
Head: Mrs C A Sibson BA(Oxon)
Type: Girls Day & Boarding 4 –18
No of pupils: 200 G200 VIth15
Fees: FB £8100–£10,062 WB £6300–£8262
DAY £3855 –£4587

WESTMINSTER ABBEY CHOIR SCHOOL
Dean's Yard, London, London SW1P 3NY
Tel: 0171 222 6151
Head: R P Overend BA, FTCL, ARCM, FRSA
Type: Boys Boarding 8 –13
No of pupils: 38 B38
Fees: FB £2919

WESTMINSTER CATHEDRAL CHOIR SCHOOL
Ambrosden Avenue, London, London SW1P 1QH
Tel: 0171 798 9081
Head: C Foulds BA
Type: Boys Day & Boarding 8 –13
No of pupils: B96
Fees: FB £3030–£3372 DAY £6120

WESTMINSTER SCHOOL
17 Dean's Yard, Westminster, London, London SW1P 3PB
Tel: 0171 963 1003
Head: D M Summerscale MA
Type: Boys Boarding & Day B13–18 G16–18
No of pupils: B320 VIth361
Fees: FB £13,530 WB £13,530 DAY £9300 –£10,125

Greater Manchester

Manchester

CHETHAM'S SCHOOL OF MUSIC
Long Millgate, Manchester, Greater Manchester M3 1SB
Tel: 0161 834 9644
Head: Canon P F Hullah BD, AKC, FRSA
Type: Co-educational Boarding & Day 8 –18
No of pupils: B126 G162 VIth125
Fees: FB £16,425 DAY £12,714

Merseyside

Wirral

KINGSMEAD SCHOOL
Bertram Drive, Hoylake, Wirral, Merseyside L47 0LL
Tel: 0151 632 3156
Head: Mr E H Bradby MA, MSc
Type: Co-educational Boarding & Day 3 –16
No of pupils: B102 G50
Fees: FB £6855–£7485 WB £6555–£7185
DAY £1650 –£4935

Middlesex

Ashford

ST DAVID'S SCHOOL FOR GIRLS
Freepost Sea 0837, Ashford, Middlesex TW15 3BR
Tel: 01784 252494
Head: Mrs Judith G Osborne BA(Hons), DipEd
Type: Girls Day & Boarding 3 –18
No of pupils: 430 B52 G430 Vlth40
Fees: FB £10,920 WB £9930 DAY £4560 –£6060

Harrow

★HARROW SCHOOL
1 High Street, Harrow, Middlesex HA1 3HW
Tel: 0181 869 1200
Head: Mr Nicholas R Bomford MA, FRSA
Type: Boys Boarding 13 –18
No of pupils: 790 B790 Vlth320
Fees: FB £15,150

Northwood

MERCHANT TAYLORS' SCHOOL
Sandy Lodge, Northwood, Middlesex HA6 2HT
Tel: 01923 820644
Head: Mr J R Gabitass MA(Oxon)
Type: Boys Day & Boarding 11 –18
No of pupils: 774 B774 Vlth251
Fees: FB £12,550 DAY £7550

ST HELEN'S SCHOOL FOR GIRLS
Eastbury Road, Northwood, Middlesex HA6 3AS
Tel: 01923 828511
Head: Mrs Diana M Jefkins MA(Cantab), Cphys
Type: Girls Day & Boarding 5 –18
No of pupils: G979 Vlth161
Fees: FB £8547–£10,101 DAY £4164 –£5361

Norfolk

Cromer

BEESTON HALL SCHOOL TRUST LIMITED
Beeston Hall School, West Runton, Cromer, Norfolk
NR27 9NQ
Tel: 01263 837324
Head: Mr I K MacAskill BEd(Hons)
Type: Co-educational Boarding & Day 7 –13
No of pupils: 170 B100 G70
Fees: FB £9615 DAY £7185

Diss

RIDDLESWORTH HALL
Garboldisham, Diss, Norfolk IP22 2TA
Tel: 01953 681246
Head: Mr D P Dean BA, CertEd
Type: Girls Boarding & Day B2–8 G2–13
No of pupils: B41 G109
Fees: FB £10,185 WB £10,095 DAY £2400 –£6495

Holt

GRESHAM'S PREPARATORY SCHOOL
Cromer Road, Holt, Norfolk NR25 6EY
Tel: 01263 712227
Head: Mr A H Cuff CertEd DPE
Type: Co-educational Day & Boarding 7 –13
No of pupils: B138 G112
Fees: FB £10,185 WB £9255 DAY £7260

GRESHAM'S SCHOOL
Holt, Norfolk NR25 6EA
Tel: 01263 713271
Head: Mr J H Arkell MA
Type: Co-educational Boarding & Day 13 –19
No of pupils: B160 G120 Vlth220
Fees: FB £13,965 DAY £9945

Hunstanton

GLEBE HOUSE SCHOOL
2 Cromer Road, Hunstanton, Norfolk PE36 6HW
Tel: 01485 532809
Head: Michael W Spinney BEd(Hons), CertEd
Type: Co-educational Boarding & Day 4 –13
No of pupils: B76 G42
Fees: WB £6390–£6900 DAY £3135 –£5850

Norwich

CAWSTON COLLEGE
Cawston, Norwich, Norfolk NR10 4JD
Tel: 01603 871204
Head: Mrs B Harrison BA(Hons), PGCE
Type: Co-educational Boarding & Day 7 –16
No of pupils: B80 G36
Fees: FB £6930–£9000 DAY £3000 –£4770

ECCLES HALL SCHOOL
Quidenham, Norwich, Norfolk NR16 2NZ
Tel: 01953 887217
Head: S A Simington
Type: Co-educational Boarding & Day 10 –16
No of pupils: 150
Fees: FB £8685 DAY £4560

HETHERSETT OLD HALL SCHOOL
Hethersett, Norwich, Norfolk NR9 3DW
Tel: 01603 810390
Head: Mrs V M Redington MA, DipEd(Oxon)
Type: Girls Boarding & Day 7 –18
No of pupils: 242 G242 VIth42
Fees: FB £8700–£10,800 WB £8700–£10,800
DAY £4125 –£5430

★LANGLEY SCHOOL
Langley Park, Loddon, Norwich, Norfolk NR14 6BJ
Tel: 01508 520210
Head: Mr J G Malcolm BSc, MA, CertEd
Type: Co-educational Boarding & Day 10 –18
No of pupils: 259 B192 G67 VIth73
Fees: FB £10,065–£12,195 WB £9405–£11,415
DAY £5190 –£6330

TAVERHAM HALL SCHOOL
Taverham, Norwich, Norfolk NR8 6HU
Tel: 01603 868206
Head: Mr Waine D Lawton MEd
Type: Co-educational Boarding & Day 3 –13
No of pupils: B128 G63
Fees: FB £8970 DAY £3105 –£6885

TOWN CLOSE HOUSE PREPARATORY SCHOOL
14 Ipswich Road, Norwich, Norfolk NR2 2LR
Tel: 01603 620180
Head: Mr S Higginson MA(Oxon)
Type: Co-educational Day & Boarding 3 –13
No of pupils: B357 G71
Fees: WB £7029 DAY £1260 –£5040

Swaffham

CONVENT OF THE SACRED HEART SCHOOL
17 Mangate Street, Swaffham, Norfolk PE37 7QW
Tel: 01760 721330/724577
Head: Sr M Francis Ridler FDC
Type: Co-educational Day & Boarding B3–11 G3–16
No of pupils: B45 G172
Fees: WB £5850 DAY £2700 –£3840

Northamptonshire

Brackley

BEACHBOROUGH SCHOOL
Westbury, Brackley, Northamptonshire NN13 5LB
Tel: 01280 700071
Head: Mr A J L Boardman CertEd
Type: Co-educational Day & Boarding 2 –13
No of pupils: B136 G75
Fees: WB £8685 DAY £4170 –£6750

WINCHESTER HOUSE
High Street, Brackley, Northamptonshire NN13 7AZ
Tel: 01280 702483
Head: J R G Griffith BA, PGCE
Type: Co-educational Boarding & Day 3 –13
No of pupils: 261 B182 G79
Fees: FB £10,080 DAY £3090 –£7575

Northampton

MAIDWELL HALL
Maidwell, Northampton, Northamptonshire NN6 9JG
Tel: 01604 686234
Head: P R Whitton BA, PGCE
Type: Boys Boarding & Day 3 –13
No of pupils: B110 G21
Fees: FB £9600 DAY £5250 –£6000

Towcester

FALCON MANOR SCHOOL
Greens Norton, Towcester, Northamptonshire NN12 8BN
Tel: 01327 350544
Head: Mr R Siewert
Type: Co-educational Boarding & Day 5 –18
No of pupils: B79 G41 VIth16
Fees: FB £6975–£8775 WB £8625 DAY £3450 –£4725

Wellingborough

WELLINGBOROUGH SCHOOL
Wellingborough, Northamptonshire NN8 2BX
Tel: 01933 222427
Head: F R Ullmann MA, ACP, FCollP
Type: Co-educational Day & Boarding 13 –18
No of pupils: B246 G134 VIth136
Fees: FB £9300 WB £8370 DAY £2490 –£5175

Northumberland

Berwick-upon-Tweed

LONGRIDGE TOWERS SCHOOL
Longridge Towers, Berwick-upon-Tweed,
Northumberland TD15 2XH
Tel: 01289 307584
Head: Dr M J Barron BSc, PhD
Type: Co-educational Day & Boarding 4 –18
No of pupils: B120 G125 VIth45
Fees: FB £7245–£8340 WB £7245–£8340
DAY £2475 –£4170

Stocksfield

MOWDEN HALL SCHOOL
Newton, Stocksfield, Northumberland NE43 7TP
Tel: 01661 842147
Head: A P Lewis MA
Type: Co-educational Boarding & Day 4 –13
No of pupils: B123 G84
Fees: FB £3015 DAY £1250 –£2160

Nottinghamshire

Newark

RODNEY SCHOOL
Kirklington, Newark, Nottinghamshire NG22 8NB
Tel: 01636 813281
Head: Miss G R T Howe BEd(Hons)
Type: Co-educational Boarding & Day 7 –18
No of pupils: B38 G37 VIth6
Fees: FB £7755–£8055 WB £7755–£8055
DAY £3855 –£4575

WELLOW HOUSE SCHOOL
Wellow, Newark, Nottinghamshire NG22 0EA
Tel: 01623 861054
Head: Dr Malcolm Tozer BSc, MEd, PhD
Type: Co-educational Day & Boarding 2 –13
No of pupils: 145 B83 G62
Fees: WB £7200 DAY £3000 –£5670

Nottingham

TRENT COLLEGE
Derby Road, Long Eaton, Nottingham NG10 4AD
Tel: 0115 9732737
Head: J S Lee MA(Oxon)
Type: Co-educational Boarding & Day 11 –18
No of pupils: B465 G237 VIth239
Fees: FB £9657–£11,445 DAY £6507 –£7026

Retford

BRAMCOTE LORNE SCHOOL
Gamston, Retford, Nottinghamshire DN22 0QQ
Tel: 01777 838636
Head: Mark L Jones CertEd, FRGS
Type: Co-educational Boarding & Day 2 –13
No of pupils: 195 B110 G85
Fees: FB £7425 DAY £2580 –£5985

RANBY HOUSE
Retford, Nottinghamshire DN22 8HX
Tel: 01777 703138
Head: D C Wansey MA(Ed)
Type: Co-educational Day & Boarding 3 –13
No of pupils: B183 G140
Fees: FB £7680 WB £7680 DAY £3300 –£5880

Worksop

WORKSOP COLLEGE
Worksop, Nottinghamshire S80 3AP
Tel: 01909 537100
Head: R A Collard MA
Type: Co-educational Boarding & Day 13 –18
No of pupils: B220 G130 VIth110
Fees: FB £11,835 DAY £8145

Oxfordshire

Abingdon

*ABINGDON SCHOOL
Park Road, Abingdon, Oxfordshire OX14 1DE
Tel: 01235 531755
Head: M St John Parker MA
Type: Boys Boarding & Day 11 –18
No of pupils: 795 B795 VIth270
Fees: FB £11,511 DAY £6246

COTHILL HOUSE
Abingdon, Oxfordshire OX13 6JL
Tel: 01865 390800
Head: Mr A D Richardson CertEd
Type: Boys Boarding 8 –13
No of pupils: B250
Fees: FB £11,100

MILLBROOK HOUSE SCHOOL
Milton, Abingdon, Oxfordshire OX14 4EL
Tel: 01235 831237
Head: Mr S R M Glazebrook BSc, EngTechAMIAgrE
Type: Co-educational Boarding & Day 8 –14
No of pupils: B45 G2
Fees: FB £11,250 DAY £5700

RADLEY COLLEGE
Radley, Abingdon, Oxfordshire OX14 2HR
Tel: 01235 543000
Head: R M Morgan MA
Type: Boys Boarding 13 –18
No of pupils: 629 B629 VIth254
Fees: FB £14,550

Banbury

BLOXHAM SCHOOL
Bloxham, Banbury, Oxfordshire OX15 4PE
Tel: 01295 720206
Head: Mr D K Exham MA
Type: Co-educational Boarding & Day 11 –18
No of pupils: 340 B360 VIth173
Fees: FB £12,735 DAY £6660 –£9990

SIBFORD JUNIOR SCHOOL
Sibford Ferris, Banbury, Oxfordshire OX15 5QN
Tel: 01295 78441
Head: J Dunston
Type: Co-educational Day

SIBFORD SCHOOL
Sibford Ferris, Banbury, Oxfordshire OX15 5QL
Tel: 01295 781200
Head: Mrs Susan Freestone GRSM, MEd, LRAM, ARCM
Type: Co-educational Boarding & Day 5 –18
No of pupils: B184 G126 VIth54
Fees: FB £8955–£11,700 WB £7935–£10,905
DAY £2970 –£5805

*TUDOR HALL SCHOOL
Wykham Park, Banbury, Oxfordshire OX16 9UR
Tel: 01295 263434
Head: Miss N Godfrey BA
Type: Girls Boarding & Day 11 –18
No of pupils: 265 G265 VIth79
Fees: FB £11,955

Chipping Norton

KINGHAM HILL SCHOOL
Kingham, Chipping Norton, Oxfordshire OX7 6TH
Tel: 01608 658999
Head: Mr M H Payne BSc, PGCE
Type: Co-educational Boarding & Day 11 –18
No of pupils: B171 G50 VIth63
Fees: FB £10,170–£10,995 DAY £6090 –£6600

Faringdon

ST HUGH'S SCHOOL
Carswell Manor, Faringdon, Oxfordshire SN7 8PT
Tel: 01367 870223
Head: D Cannon MA
Type: Co-educational Day & Boarding 4 –13
No of pupils: B158 G72
Fees: FB £8250–£8730 WB £7500 DAY £3810 –£6930

Henley-on-Thames

SHIPLAKE COLLEGE
Henley-on-Thames, Oxfordshire RG9 4BS
Tel: 0118 940 2455
Head: Mr N V Bevan MA(Oxon)
Type: Boys Boarding & Day B13–18 G16–18
No of pupils: B280 VIth90
Fees: FB £12,300 DAY £8280

Oxford

CHRIST CHURCH CATHEDRAL SCHOOL
3 Brewer Street, Oxford OX1 1QW
Tel: 01865 242561
Head: Allan H Mottram MA(Cantab)
Type: Boys Day & Boarding 2 –13
No of pupils: B141
Fees: FB £7596 DAY £2961 –£4977

*D'OVERBROECK'S COLLEGE
Beechlawn House, Park Town, Oxford OX2 6SN
Tel: 01865 310000/311902
Principals: Mr S Cohen BSc & Dr R Knowles MA,
DPhil(Oxon)
Type: Co-educational Day & Boarding 13 –19
No of pupils: 270 B130 G140
Fees: FB £10,350–£15,315 DAY £6750 –£10,215

★DRAGON SCHOOL
Bardwell Road, Oxford OX2 6SS
Tel: 01865 315400
Head: Mr R S Trafford MA(Oxon)
Type: Co-educational Boarding & Day 3 –13
No of pupils: 815 B615 G200
Fees: FB £11,235 DAY £4290 –£7545

HEADINGTON SCHOOL
Oxford OX3 7TD
Tel: 01865 741968
Head: Mrs H A Fender BA(Exeter)
Type: Girls Day & Boarding B4–7 G4–18
No of pupils: B15 G600 VIth154
Fees: FB £8070–£9600 WB £7974–£9504
DAY £2550 –£4830

RYE ST ANTONY SCHOOL
Pullens Lane, Headington Hill, Oxford OX3 0BY
Tel: 01865 762802
Head: Miss A M Jones BA, PGCE
Type: Girls Boarding & Day 8 –18
No of pupils: G400
Fees: FB £7185–£7950 WB £6885–£7575
DAY £2775 –£4875

★ST EDWARD'S, OXFORD
Woodstock Road, Oxford OX2 7NN
Tel: 01865 319200
Head: David Christie BA, BSc(Econ)
Type: Co-educational Boarding & Day 13 –18
No of pupils: 568 B468 G100
Fees: FB £13,425 DAY £9600

SUMMER FIELDS
Mayfield Road, Oxford OX2 7EN
Tel: 01865 554433
Head: Mr R F Badham-Thornhill BA, PGCE
Type: Boys Boarding & Day 8 –13
No of pupils: B254
Fees: FB £10,620 DAY £7010

★WYCHWOOD SCHOOL
74 Banbury Road, Oxford OX2 6JR
Tel: 01865 557976
Head: Mrs S Wingfield Digby BA(Hons)Oxon,
PGCE(London)
Type: Girls Boarding & Day 11 –18
No of pupils: 170 G170 VIth30
Fees: FB £8040 DAY £5070

Wallingford

MOULSFORD PREPARATORY SCHOOL
Moulsford, Wallingford, Oxfordshire OX10 9HR
Tel: 01491 651438
Head: M J Higham BA, CertEd
Type: Boys Day & Boarding 5 –13
No of pupils: 220 B220
Fees: WB £7020–£8475 DAY £4020 –£6750

Wantage

ST MARY'S SCHOOL, WANTAGE
Newbury Street, Wantage, Oxfordshire OX12 8BZ
Tel: 01235 763571
Head: Mrs S Bodinham BSc, AKC, AdvDipEd
Type: Girls Boarding 11 –18
No of pupils: G220 VIth73
Fees: FB £12,300 DAY £8200

Witney

COKETHORPE SCHOOL
Cokethorpe, Witney, Oxfordshire OX8 7PU
Tel: 01993 703921
Head: P J S Cantwell BA
Type: Co-educational Boarding & Day 7 –18
No of pupils: 300 B230 G70 VIth41
Fees: FB £9300–£13,200 DAY £4200 –£8700

Rutland

Oakham

OAKHAM SCHOOL
Chapel Close, Oakham, Rutland LE15 6DT
Tel: 01572 722487
Head: Mr A R M Little MA
Type: Co-educational Boarding & Day 10 –18
No of pupils: B405 G405 VIth330
Fees: FB £12,240–£13,530 DAY £7800 –£8100

Uppingham

UPPINGHAM SCHOOL
Uppingham, Rutland LE15 9QE
Tel: 01572 822216
Head: Dr S C Winkley MA, DPhil
Type: Boys Boarding & Day B11–18 G16–18
No of pupils: 642 B514 G128 VIth340
Fees: FB £13,920 DAY £9000

Shropshire

Bucknell

BEDSTONE COLLEGE
Bedstone, Bucknell, Shropshire SY7 0BG
Tel: 01547 530303
Head: Mr M S Symonds BSc, PGCE
Type: Co-educational Boarding & Day 7 –18
No of pupils: B75 G75 VIth50
Fees: FB £6519–£9639 DAY £4335 –£6000

Ellesmere

ELLESMERE COLLEGE
Ellesmere, Shropshire SY12 9AB
Tel: 01691 622321
Head: Mr B J Wignall MA, MIMgt
Type: Co-educational Boarding & Day 9 –18
No of pupils: 402 B264 G138 VIth126
Fees: FB £9048–£11,652 DAY £4452 –£7716

Ludlow

MOOR PARK SCHOOL
Ludlow, Shropshire SX8 4EA
Tel: 01584 876061
Head: J R Badham BA, BEd(Oxon)
Type: Co-educational Boarding & Day 3 –13
No of pupils: 304 B166 G138
Fees: FB £7695–£9090 DAY £900 –£6570

Oswestry

★MORETON HALL
Weston Rhyn, Oswestry, Shropshire SY11 3EW
Tel: 01691 773671
Head: Mr Jonathan Forster BA, FRSA
Type: Girls Boarding & Day 11 –18
No of pupils: 261 VIth90
Fees: FB £13,320 DAY £9135

OSWESTRY SCHOOL
Upper Brook Street, Oswestry, Shropshire SY11 2TL
Tel: 01691 655711
Head: Mr P K Smith MA(Cantab), MEd, FRGS
Type: Co-educational Boarding & Day 9 –18
No of pupils: B179 G103
Fees: FB £10,452–£11,442 DAY £5856 –£6816

Shrewsbury

ADCOTE SCHOOL FOR GIRLS
Little Ness, Shrewsbury, Shropshire SY4 2JY
Tel: 01939 260202
Head: Mrs A E Read MA, BSc, PGCE
Type: Girls Boarding & Day 4 –18
No of pupils: G100 VIth15
Fees: FB £8670–£10,710 WB £7875–£9765
DAY £3315 –£6150

CONCORD COLLEGE
Acton Burnell Hall, Shrewsbury, Shropshire SY5 7PF
Tel: 01694 731631
Head: A L Morris BA, DipEd
Type: Co-educational Day & Boarding 12 –19
No of pupils: 280 B170 G110 VIth200
Fees: FB £13,500 DAY £4800

KINGSLAND GRANGE
Old Roman Road, Shrewsbury, Shropshire SY3 9AH
Tel: 01743 232132
Head: Mr M C James MSc
Type: Boys Day & Boarding 4 –13
No of pupils: B150
Fees: WB £5880 DAY £2985 –£4980

★PACKWOOD HAUGH
Ruyton XI Towns, Shrewsbury, Shropshire SY4 1HX
Tel: 01939 260217
Head: Mr P J F Jordan MA(Cantab)
Type: Co-educational Boarding & Day 7 –13
No of pupils: 226 B144 G82
Fees: FB £9468 DAY £3150 –£7362

PRESTFELDE PREPARATORY SCHOOL
London Road, Shrewsbury, Shropshire SY2 6NZ
Tel: 01743 356500
Head: Mr J R Bridgeland MA
Type: Co-educational Boarding & Day 3 –13
No of pupils: B242 G38
Fees: FB £7650 DAY £1800 –£5940

★SHREWSBURY SCHOOL
The Schools, Shrewsbury, Shropshire SY3 7BA
Tel: 01743 344537
Head: Mr F E Maidment MA
Type: Boys Boarding & Day 13 –18
No of pupils: 700 B700 VIth302
Fees: FB £14,325 DAY £10,080

Telford

THE OLD HALL SCHOOL
Holyhead Road, Wellington, Telford, Shropshire TF1 2DN
Tel: 01952 223117
Head: R J Ward MA
Type: Co-educational Day & Boarding 3 –13
No of pupils: B182 G151
Fees: WB £5655 DAY £2775 –£4410

WREKIN COLLEGE
Wellington, Telford, Shropshire TF1 3BG
Tel: 01952 240131
Head: Mr S G Drew MA
Type: Co-educational Boarding & Day 11–18
No of pupils: B190 G130 Vlth108
Fees: FB £3960–£4360 DAY £2280–£2640

Somerset

Bath

DOWNSIDE SCHOOL
Stratton-on-the-Fosse, Bath, Somerset BA3 4RJ
Tel: 01761 235100
Head: Dom Antony Sutch MA
Type: Boys Boarding & Day 9–19
No of pupils: B300 Vlth120
Fees: FB £9768–£12,180 DAY £5556–£6180

KINGSWOOD SCHOOL
Lansdown, Bath, Somerset BA1 5RG
Tel: 01225 734200
Head: G M Best MA
Type: Co-educational Boarding & Day 11–18
No of pupils: B184 G136 Vlth133
Fees: FB £9321–£11,829 WB £9321–£11,829
DAY £5757–£7350

MONKTON COMBE JUNIOR SCHOOL
Combe Down, Bath, Somerset BA2 7ET
Tel: 01225 837912
Head: Mr C J Stafford BA, CertEd
Type: Co-educational Day & Boarding 2–13
No of pupils: B191 G80
Fees: FB £9075–£9510 DAY £5625–£6660

MONKTON COMBE SENIOR SCHOOL
Bath, Somerset BA2 7HG
Tel: 01225 721102
Head: M J Cuthbertson MA
Type: Co-educational Boarding & Day 11–19
No of pupils: 332 B222 G110 Vlth131
Fees: FB £11,235–£13,725 WB £11,235–£13,725
DAY £7560–£9375

PRIOR PARK COLLEGE
Bath, Somerset BA2 5AH
Tel: 01225 835353
Head: Dr Giles Mercer MA, Dphil
Type: Co-educational Boarding & Day 11–18
No of pupils: B288 G227 Vlth154
Fees: FB £12,054WB £12,054 DAY £6384–£6669

Bruton

BRUTON SCHOOL FOR GIRLS
Sunny Hill, Bruton, Somerset BA10 0NT
Tel: 01749 812277
Head: Mrs A Napier
Type: Girls Boarding & Day 8–18
No of pupils: G540 Vlth94
Fees: FB £7761 DAY £4011

KING'S BRUTON
Bruton, Somerset BA10 0ED
Tel: 01749 813326
Head: Mr R I Smyth MA
Type: Co-educational Boarding & Day 13 –18
No of pupils: B311 G50 VIth157
Fees: FB £12,360 DAY £8850

Crewkerne

PERROTT HILL SCHOOL
North Perrott, Crewkerne, Somerset TA18 7SL
Tel: 01460 72051
Head: Michael Davies BA(Hons), PGCE
Type: Co-educational Boarding & Day 3 –13
No of pupils: 163 B98 G65
Fees: FB £8520 DAY £1830 –£6129

Glastonbury

MILLFIELD PREPARATORY SCHOOL
Glastonbury, Somerset BA6 8LD
Tel: 01458 832446
Head: S P J Cummins MA
Type: Co-educational Boarding & Day 7 –13
No of pupils: 513 B322 G191
Fees: FB £10,485 DAY £7050

Highbridge

ROSSHOLME SCHOOL
East Brent, Highbridge, Somerset TA9 4JA
Tel: 01278 760219
Head: Mrs S J B Webb FRSA
Type: Girls Day & Boarding B3–7 G3–16
No of pupils: B5 G71
Fees: FB £6150–£7650 DAY £2250

Shepton Mallet

ALL HALLOWS SCHOOL
Cranmore Hall, Shepton Mallet, Somerset BA4 4SF
Tel: 01749 880227
Head: Mr Christopher J Bird BA(Cardiff), PGCE(Exeter)
Type: Co-educational Boarding & Day 4 –13
No of pupils: 245 B150 G95
Fees: FB £9345 DAY £3120 –£6225

Taunton

KING'S COLLEGE
Taunton, Somerset TA1 3DX
Tel: 01823 334222
Head: R S Funnell MA(Cantab)
Type: Co-educational Boarding & Day 13 –18
No of pupils: B279 G153 VIth190
Fees: FB £13,215 DAY £8700

KING'S HALL SCHOOL
Pyrland, Taunton, Somerset TA2 8AA
Tel: 01823 272431
Head: Mrs M Willson CertEd
Type: Co-educational Boarding & Day 3 –13
No of pupils: B230 G180
Fees: FB £5235–£9300 DAY £2160 –£6600

QUEEN'S COLLEGE
Trull Road, Taunton, Somerset TA1 4QS
Tel: 01823 272559
Head: Mr Christopher T Bradnock MA, FRSA
Type: Co-educational Boarding & Day 2 –18
No of pupils: B332 G303 VIth141
Fees: FB £5010–£10,590 DAY £2520 –£6945

QUEEN'S COLLEGE JUNIOR SCHOOL
Trull Road, Taunton, Somerset TA1 4QR
Tel: 01823 272990
Head: Peter N Lee-Smith BA, CertEd
Type: Co-educational Day & Boarding 8 –12
No of pupils: B93 G80
Fees: FB £4770–£8613 DAY £3096 –£5688

TAUNTON PREPARATORY SCHOOL
Staplegrove Road, Taunton, Somerset TA1 1DW
Tel: 01823 349209
Head: J H Gibson BEd
Type: Co-educational Boarding & Day 3 –13
No of pupils: B261 G206
Fees: FB £1430–£2770 DAY £440 –£1830

TAUNTON SCHOOL
Staplegrove Road, Taunton, Somerset TA2 6AD
Tel: 01823 349200
Head: Mr J P Whitely BSc, MBA
Type: Co-educational Boarding & Day 13 –18
No of pupils: B611 G482 VIth185
Fees: FB £12,150 DAY £7785

Wellington

WELLINGTON SCHOOL
South Street, Wellington, Somerset TA21 8NT
Tel: 01823 668800
Head: Mr A J Rogers MA, FRSA
Type: Co-educational Boarding & Day 10 –18
No of pupils: B441 G360 VIth187
Fees: FB £9300 DAY £5088

Wells

WELLS CATHEDRAL JUNIOR SCHOOL
8 New Street, Wells, Somerset BA5 2LQ
Tel: 01749 672291
Head: Mr N M Wilson BA, PGCE
Type: Co-educational Boarding & Day 3 –11
No of pupils: B105 G78
Fees: FB £9705 DAY £3114 –£5985

WELLS CATHEDRAL SCHOOL
Wells, Somerset BA5 2ST
Tel: 01749 672117
Head: Mr John S Baxter BA(Dunelm), DipEd(Oxon), MBIM, FRSA
Type: Co-educational Boarding & Day 3–18
No of pupils: 789 B411 G378 Vlth197
Fees: FB £9705–£11,502 DAY £3114 –£6831

Winscombe

SIDCOT SCHOOL
Winscombe, Somerset BS25 1PD
Tel: 01934 843102
Head: Angus Slesser MA
Type: Co-educational Boarding & Day 9–18
No of pupils: 396 B243 G153 Vlth117
Fees: FB £11,175 DAY £4800 –£6450

Yeovil

CHILTON CANTELO SCHOOL
Chilton Cantelo, Yeovil, Somerset BA22 8BG
Tel: 01935 850555
Head: D S von Zeffman LLB Barrister
Type: Co-educational Boarding & Day 7–18
No of pupils: B60 G60
Fees: FB £6555–£8160 WB £6555–£8160
DAY £3315 –£4410

HAZLEGROVE
(King's Bruton Preparatory School), Hazlegrove Hse, Sparkford, Yeovil, Somerset BA22 7JA
Tel: 01963 440314
Head: Revd Bramwell Bearcroft BEd(Hons)(Cantab)
Type: Co-educational Boarding & Day 3–13
No of pupils: B284 G136
Fees: FB £8250–£9405 DAY £3270 –£6735

THE PARK SCHOOL
Yeovil, Somerset BA20 1DH
Tel: 01935 423514/75468
Head: Mr P W Bate BA(Econ), PGCE, AdvDipMkt
Type: Co-educational Day & Boarding 3–17
No of pupils: B62 G98 Vlth4
Fees: FB £4425–£8970 DAY £1830 –£5130

Staffordshire

Cannock

CHASE ACADEMY
Lyncroft House, St John's Road, Cannock, Staffordshire WS11 3UR
Tel: 01543 502388
Head: Mr R Edgar BSc,PGCE, CPhys, MInstP
Type: Co-educational Day & Boarding 3–18
No of pupils: B80 G57 Vlth12
Fees: FB £9138 DAY £2988 –£4872

Lichfield

LICHFIELD CATHEDRAL SCHOOL
The Palace, Lichfield, Staffordshire WS13 7LH
Tel: 01543 306170
Head: The Rev A F Walters ACP, CertEd
Type: Co-educational Day & Boarding 4–13
No of pupils: 254 B169 G85
Fees: FB £6735–£7680 DAY £3210 –£5265

Nr Lichfield

ABBOTS BROMLEY
School of S Mary & S Anne, Nr Lichfield, Staffordshire WS15 3BW
Tel: 01283 840232
Head: Mrs M Steel BA
Type: Girls Boarding & Day 4–18
No of pupils: G273 Vlth66
Fees: FB £5075–£12,120 DAY £2840 –£8095

Stafford

ST BEDE'S SCHOOL
Bishton Hall, Wolseley Bridge, Stafford ST17 0XN
Tel: 01889 881277
Head: Mr A H & Mrs H C Stafford Northcote MA(Oxon), MA(Cantab)
Type: Co-educational Day & Boarding 3–13
No of pupils: B65 G50
Fees: FB £7200 DAY £5550

THE YARLET SCHOOLS
Yarlet, Stafford ST18 9SU
Tel: 01889 508240
Head: Mr R S Plant MA(Cambridge)
Type: Co-educational Boarding & Day 3–13
No of pupils: 140
Fees: FB £7800 DAY £3060 –£6420

Uttoxeter

ABBOTSHOLME SCHOOL
Rocester, Uttoxeter, Staffordshire ST14 5BS
Tel: 01889 590217
Head: I M Allison MA, PGCE
Type: Co-educational Boarding & Day 10 –18
No of pupils: B121 G88 VIth65
Fees: FB £12,525–£13,011 DAY £6075 –£8355

DENSTONE COLLEGE
Uttoxeter, Staffordshire ST14 5HN
Tel: 01889 590484
Head: Mr David Derbyshire MSc, BA
Type: Co-educational Boarding & Day 11 –18
No of pupils: 336 B227 G109 VIth90
Fees: FB £9219–£10,248 DAY £4635 –£6798

SMALLWOOD MANOR PREP SCHOOL
Smallwood Manor, Uttoxeter, Staffordshire ST14 8NS
Tel: 01889 562083
Head: Reverend C J Cann MA, BA, CertTheol
Type: Co-educational Day 3 –11
No of pupils: 102 B57 G45
Fees: DAY £2775 –£3675

Suffolk

Bury St Edmunds

CULFORD SCHOOL
Culford, Bury St Edmunds, Suffolk IP28 6TX
Tel: 01284 728615
Head: Mr J S Richardson MA
Type: Co-educational Boarding & Day 2 –18
No of pupils: B361 G275 VIth123
Fees: FB £9504–£12,330 DAY £6105 –£8022

MORETON HALL
Mount Road, Bury St Edmunds, Suffolk IP32 7BJ
Tel: 01284 753532
Head: Mr M E Higgins BEd(Hons), MA
Type: Co-educational Boarding & Day 3 –13
No of pupils: B61 G33
Fees: FB £9075 WB £8085 DAY £3930 –£6585

Haverhill

BARNARDISTON HALL PREP SCHOOL
Barnardiston, Haverhill, Suffolk CB9 7TG
Tel: 01440 786316
Head: Lt Col K A Boulter MA(Cantab), PGCE
Type: Co-educational Day & Boarding 1 –13
No of pupils: 300 B150 G150
Fees: FB £8400 WB £7800 DAY £4050 –£5025

Ipswich

IPSWICH SCHOOL
Henley Road, Ipswich, Suffolk IP1 3SG
Tel: 01473 408300
Head: Mr Ian Galbraith MA
Type: Co-educational Day & Boarding 11 –18
No of pupils: B495 G88 VIth200
Fees: FB £8604–£10,026 WB £8454–£9738
DAY £5250 –£5823

★OLD BUCKENHAM HALL SCHOOL
Brettenham, Ipswich, Suffolk IP7 7PH
Tel: 01449 740252
Head: Mr M A Ives BEd(Hons)
Type: Boys Day & Boarding 2 –13
No of pupils: 182
Fees: FB £9600 WB £9750 DAY £3750 –£7800

★ORWELL PARK SCHOOL
Nacton, Ipswich, Suffolk IP10 0ER
Tel: 01473 659225
Head: Mr Andrew H Auster BA(Hons), DipEd(Cantab), Hon
FLCM, FRSA
Type: Co-educational Boarding & Day 3 –13
No of pupils: B156 G89
Fees: FB £9420–£10,590 WB £9420–£10,590
DAY £2805 –£7830

ROYAL HOSPITAL SCHOOL
Holbrook, Ipswich, Suffolk IP9 2RX
Tel: 01473 326200
Head: Mr N K D Ward BSc
Type: Co-educational Boarding 11–18
No of pupils: B430 G220 VIth150
Fees: FB £8600–£12,054 DAY £6450

Leiston

SUMMERHILL SCHOOL
Westward Ho, Leiston, Suffolk IP16 4HY
Tel: 01728 830540
Head: Mrs Z S Readhead
Type: Co-educational Boarding & Day 5–18
No of pupils: B42 G26
Fees: FB £6897 DAY £2046

Southwold

SAINT GEORGE'S SCHOOL
Southwold, Suffolk IP18 6SD
Tel: 01502 723314
Head: Mrs W H Holland ARCM, LRAM, GRSM, CertEd, FCollP
Type: Co-educational Boarding & Day 2–11
No of pupils: 150 B55 G95
Fees: FB £7500 WB £7500 DAY £1980–£4398

ST FELIX SCHOOL
Southwold, Suffolk IP18 6SD
Tel: 01502 722175
Head: Mr R W Williams, BSc, Adv Dip EM
Type: Girls Boarding & Day 11–18
No of pupils: G155 VIth35
Fees: FB £11,550 DAY £7650

Stowmarket

FINBOROUGH SCHOOL
Great Finborough, Stowmarket, Suffolk IP14 3EF
Tel: 01449 773600
Head: Mr J Sinclair BSc(Econ), FCA
Type: Co-educational Boarding & Day 2–18
No of pupils: B102 G78 VIth34
Fees: FB £4800–£9300 DAY £2400–£5100

Sudbury

STOKE COLLEGE
Stoke-by-Clare, Sudbury, Suffolk CO10 8JE
Tel: 01787 278141
Head: Mr John Gibson BA, CertEd
Type: Co-educational Day & Boarding 3–16
No of pupils: B143 G98
Fees: FB £8520–£9480 DAY £3900–£5625

Woodbridge

ALEXANDERS INTERNATIONAL SCHOOL
Bawdsey Manor, Woodbridge, Suffolk IP12 3AZ
Tel: 01394 411633
Head: Dr Graham Platts
Type: Co-educational Boarding 11–18
No of pupils: B60 G40
Fees: FB £9000

★FRAMLINGHAM COLLEGE
Framlingham, Woodbridge, Suffolk IP13 9EY
Tel: 01728 723789
Head: Mrs G M Randall BA
Type: Co-educational Boarding & Day 4–18
No of pupils: 714 B440 G214
Fees: FB £11,373 DAY £8970

★FRAMLINGHAM COLLEGE JUNIOR SCHOOL
Brandeston Hall, Woodbridge, Suffolk IP13 7AQ
Tel: 01728 685331
Head: N Johnson BA
Type: Co-educational Boarding & Day 4–18
No of pupils: B306 G199 VIth212
Fees: FB £8426–£10,648 DAY £5226–£6855

Surrey

Ashtead

CITY OF LONDON FREEMEN'S SCHOOL
Ashtead Park, Ashtead, Surrey KT21 1ET
Tel: 01372 277933
Head: Mr David C Haywood MA
Type: Co-educational Day & Boarding 7 –18
No of pupils: B363 G407 Vlth170
Fees: FB £10,827–£11,187 WB £9045–£11,187
DAY £5520 –£7002

Camberley

ELMHURST BALLET SCHOOL
Heathcote Road, Camberley, Surrey GU15 2EV
Tel: 01276 65301
Head: John McNamara BA, MPhil
Type: Co-educational Boarding & Day 9 –19
No of pupils: B15 G134 Vlth72
Fees: FB £9570 DAY £7020

Caterham

CATERHAM SCHOOL
Harestone Valley, Caterham, Surrey CR3 6YA
Tel: 01883 343028
Head: Mr R A E Davey MA(Dublin)
Type: Co-educational Day & Boarding 11 –18
No of pupils: B486 G202 Vlth188
Fees: FB £12,507–£13,182 DAY £2160 –£7065

Cobham

FELTONFLEET SCHOOL
Cobham, Surrey KT11 1DR
Tel: 01932 862264
Head: D T Cherry
Type: Co-educational Day & Boarding 3 –13
No of pupils: B211 G30
Fees: FB £8400 DAY £2025 –£6300

PARKSIDE SCHOOL
The Manor, Stoke d'Abernon, Cobham, Surrey KT11 3PX
Tel: 01932 862749
Head: R L Shipp FCP, BA, CertEd
Type: Boys Day & Boarding B2–14 G3–5
No of pupils: B290 G20
Fees: FB £8820 DAY £4005 –£6090

REED'S SCHOOL
Sandy Lane, Cobham, Surrey KT11 2ES
Tel: 01932 863076
Head: Mr D W Jarrett MA
Type: Boys Boarding & Day B11–18 G16–18
No of pupils: B381 G20 Vlth126
Fees: FB £10,110–£11,970 DAY £7581 –£9048

Cranleigh

CRANLEIGH PREPARATORY SCHOOL
Horseshoe Lane, Cranleigh, Surrey GU6 8QH
Tel: 01483 274199
Head: Mr Malcolm R Keppie MA, PGCE
Type: Boys Boarding & Day 7 –13
No of pupils: 186 B186
Fees: FB £9735 DAY £7230

CRANLEIGH SCHOOL
Horseshoe Lane, Cranleigh, Surrey GU6 8QQ
Tel: 01483 273666
Head: Mr G de W Waller MA, MSc, FRSA
Type: Boys Boarding & Day B13–18 G16–18
No of pupils: B406 G78 Vlth244
Fees: FB £13,710 DAY £10,140

DUKE OF KENT SCHOOL
Peaslake Road, Ewhurst, Cranleigh, Surrey GU6 7NS
Tel: 01483 277313
Head: Mr R K Wilson MA
Type: Co-educational Boarding & Day 4 –13
No of pupils: B110 G60
Fees: FB £8400–£9870 DAY £2910 –£6765

Croydon

ROYAL RUSSELL PREP SCHOOL
Coombe Lane, Croydon, Surrey CR9 5BX
Tel: 0181 651 5884
Head: Mr C L Hedges BA, CertEd
Type: Co-educational Day 3 –11
No of pupils: B150 G130
Fees: DAY £480 –£1460

Dorking

BELMONT PREPARATORY SCHOOL
Feldemore, Holmbury St Mary, Dorking, Surrey RH5 6LQ
Tel: 01306 730852
Head: D St Clair Gainer BEd(Hons)(London)
Type: Co-educational Boarding & Day 4 –13
No of pupils: 250 B187 G63
Fees: WB £2730 DAY £3105 –£5925

BOX HILL SCHOOL
Mickleham, Dorking, Surrey RH5 6EA
Tel: 01372 373382
Head: Dr R A S Atwood BA, PhD
Type: Co-educational Boarding & Day 11 –18
No of pupils: B176 G93
Fees: FB £10,530 WB £10,080 DAY £5100 –£6300

ST TERESA'S SCHOOL
Effingham Hill, Dorking, Surrey RH5 6ST
Tel: 01372 452037
Head: Mrs Mary Prescott BA(Hons), PGCE, FRSA
Type: Girls Boarding & Day 11 –18
No of pupils: G360
Fees: FB £11,700 DAY £6450

Epsom

EPSOM COLLEGE
Epsom, Surrey KT17 4JQ
Tel: 01372 821004
Head: A H Beadles MA
Type: Co-educational Boarding & Day 13 –18
No of pupils: B549 G99 VIth314
Fees: FB £12,825 WB £12,645 DAY £9525

Esher

CLAREMONT FAN COURT MIDDLE SCHOOL
Claremont Drive, Esher, Surrey KT10 9LY
Tel: 01372 465380
Head: Mr F Clark-Brown BSc, HDE, BEd(Hons)
Type: Co-educational Day 7 –11
No of pupils: 137 B65 G72
Fees: DAY £5205

Farnham

EDGEBOROUGH
Frensham, Farnham, Surrey GU10 3AH
Tel: 01252 792495
Head: Mr R A Jackson MA(Cantab), PGCE
Type: Co-educational Boarding & Day 3 –13
No of pupils: 300 B214 G86
Fees: FB £8475–£10,020 DAY £4245 –£7575

★FRENSHAM HEIGHTS SCHOOL
Rowledge, Farnham, Surrey GU10 4EA
Tel: 01252 792134
Head: Peter M de Voil MA, FRSA
Type: Co-educational Boarding & Day 4 –18
No of pupils: 342 B160 G176 VIth90
Fees: FB £12,600–£13,800 DAY £8100 –£9150

Godalming

ALDRO SCHOOL
Shackleford, Godalming, Surrey GU8 6AS
Tel: 01483 409020
Head: Mr I M Argyle BEd
Type: Boys Boarding & Day 7 –13
No of pupils: B220
Fees: FB £9975 DAY £7590

CHARTERHOUSE
Godalming, Surrey GU7 2DX
Tel: 01483 291601
Head: Rev John Witheridge MA
Type: Boys Boarding & Day B13–18 G16–18
No of pupils: B627 G78
Fees: FB £13,341 DAY £11,022

★KING EDWARD'S SCHOOL WITLEY
Petworth Road, Wormley, Godalming, Surrey GU8 5SG
Tel: 01428 682572
Head: R J Fox MA, CMath, FIMA
Type: Co-educational Boarding & Day 11 –18
No of pupils: 472 B282 G190 VIth127
Fees: FB £10,695 DAY £7320

★PRIOR'S FIELD SCHOOL
Priorsfield Road, Godalming, Surrey GU7 2RH
Tel: 01483 810551
Head: Mrs J M McCallum BA(Hons)
Type: Girls Boarding & Day 11 –18
No of pupils: 234 G234 VIth56
Fees: FB £11,670 DAY £7800

Guildford

★ST CATHERINE'S SCHOOL
Bramley, Guildford, Surrey GU5 0DF
Tel: 01483 893363
Head: Mrs C M Oulton MA(Oxon)
Type: Girls Day & Boarding 4 –18
No of pupils: 693 VIth102
Fees: FB £10,680–£11,985 DAY £3615 –£7230

Haslemere

THE ROYAL SCHOOL
Farnham Lane, Haslemere, Surrey GU27 1HQ
Tel: 01428 605407
Head: Miss Linda Inniss MA
Type: Girls Day & Boarding 4 –18
No of pupils: 313 VIth50
Fees: FB £8829–£11,214 DAY £4185 –£7146

WISPERS SCHOOL
High Lane, Haslemere, Surrey GU27 1AD
Tel: 01428 643646
Head: Henry Beltran BA(Hons), PGCE
Type: Girls Boarding & Day 11 –18
No of pupils: 130
Fees: FB £10,350 DAY £6660

Hindhead

AMESBURY SCHOOL
Hazel Grove, Hindhead, Surrey GU26 6BL
Tel: 01428 604322
Head: Mr Nigel Taylor MA
Type: Co-educational Day & Boarding 3 –13
No of pupils: 250 B158 G92
Fees: WB £8655 DAY £4350 –£6960

ST EDMUND'S SCHOOL TRUST LTD
Portsmouth Road, Hindhead, Surrey GU26 6BH
Tel: 01428 604808
Head: Mr A J Fowler-Watt MA(Cantab)
Type: Co-educational Boarding & Day 2 –13
No of pupils: 180 B160 G20
Fees: FB £6440–£8390 DAY £5550 –£7500

Leatherhead

ST JOHN'S SCHOOL
Epsom Road, Leatherhead, Surrey KT22 8SP
Tel: 01372 372021
Head: C H Tongue MA(Cantab)
Type: Boys Boarding & Day B13–18 G16–18
No of pupils: B350 G50 Vlth186
Fees: FB £11,700 WB £11,700 DAY £8100

Oxted

HAZELWOOD SCHOOL
Wolf's Hill, Limpsfield, Oxted, Surrey RH8 0QU
Tel: 01883 712194
Head: A M Synge MA(Oxon), PGCE
Type: Co-educational Day & Boarding 3 –13
No of pupils: 339 B234 G105
Fees: WB £7860 DAY £1755 –£5940

Windlesham

WOODCOTE HOUSE SCHOOL
Snows Ride, Windlesham, Surrey GU20 6PF
Tel: 01276 472115
Head: Mr N H K Paterson BA(Hons), PGCE
Type: Boys Boarding & Day 7 –14
No of pupils: B100
Fees: FB £8700 DAY £6000

Woking

HOE BRIDGE AND THE TREES SCHOOL
Hoe Place, Old Woking Road, Woking, Surrey GU22 8JE
Tel: 01483 760018
Head: Mr R W K Barr BEd(Oxon)
Type: Co-educational Boarding & Day 2 –14
No of pupils: 434 B339 G95
Fees: FB £8250–£9105 DAY £780 –£6345

Woldingham

WOLDINGHAM SCHOOL
Marden Park, Woldingham, Surrey CR3 7YA
Tel: 01883 349431
Head: Mrs Maureen Ribbins MA, MSc, BSc
Type: Girls Boarding & Day 11 –18
No of pupils: G410 Vlth140
Fees: FB £13,431 DAY £8124

East Sussex

Battle

BATTLE ABBEY SCHOOL
Battle, East Sussex TN33 0AD
Tel: 01424 772385
Head: Mr R C Clark
Type: Co-educational Day & Boarding 2 –18
No of pupils: B94 G110 Vlth36
Fees: FB £8400–£10,485 DAY £3570 –£6570

Brighton

BRIGHTON COLLEGE
Eastern Road, Brighton, East Sussex BN2 2AL
Tel: 01273 704202
Head: Dr A F Seldon MA, PhD, FRSA, MBA, FR, HISS
Type: Co-educational Day & Boarding 13 –18
No of pupils: B340 G139 Vlth197
Fees: FB £13,695–£14,055 WB £11,985–£12,345
DAY £8700 –£9066

HAWKHURST COURT SCHOOL
Brighton College, 161 Eastern Road, Brighton,
East Sussex BN2 2AG
Tel: 01273 681484
Head: Mrs M F Hollinshead CertEd, RSA, DipSpLD
Type: Co-educational Day & Boarding 7 –13
No of pupils: B33 G5
Fees: WB £8850 DAY £7455

ROEDEAN SCHOOL
Brighton, East Sussex BN2 5RQ
Tel: 01273 603181
Head: Mrs P Metham BA
Type: Girls Boarding & Day 11 –18
No of pupils: 410 G410 Vlth170
Fees: FB £14,925 DAY £9720 –£9720

ST AUBYNS
76 High Street, Rottingdean, Brighton,
East Sussex BN2 7JN
Tel: 01273 302170
Head: Mr Adrian Gobat BSc Hons, PGCE
Type: Co-educational Boarding & Day 4 –13
No of pupils: B102 G15
Fees: FB £9630 DAY £7020

*ST MARY'S HALL
Eastern Road, Brighton, East Sussex BN2 5JF
Tel: 01273 606061
Head: Mrs S M Meek MA
Type: Girls Day & Boarding B3–8 G3–18
No of pupils: 403 B7 G369 Vlth40
Fees: FB £7875–£10,215 DAY £4089 –£6675

Eastbourne

EASTBOURNE COLLEGE
Old Wish Road, Eastbourne, East Sussex BN21 4JX
Tel: 01323 452300
Head: Mr C M P Bush MA
Type: Co-educational Boarding & Day 13–18
No of pupils: B368 G141 VIth230
Fees: FB £13,590 DAY £9360 –£9360

MOIRA HOUSE JUNIOR SCHOOL
Upper Carlisle Road, Eastbourne, East Sussex BN20 7TE
Tel: 01323 644144
Head: Mrs Jane Booth-Clibborn CertEd, CertEng
Type: Girls Day & Boarding 2–11
No of pupils: 95 G95
Fees: FB £9045–£9915 DAY £3465 –£6390

MOIRA HOUSE SCHOOL
Upper Carlisle Road, Eastbourne, East Sussex BN20 7TD
Tel: 01323 644144
Head: Mrs Ann Harris BEd(Hons), ARCM
Type: Girls Boarding & Day 11–18
No of pupils: 320 VIth70
Fees: FB £9915–£12,935 WB £9045–£11,395
DAY £3465 –£8190

ST ANDREW'S SCHOOL
Meads, Eastbourne, East Sussex BN20 7RP
Tel: 01323 733203
Head: H Davies Jones MA
Type: Co-educational Day & Boarding 3–13
No of pupils: B262 G175
Fees: FB £9225 WB £8625 DAY £1890 –£6390

ST BEDE'S PREPARATORY SCHOOL
Duke's Drive, Eastbourne, East Sussex BN20 7XL
Tel: 01323 734222
Head: Mr C Pyemont DipEd
Type: Co-educational Day & Boarding 2–13
No of pupils: 360 B210 G150
Fees: FB £10,485 DAY £6720

Forest Row

ASHDOWN HOUSE SCHOOL
Forest Row, East Sussex RH18 5JY
Tel: 01342 822574
Head: M V C Williams MA(Cantab)
Type: Co-educational Boarding & Day 8–13
No of pupils: B148 G54
Fees: FB £8010 DAY £7200

GREENFIELDS SCHOOL
Priory Road, Forest Row, East Sussex RH18 5JD
Tel: 01342 822845
Head: Mr A M McQuade MA(Oxon)
Type: Co-educational Day & Boarding 3–18
No of pupils: B99 G76 VIth14
Fees: FB £9312–£9947 DAY £2933 –£5441

MICHAEL HALL SCHOOL
Kidbrooke Park, Forest Row, East Sussex RH18 5JB
Tel: 01342 822275
Head: Chair of the College of Teachers
Type: Co-educational Day & Boarding 1–19
No of pupils: 407 B202 G205 VIth28
Fees: FB £4200–£5580 DAY £2100 –£4650

Hailsham

*ST BEDE'S SCHOOL
The Dicker, Hailsham, East Sussex BN27 3QH
Tel: 01323 843252
Head: Mr R A Perrin MA
Type: Co-educational Boarding & Day 12½–18
No of pupils: 532 B350 G182 VIth203
Fees: FB £13,050 DAY £7875

Hastings

BROOMHAM SCHOOL
Guestling, Hastings, East Sussex TN35 4LT
Tel: 01424 814456
Head: Mr S Prince BA(Hons), DipSLC
Type: Co-educational Boarding & Day 2–18
No of pupils: B67 G58 VIth4
Fees: FB £7377–£12,540 DAY £3175 –£8640

Hove

MOWDEN SCHOOL
The Droveway, Hove, East Sussex BN3 6LU
Tel: 01273 503452
Head: C E M Snell
Type: Boys Day & Boarding 7–13
No of pupils: B101
Fees: WB £6360 DAY £5325

Mayfield

ST LEONARDS-MAYFIELD SCHOOL
The Old Palace, Mayfield, East Sussex TN20 6PH
Tel: 01435 873055
Head: Sister J Sinclair BSc, PGCE
Type: Girls Boarding & Day 11–18
No of pupils: G500 VIth165
Fees: FB £12,213 DAY £8142

Robertsbridge

VINEHALL SCHOOL
Robertsbridge, East Sussex TN32 5JL
Tel: 01580 880413
Head: D C Chaplin BA, CertEd
Type: Co-educational Boarding & Day 2–13
No of pupils: 389 B239 G150
Fees: FB £9330 DAY £4020

Seaford

*NEWLANDS SCHOOL
Eastbourne Road, Seaford, East Sussex BN25 4NP
Tel: 01323 892334
Head: Mr Oliver T Price BEd(Hons)
Type: Co-educational Boarding & Day 2 –18
No of pupils: 550 B350 G200 VIth68
Fees: FB £8850–£9765 DAY £4650 –£6195

Uckfield

TEMPLE GROVE SCHOOL
Heron's Ghyll, Uckfield, East Sussex TN22 4DA
Tel: 01825 712112
Head: Mrs J E Lee BA, CertEd
Type: Co-educational Day & Boarding 3 –13
No of pupils: B71 G70
Fees: FB £7560–£8910 DAY £4260 –£7110

Wadhurst

BELLERBYS COLLEGE MAYFIELD AND WADHURST
(Central Admissions), Mayfield Lane, Wadhurst, East
Sussex TN5 6JA
Tel: 01892 782000
Head: Geoffrey Hazell MA(Cantab), PGCE & Mrs Margaret
Burnett Ward
Type: Co-educational Boarding & Day 11 –18
No of pupils: B133 G184 VIth71
Fees: FB £4200 DAY £1000 –£2140

West Sussex

Arundel

SLINDON COLLEGE
Slindon House, Slindon, Arundel, West Sussex BN18 0RH
Tel: 01243 814320
Head: Mr P D Morris BEd, MA(Oxon)
Type: Boys Boarding & Day 11 –18
No of pupils: 110 B110 VIth10
Fees: FB £10,365 DAY £6420

Burgess Hill

BURGESS HILL SCHOOL
Keymer Road, Burgess Hill, West Sussex RH15 0EG
Tel: 01444 241050
Head: Mrs Rosemary Lewis BSc
Type: Girls Day & Boarding 4 –18
No of pupils: 581 G581 VIth95
Fees: FB £10,635 DAY £2925 –£6285

Chichester

GREAT BALLARD SCHOOL
Eartham, Chichester, West Sussex PO18 0LR
Tel: 01243 814236
Head: Mr Richard E T Jennings CertEd
Type: Co-educational Boarding & Day 2 –13
No of pupils: 181
Fees: FB £7875–£8424 DAY £1623 –£6000

LAVANT HOUSE ROSEMEAD
Chichester, West Sussex PO18 9AB
Tel: 01243 527211
Head: Mrs S E Watkins BA
Type: Girls Day & Boarding 5 –18
No of pupils: G150 VIth20
Fees: FB £9180–£11,490 DAY £3210 –£6450

LITTLEMEAD GRAMMAR SCHOOL
Woodfield House, Oving, Chichester,
West Sussex PO20 6EU
Tel: 01243 787551
Head: Mr I F A Bowler
Type: Co-educational Day & Boarding 3 –16
No of pupils: B61 G35
Fees: FB £6630–£7800 WB £6120–£7290
DAY £1248 –£4800

OAKWOOD SCHOOL
Oakwood, Chichester, West Sussex PO18 9AN
Tel: 01243 575209
Head: Mr Andrew H Cowell BEd
Type: Co-educational Boarding & Day 2 –11
No of pupils: B86 G74
Fees: WB £7818 DAY £2652 –£5898

THE PREBENDAL SCHOOL
53 West Street, Chichester, West Sussex PO19 1RT
Tel: 01243 782026
Head: Rev Canon Godfrey C Hall MA(Oxon)
Type: Co-educational Day & Boarding 3 –13
No of pupils: 286 B165 G121
Fees: FB £7860 WB £7500 DAY £1425 –£5760

WESTBOURNE HOUSE SCHOOL
Shopwyke, Chichester, West Sussex PO20 6BH
Tel: 01243 782739
Head: S L Rigby BA, PGCE
Type: Co-educational Boarding & Day 3 –13
No of pupils: 285 B191 G94
Fees: FB £8880 DAY £3675 –£7155

Crawley

COPTHORNE SCHOOL TRUST
Effingham Lane, Copthorne, Crawley,
West Sussex RH10 3HR
Tel: 01342 712311
Head: Mr David Newton BA(Hons)
Type: Co-educational Day & Boarding 2 –13
No of pupils: 248 B156 G92
Fees: WB £7860 DAY £3660 –£6690

WORTH SCHOOL
Turners Hill, Crawley, West Sussex RH10 4SD
Tel: 01342 710200
Head: Rev P C Jamison MA(Oxon)
Type: Boys Boarding & Day 11 –18
No of pupils: B405 VIth125
Fees: FB £9630–£13,179 DAY £6681 –£9024

East Grinstead

BRAMBLETYE
Brambletye, East Grinstead, West Sussex RH19 3PD
Tel: 01342 321004
Head: Mr H Cocke BA
Type: Boys Boarding & Day 7 –13
No of pupils: 168 B168
Fees: FB £10,185 DAY £7485

Hassocks

HURSTPIERPOINT COLLEGE
Hassocks, West Sussex BN6 9JS
Tel: 01273 833636
Head: Mr S D A Meek MA
Type: Co-educational Boarding & Day 7 –18
No of pupils: B385 G125 VIth170
Fees: FB £8850–£13,170 DAY £5175 –£10,200

HURSTPIERPOINT JUNIOR SCHOOL
Hurstpierpoint, Hassocks, West Sussex BN6 9JS
Tel: 01273 834975
Head: S J Andrews BA, LĒsL
Type: Co-educational Day & Boarding 7 –13
No of pupils: B122 G39
Fees: FB £8430 DAY £4920 –£6255

Haywards Heath

ARDINGLY COLLEGE
Haywards Heath, West Sussex RH17 6SQ
Tel: 01444 892577/892429
Head: J W Flecker MA
Type: Co-educational Boarding & Day 13 –18
No of pupils: B256 G191
Fees: FB £11,085 DAY £8805

ARDINGLY COLLEGE JUNIOR SCHOOL
Haywards Heath, West Sussex RH17 6SQ
Tel: 01444 892279
Head: Peter Thwaites
Type: Co-educational Day & Boarding 2 –13
No of pupils: B70 G75
Fees: FB £8250 DAY £1200 –£5400

CUMNOR HOUSE SCHOOL
Danehill, Haywards Heath, West Sussex RH17 7HT
Tel: 01825 790347
Head: N J Milner-Gulland MA(Cantab), CertEd
Type: Co-educational Boarding & Day 4 –13
No of pupils: 244 B131 G113
Fees: FB £3415 DAY £1340 –£2620

GREAT WALSTEAD SCHOOL
Lindfield, Haywards Heath, West Sussex RH16 2QL
Tel: 01444 483528
Head: Mr H J Lowries BA(Bristol)
Type: Co-educational Boarding & Day 2 –13
No of pupils: B235 G144
Fees: FB £7275–£7905 WB £7080–£7710
DAY £480 –£6405

HANDCROSS PARK SCHOOL
Handcross, Haywards Heath, West Sussex RH17 6HF
Tel: 01444 400526
Head: Mr W J Hilton BA, CertEd
Type: Co-educational Day & Boarding 2 –13
No of pupils: 263 B157 G106
Fees: WB £8100 DAY £1890 –£6912

Horsham

CHRIST'S HOSPITAL
Horsham, West Sussex RH13 7LS
Tel: 01403 211293
Head: Dr Peter C D Southern MA, PhD
Type: Co-educational Boarding 11 –18
No of pupils: B479 G334 VIth244
Fees: FB £12,135

★FARLINGTON SCHOOL
Strood Park, Horsham, West Sussex RH12 3PN
Tel: 01403 254967
Head: Mrs P M Mawer BA
Type: Girls Day & Boarding 4 –18
No of pupils: 360 VIth60
Fees: FB £8745–£11,040 DAY £3045 –£6795

Lancing

LANCING COLLEGE
Lancing, West Sussex BN15 0RW
Tel: 01273 452213
Head: Mr P M Tinniswood MA, MBA
Type: Boys Boarding & Day B13–18 G16–18
No of pupils: B430 G70
Fees: FB £14,070 DAY £10,575

SOMPTING ABBOTTS PREPARATORY SCHOOL
Church Lane, Sompting, Lancing, West Sussex BN15 0AZ
Tel: 01903 235960
Head: Mr R J Johnson CertEd
Type: Boys Day & Boarding 3 –13
No of pupils: 165 B140 G25
Fees: WB £6495 DAY £2475 –£4470

Pease Pottage

★COTTESMORE SCHOOL
Buchan Hill, Pease Pottage, West Sussex RH11 9AU
Tel: 01293 520648
Head: Mr M A Rogerson MA(Cantab)
Type: Co-educational Boarding 7 –13
No of pupils: 145 B100 G45
Fees: FB £10,110

Petworth

SEAFORD COLLEGE
Lavington Park, Petworth, West Sussex GU28 0NB
Tel: 01798 867392
Head: T J Mullins BA(Hons)
Type: Co-educational Boarding & Day 11 –18
No of pupils: B280 G30 VIth96
Fees: FB £8850–£10,830 WB £8850–£10,830
DAY £5940 –£7125

Pulborough

DORSET HOUSE SCHOOL
The Manor, Church Lane, Bury, Pulborough, West Sussex
RH20 1PB
Tel: 01798 831456
Head: A L James BA(Oxon)
Type: Boys Boarding & Day 4 –13
No of pupils: 140 B140
Fees: FB £8280–£9330 WB £8280–£9330
DAY £3870 –£7800

★WINDLESHAM HOUSE
Washington, Pulborough, West Sussex RH20 4AY
Tel: 01903 873207
Head: Philip J Lough MA(Oxon), PGCE(Dunelm)
Type: Co-educational Boarding 4 –13
No of pupils: 285 B160 G125
Fees: FB £10,350

Steyning

THE TOWERS
Convent of the Blessed Sacrement, Upper Beeding,
Steyning, West Sussex BN44 3TF
Tel: 01903 812185
Head: Sister M Andrew RSS BA
Type: Co-educational Day & Boarding B3–8 G3–16
No of pupils: 190 B3 G200
Fees: FB £5850–£6150 WB £5520–£5820
DAY £900 –£3450

Warwickshire

West Midlands

Leamington Spa

ARNOLD LODGE SCHOOL
Kenilworth Road, Leamington Spa, Warwickshire CV32 5TW
Tel: 01926 424737
Head: Graham Hill MA(Oxon)
Type: Co-educational Day & Boarding 3 –13
No of pupils: 347
Fees: FB £6315 DAY £1215 –£4080

Rugby

BILTON GRANGE
Dunchurch, Rugby, Warwickshire CV22 6QU
Tel: 01788 810217
Head: Q G Edwards MA(Oxon), PGCE
Type: Co-educational Boarding & day 4 –13
No of pupils: 334 B211 G123
Fees: FB £9753 WB £9753 DAY £2898 –£7800

PRINCETHORPE COLLEGE
Leamington Road, Princethorpe, Rugby,
Warwickshire CV23 9PX
Tel: 01926 632147
Head: Rev Alan Whelan BA
Type: Boys Day & Boarding B11–18 G16–18
No of pupils: B399 G8
Fees: FB £6912–£7659 DAY £3570

RUGBY SCHOOL
Rugby, Warwickshire CV22 5EH
Tel: 01788 543465
Head: M B Mavor
Type: Co-educational Boarding & day 13 –18
No of pupils: 679 B508 G171
Fees: FB £12,270 DAY £4380 –£9195

Warwick

★WARWICK SCHOOL
Myton Road, Warwick CV34 6PP
Tel: 01926 776400
Head: Dr P J Cheshire BSc, PhD
Type: Boys Day & Boarding 7 –19
No of pupils: 1014 VIth200
Fees: FB £11,031–£11,667 WB £10,263–£10,899
DAY £4830 –£5466

Stourbridge

ELMFIELD RUDOLF STEINER SCHOOL
14 Love Lane, Stourbridge, West Midlands DY8 2EA
Tel: 01384 394633
Head: Mr W A Steffen
Type: Co-educational Day & Boarding 3 –17
No of pupils: B134 G129
Fees: FB £4650–£6300 DAY £2070 –£3720

Wolverhampton

BIRCHFIELD SCHOOL
Albrighton, Wolverhampton, West Midlands WV7 3AF
Tel: 01902 372534
Head: Mr J F N Benwell MSc, BA, CertEd
Type: Boys Day & Boarding 3 –13
No of pupils: 250 B250
Fees: WB £6285 DAY £2670 –£5235

TETTENHALL COLLEGE
Wood Road, Tettenhall, Wolverhampton,
West Midlands WV6 8QX
Tel: 01902 751119
Head: Dr P C Bodkin BSc, PhD
Type: Co-educational Day & Boarding 7 –18
No of pupils: B231 G109 VIth92
Fees: FB £8043–£9798 WB £6525–£8151
DAY £4833 –£6039

★THE ROYAL WOLVERHAMPTON JUNIOR SCHOOL
Penn Road, Wolverhampton, West Midlands WV3 0EF
Tel: 01902 341230
Head: Mrs M Saunders CertEd
Type: Co-educational Day & Boarding 2 –11
No of pupils: B167 G100
Fees: FB £9045 DAY £2685 –£4134

★THE ROYAL WOLVERHAMPTON SCHOOL
Penn Road, Wolverhampton, West Midlands WV3 0EG
Tel: 01902 341230
Head: Mrs B A Evans BSc, HNC
Type: Co-educational Day & Boarding 2 –18
No of pupils: 673 B406 G267 VIth100
Fees: FB £9525–£11,625 DAY £2820 –£5880

Wiltshire

Calne

*ST MARY'S SCHOOL
Calne, Wiltshire SN11 0DF
Tel: 01249 857200
Head: Mrs C J Shaw BA(London)
Type: Girls Boarding & Day 11 –18
No of pupils: 388 G388 VIth88
Fees: FB £13,620 DAY £8370

Devizes

*DAUNTSEY'S SCHOOL
High Street, West Lavington, Devizes, Wiltshire SN10 4HE
Tel: 01380 818441
Head: Mr Stewart B Roberts MA
Type: Co-educational Day & Boarding 11 –18
No of pupils: 665 B364 G301 VIth236
Fees: FB £12,318 DAY £7512

Marlborough

MARLBOROUGH COLLEGE
Marlborough, Wiltshire SN8 1PA
Tel: 01672 892300
Head: Mr E J H Gould MA
Type: Co-educational Boarding & Day 13 –18
No of pupils: B496 G320 VIth340
Fees: FB £14,100 DAY £10,140

Marshfield

*THE INTERNATIONAL SCHOOL OF CHOUEIFAT
Ashwicke Hall, Marshfield, Wiltshire SN14 8AG
Tel: 01225 891841
Director: Salah Ayche BSc, MSc
Type: Co-educational Boarding 10 –18
No of pupils: B76 G14 VIth44
Fees: FB £9900–10,299

Melksham

STONAR SCHOOL
Cottles Park, Atworth, Melksham, Wiltshire SN12 8NT
Tel: 01225 702309/702795
Head: Mrs C Homan MA
Type: Girls Boarding & Day 2 –18
No of pupils: B2 G400 VIth110
Fees: FB £9819–£10,722 DAY £2634 –£5955

Salisbury

CHAFYN GROVE SCHOOL
Bourne Avenue, Salisbury, Wiltshire SP1 1LR
Tel: 01722 333423
Head: D P Duff-Mitchell BA, CertEd
Type: Co-educational Day & Boarding 4 –13
No of pupils: B180 G92
Fees: FB £8481 DAY £2973 –£6336

*LEADEN HALL SCHOOL
70 The Close, Salisbury, Wiltshire SP1 2EP
Tel: 01722 334700
Head: Mrs Diana Watkins MA
Type: Girls Day & Boarding 3 –13
No of pupils: 227
Fees: FB £8070 WB £6885 DAY £2634 –£4515

NORMAN COURT PREPARATORY SCHOOL
West Tytherley, Salisbury, Wiltshire SP5 1NH
Tel: 01980 862345/862082
Head: Mr Kevin Foyle BA
Type: Co-educational Boarding & Day 3 –13
No of pupils: B162 G108
Fees: FB £9402 DAY £3435 –£6963

SALISBURY CATHEDRAL SCHOOL
The Old Palace, 1 The Close, Salisbury, Wiltshire SP1 2EQ
Tel: 01722 322652
Head: R M Thackray BSc
Type: Co-educational Day & Boarding 3 –13
No of pupils: 221 B138 G83
Fees: FB £9285 DAY £1785 –£6585

SANDROYD SCHOOL
Rushmore, Tollard Royal, Salisbury, Wiltshire SP5 5QD
Tel: 01725 516264
Head: Mr M J Hatch MA(Oxon), AFIMA
Type: Boys Boarding & Day 7 –13
No of pupils: B150
Fees: FB £10,200 DAY £8400

THE GODOLPHIN SCHOOL
Milford Hill, Salisbury, Wiltshire SP1 2RA
Tel: 01722 333059
Head: Miss M J Horsburgh MA(Oxon)
Type: Girls Boarding & Day 5 –18
No of pupils: G384 VIth100
Fees: FB £11,886 DAY £7119

Swindon

PINEWOOD SCHOOL
Bourton, Swindon, Wiltshire SN6 8HZ
Tel: 01793 782205
Head: J S Croysdale BA
Type: Co-educational Day & Boarding 4 –13
No of pupils: 213 B128 G85
Fees: FB £9120 DAY £3465 –£6852

PRIOR PARK PREPARATORY SCHOOL
Calcutt Street, Cricklade, Swindon, Wiltshire SN6 6BB
Tel: 01793 750275
Head: Mr G B Hobern BA
Type: Co-educational Boarding & Day 7 –13
No of pupils: B115 G60
Fees: FB £8034 DAY £5619

Warminster

WARMINSTER PREPARATORY SCHOOL
Vicarage Street, Warminster, Wiltshire BA12 8JG
Tel: 01985 210152
Head: A M T Palmer MA, BEd
Type: Co-educational Day & Boarding 4 –12
No of pupils: B68 G46
Fees: FB £9210–£10,110 DAY £2595 –£5850

WARMINSTER SCHOOL
Church Street, Warminster, Wiltshire BA12 8PJ
Tel: 01985 210100
Head: Mr David Dowdles MA
Type: Co-educational Day & Boarding 3 –18
No of pupils: B234 G136 VIth72
Fees: FB £9225–£10,605 DAY £2685 –£5985

Worcestershire

Bewdley

MOFFATS SCHOOL
Kinlet Hall, Kinlet, Bewdley, Worcestershire DY12 3AY
Tel: 01299 841230
Head: M H Daborn MA(Cantab) & Mrs M H Daborn CertEd
Type: Co-educational Boarding 4 –13
No of pupils: 79 B45 G34
Fees: FB £6825 DAY £2730 –£4140

Bromsgrove

BROMSGROVE LOWER SCHOOL
Cobham House, Conway Road, Bromsgrove,
Worcestershire B60 2AD
Tel: 01527 579600
Head: E J Ormerod
Type: Co-educational Day & Boarding 7 –13
No of pupils: B238 G167
Fees: FB £7605–£8700 DAY £4455 –£5745

BROMSGROVE SCHOOL
Bromsgrove, Worcestershire B61 7DU
Tel: 01527 579679
Head: Mr T M Taylor MA, DipEd
Type: Co-educational Day & Boarding 3 –18
No of pupils: 1089 B624 G465 VIth290
Fees: FB £11,640 DAY £7410

Evesham

GREEN HILL SCHOOL
Evesham, Worcestershire WR11 4NG
Tel: 01386 442364
Head: Mr Oliver Lister MA
Type: Co-educational Day & Boarding 3 –13
No of pupils: B46 G49
Fees: DAY £2250 –£3450

Malvern

CROFTDOWN SCHOOL
Abbey Road, Malvern, Worcestershire WR14 3HE
Tel: 01684 575083
Head: Mrs J D Myring BSc, DipEd
Type: Girls Day B3–7 G3–11
No of pupils: B3 G40
Fees: FB £7350 DAY £1620 –£4860

HILLSTONE MALVERN COLLEGE
Abbey Road, Malvern, Worcestershire WR14 3HF
Tel: 01684 573057
Head: Mr P H Moody MA(Cantab)
Type: Co-educational Day & Boarding 3 –13
No of pupils: 205 B111 G94
Fees: FB £5670–£9255 DAY £2595 –£6990

MALVERN COLLEGE
College Road, Malvern, Worcestershire WR14 3DF
Tel: 01684 892333
Head: Mr Hugh C K Carson BA
Type: Co-educational Boarding & Day 2 –18
No of pupils: 722 B476 G246 VIth296
Fees: FB £14,175 DAY £8985 –£10,305

MALVERN GIRLS' COLLEGE
15 Avenue Road, Malvern, Worcestershire WR14 3BA
Tel: 01684 892288
Head: Mrs Philippa Leggate BA, MEd, PGCE
Type: Girls Boarding & Day 11 –18
No of pupils: G421 VIth171
Fees: FB £13,020–£13,815 DAY £8685 –£9480

ST JAMES'S AND THE ABBEY
185 West Malvern Road, West Malvern, Malvern,
Worcestershire WR14 4DF
Tel: 01684 560851
Head: Mrs S Kershaw BA
Type: Girls Boarding & Day 11 –18
No of pupils: G150 VIth40
Fees: FB £12,366 DAY £7722

THE DOWNS SCHOOL
Colwall, Malvern, Worcestershire WR13 6EY
Tel: 01684 540277
Head: Mrs J M Griggs BEd(Hons)
Type: Co-educational Day & Boarding 3 –13
No of pupils: B79 G63
Fees: FB £7935 WB £7935 DAY £1860 –£5835

THE ELMS
Colwall, Malvern, Worcestershire WR13 6EF
Tel: 01684 540344
Head: Mr L A C Ashby BA, CertEd
Type: Co-educational Day & Boarding 3 –13
No of pupils: B95 G65
Fees: FB £9435 DAY £1740 –£8160

Tenbury Wells

SAINT MICHAEL'S COLLEGE
Oldwood Road, Tenbury Wells, Worcestershire WR15 8PH
Tel: 01584 811300
Head: Stuart Higgins BA, MEd
Type: Co-educational Boarding 14 –19
No of pupils: 150 B75 G75
Fees: FB £11,199

Worcester

ABBERLEY HALL
Abberley Hall, Worcester, Worcestershire WR6 6DD
Tel: 01299 896275
Head: J G W Walker BSc(Sussex)
Type: Co-educational Boarding & Day 2 –13
No of pupils: B200 G30
Fees: FB £9330 DAY £2580

KING'S JUNIOR SCHOOL
Mill Street, Worcester, Worcestershire WR1 2NJ
Tel: 01905 354906
Head: Mr J A Allcott MSc, Bed
Type: Co-educational Day 7 –11
No of pupils: B111 G73
Fees: DAY £3651 –£5148

North Yorkshire

Bedale

AYSGARTH SCHOOL
Bedale, North Yorkshire DL8 1TF
Tel: 01677 450240
Head: J C Hodgkinson MA
Type: Boys Boarding B3–13 G3–8
No of pupils: B125 G13
Fees: FB £8226 DAY £324 –£5760

Harrogate

ASHVILLE COLLEGE
Green Lane, Harrogate, North Yorkshire HG2 9JP
Tel: 01423 566358
Head: M H Crosby MA(Cantab)
Type: Co-educational Day & Boarding 4 –18
No of pupils: B458 G312 VIth60
Fees: FB £7974–£8754 DAY £2400 –£4680

GROSVENOR HOUSE SCHOOL
Swarcliffe Hall, Birstwith, Harrogate,
North Yorkshire HG3 2JG
Tel: 01423 771029
Head: Mr G J Raspin MA(Cantab), PGCE(Leeds)
Type: Boys Day & Boarding 3 –13
No of pupils: B170 G45
Fees: FB £7560 DAY £1635 –£4800

HARROGATE LADIES' COLLEGE
Clarence Drive, Harrogate, North Yorkshire HG1 2QG
Tel: 01423 504543
Head: Dr Margaret J Hustler BSc, PhD
Type: Girls Boarding & Day 9 –18
No of pupils: 380 G380 VIth120
Fees: FB £10,935 DAY £6900

Malton

WOODLEIGH SCHOOL LANGTON
Langton Hall, Malton, North Yorkshire YO17 9QN
Tel: 01653 658215
Head: Mr D M England BSc
Type: Co-educational Boarding & Day 3 –13
No of pupils: B63 G38
Fees: FB £6300 WB £6300 DAY £2190 –£4875

Ripon

RIPON CATHEDRAL CHOIR SCHOOL
Whitcliffe Lane, Ripon, North Yorkshire HG4 2LA
Tel: 01765 602134
Head: Mr R H Moore BA
Type: Co-educational Day & Boarding 4 –13
No of pupils: B70 G50
Fees: FB £7020–£7590 DAY £3780 –£5565

Scarborough

BRAMCOTE SCHOOL
Filey Road, Scarborough, North Yorkshire YO11 2TT
Tel: 01723 373086
Head: J P Kirk BSc, FRSA
Type: Co-educational Boarding & Day 5 –13
No of pupils: 95 B70 G25
Fees: FB £8640 DAY £6000

SCARBOROUGH COLLEGE & LISVANE JUNIOR SCHOOL
Filey Road, Scarborough, North Yorkshire YO11 3BA
Tel: 01723 360620
Head: Mr T L Kirkup MA, ARCM
Type: Co-educational Day & Boarding 3 –18
No of pupils: B292 G224 VIth103
Fees: FB £10,539 WB £7893 DAY £2970 –£5715

SCARBOROUGH COLLEGE JUNIOR SCHOOL
Lisvane, Sandybed Lane, Scarborough,
North Yorkshire YO12 5LJ
Tel: 01723 361595
Head: Mr Coston BEd,DipEd,CertEd,ACP,FColP
Type: Co-educational Day 3 –11
No of pupils: B61 G68
Fees: DAY £2970 –£4149

Selby

READ SCHOOL
Drax, Selby, North Yorkshire YO8 8NL
Tel: 01757 618248
Head: R A Hadfield BA, CertEd
Type: Co-educational Day & Boarding 3 –18
No of pupils: B163 G57 VIth24
Fees: FB £6993–£8220 WB £6993–£8220
DAY £2865 –£3984

Settle

CATTERAL HALL
Giggleswick, Settle, North Yorkshire BD24 0DG
Tel: 01729 822527
Head: Mr Martin J Morris BEd, BA
Type: Co-educational Boarding & Day 3 –13
No of pupils: B101 G51
Fees: FB £9690–£10,410 DAY £3300 –£6960

★GIGGLESWICK SCHOOL
Giggleswick, Settle, North Yorkshire BD24 0DE
Tel: 01729 823545
Head: Mr A P Millard BSc(Econ), FRSA
Type: Co-educational Boarding & Day 7 –18
No of pupils: 440 B289 G151 VIth157
Fees: FB £10,269–£13,515 DAY £6870 –£8970

Skipton

MALSIS SCHOOL
Cross Hills, Skipton, North Yorkshire BD20 8DT
Tel: 01535 633027
Head: John Elder MA(Hons)Edin, PGCE
Type: Boys Boarding 3 –13
No of pupils: 160 B140 G20
Fees: FB £9120 DAY £5460 –£6840

Thirsk

QUEEN MARY'S SCHOOL
Baldersby Park, Topcliffe, Thirsk, North Yorkshire YO7 3BZ
Tel: 01845 577425
Head: Mr & Mrs I H Angus MA, HDipEd, MSc, CertEd
Type: Girls Boarding & Day 3 –16
No of pupils: 232 B1 G231
Fees: FB £3250 DAY £730 –£2035

Whitby

FYLING HALL SCHOOL
Robin Hood's Bay, Whitby, North Yorkshire YO22 4QD
Tel: 01947 880353
Head: Mr Michael Bayes BA, MA
Type: Co-educational Boarding & Day 5 –19
No of pupils: B120 G115 Vlth38
Fees: FB £7797 DAY £2835 –£3525

York

AMPLEFORTH COLLEGE
York, North Yorkshire YO62 4ER
Tel: 01439 766000
Head: Rev G F L Chamberlain OSB, MA
Type: Boys Boarding & Day 13 –18
No of pupils: 610 B610 Vlth220
Fees: FB £13,305 DAY £6870

AMPLEFORTH COLLEGE JUNIOR SCHOOL
The Castle, Gilling East, York, North Yorkshire YO6 4HP
Tel: 01439 788238
Head: Fr Jeremy Sierla, OSB, MA(Oxon)
Type: Boys Boarding & Day 8 –13
No of pupils: B123
Fees: FB £9318 DAY £5724 –£7251

BOOTHAM SCHOOL
York, North Yorkshire YO3 7BU
Tel: 01904 623636
Head: Mr Ian M Small BA, FRSA
Type: Co-educational Boarding & Day 11 –18
No of pupils: B184 G103 Vlth89
Fees: FB £10,995 DAY £7155

CHAPTER HOUSE PREPARATORY SCHOOL
Thorpe Underwood Hall, Ouseburn, York,
North Yorkshire YO5 9SZ
Tel: 01423 330859
Head: Ms Erica Taylor
Type: Co-educational Boarding & Day 2 –11
No of pupils: B22 G60
Fees: FB £6525–£7890 DAY £1425 –£4050

CUNDALL MANOR SCHOOL
Helperby, York, North Yorkshire YO6 2RW
Tel: 01423 360200
Head: Mr J F Napier MA(Hons), CertEd
Type: Co-educational Day & Boarding 2 –13
No of pupils: B100 G56
Fees: FB £7200 –£8000 DAY £2400 –£5500

HOWSHAM HALL
York, North Yorkshire YO6 7PJ
Tel: 01653 618374
Head: S J Knock CertEd
Type: Boys Day & Boarding 5 –14
No of pupils: B75
Fees: FB £5940 –£6300 DAY £2400 –£3900

*POCKLINGTON SCHOOL
West Green, Pocklington, York, North Yorkshire YO42 2NJ
Tel: 01759 303125
Head: Mr J N D Gray BA
Type: Co-educational Day & Boarding 7 –18
No of pupils: 751 B447 G304 Vlth165
Fees: FB £8526–£9900 DAY £5127 –£5955

QUEEN ETHELBURGA'S COLLEGE
Thorpe Underwood Hall, Ouseburn, York, North Yorkshire YO5 9SZ
Tel: 01423 331480
Head: Ms Erica Taylor
Type: Girls Boarding & Day 2 –18
No of pupils: B25 G270
Fees: FB £6525–£9585 DAY £1425 –£6075

QUEEN MARGARET'S SCHOOL
Escrick Park, York, North Yorkshire YO4 6EU
Tel: 01904 728261
Head: Dr G A H Chapman MA(Oxon), DLitt et Phil(SA), FRSA
Type: Girls Boarding & Day 11 –18
No of pupils: G265 Vlth100
Fees: FB £10,218 DAY £6474

RED HOUSE PREP SCHOOL
Moor Monkton, York, North Yorkshire YO5 8JQ
Tel: 01904 738256
Head: Major A V Gordon
Type: Co-educational Boarding & Day 3 –13
No of pupils: 40 B25 G15
Fees: FB £6555–£6870 DAY £1650 –£4635

ST MARTIN'S SCHOOL
Kirkdale Manor, Nawton, York, North Yorkshire YO6 5UA
Tel: 01439 771215
Head: S M Mullen BEd(Hons)
Type: Co-educational Boarding & Day 3 –13
No of pupils: B61 G49
Fees: FB £6867 DAY £2211 –£4635

ST OLAVES SCHOOL (JUNIOR OF ST PETER'S)
Clifton, York, North Yorkshire YO30 6AB
Tel: 01904 623269
Head: Mr T Mulryne MA, BEd, DPE
Type: Co-educational Day & Boarding 8 –13
No of pupils: B192 G118
Fees: FB £8592–£9801 DAY £4299 –£5880

ST PETER'S SCHOOL
Clifton, York, North Yorkshire YO3 6AB
Tel: 01904 623213
Head: Mr A F Trotman MA
Type: Co-educational Day & Boarding 13 –18
No of pupils: B314 G187 VIth215
Fees: FB £11,376–£11,679 DAY £6621 –£6954

TERRINGTON HALL
Terrington, York, North Yorkshire YO6 4PR
Tel: 01653 648227
Head: M J Glen BA, PGCE
Type: Co-educational Boarding & Day 3 –13
No of pupils: B65 G55
Fees: FB £7650 DAY £2190 –£5205

THE MOUNT SCHOOL, YORK
Dalton Terrace, York, North Yorkshire YO2 4DD
Tel: 01904 667500
Head: Miss B J Windle MA(Cantab)
Type: Girls Boarding & Day 11 –18
No of pupils: G265 VIth75
Fees: FB £10,794 DAY £6645

West Yorkshire

Apperley Bridge

WOODHOUSE GROVE SCHOOL
Apperley Bridge, West Yorkshire BD10 0NR
Tel: 0113 2502477
Head: David C Humphreys BA
Type: Co-educational Day & Boarding 3 –18
No of pupils: 875 B528 G347 VIth150
Fees: FB £9435–£10,500 DAY £3525 –£6120

Bradford

BRONTE HOUSE SCHOOL
Apperley Bridge, Bradford, West Yorkshire BD10 0PQ
Tel: 0113 2502811
Head: Mr F F Watson CertEd, AIST, MCollP
Type: Co-educational Day & Boarding 3 –11
No of pupils: B210 G95
Fees: FB £9435 DAY £3525 –£5280

Halifax

*RISHWORTH SCHOOL
Rishworth, Halifax, West Yorkshire HX6 4QA
Tel: 01422 822217
Head: Mr R A Baker MA
Type: Co-educational Day & Boarding 4 –18
No of pupils: 485 B255 G230
Fees: FB £9720–£10,560 DAY £2790 –£5460

Ilkley

CLEVEDON HOUSE
The Drive, Ben Rhydding, Ilkley, West Yorkshire LS29 8BJ
Tel: 01943 608515
Head: Mr J C Mackay BSc, PGCE
Type: Co-educational Day & Boarding 3 –16
No of pupils: B115 G60
Fees: FB £2900–£9150 DAY £3840 –£5025

Leeds

FULNECK SCHOOL
Fulneck, Pudsey, Leeds, West Yorkshire LS28 8DS
Tel: 0113 2570235
Head: Mrs H S Gordon BA(Hons), PGCE
Type: Co-educational Day & Boarding 3 –18
No of pupils: B238 G215 VIth73
Fees: FB £7575–£9540 DAY £3195 –£3985

Pontefract

ACKWORTH SCHOOL
Barnsley Road, Ackworth, Pontefract,
West Yorkshire WF7 7LT
Tel: 01977 611401
Head: Martin J Dickinson MA(Cantab)
Type: Co-educational Day & Boarding 7–18
No of pupils: B184 G194 VIth85
Fees: FB £10,761 DAY £3294–£6120

Northern Ireland

County Antrim

Belfast

CABIN HILL SCHOOL
562-594 Upper Newtownards Road, Knock,
Belfast BT4 3HJ
Tel: 01232 653368
Head: N I Kendrick
Type: Boys Day & Boarding 4 –13
No of pupils: B392
Fees: FB £4611–£6231 WB £4512–£6132
DAY £861–£2829

CAMPBELL COLLEGE
Belfast BT4 2ND
Tel: 01232 763076
Head: Dr R J I Pollock BSc, MEd, PhD
Type: Boys Day & Boarding 11 –18
No of pupils: 731 B731 VIth213
Fees: FB £5823–£5997 WB £5823–£5997
DAY £996–£1170

HUNTERHOUSE COLLEGE
Finaghy, Belfast BT10 0LE
Tel: 01232 612293
Head: Mrs M Clark BA, PGCE
Type: Girls Day & Boarding 5 –18
No of pupils: G699 VIth162
Fees: FB £3255 DAY £1051–£1294

METHODIST COLLEGE
1 Malone Road, Belfast BT9 6BY
Tel: 01232 205205
Head: Dr T W Mulryne MA
Type: Co-educational Day & Boarding 4 –18
No of pupils: B1046 G851 VIth556
Fees: FB £3740–£6525 DAY £240–£3005

VICTORIA COLLEGE BELFAST
Cranmore Park, Belfast BT9 6JA
Tel: 01232 661506
Head: Mrs M Andrews BSc, PGDICE
Type: Girls Day & Boarding 3 –18
No of pupils: G860 VIth120
Fees: FB £4200 DAY £252

Lisburn

FRIENDS' SCHOOL LISBURN
6 Magheralave Road, Lisburn, County Antrim BT28 3BH
Tel: 01846 662156
Head: J T Green MA, DipEd
Type: Co-educational Day & Boarding 5 –18
No of pupils: 948 B453 G495
Fees: FB £3400–£5935 DAY £72–£2607

County Armagh

Armagh

THE ROYAL SCHOOL
College Hill, Armagh, County Armagh BT61 9DH
Tel: 01861 522807
Head: T Duncan MA, BSc, DASE
Type: Co-educational Boarding & Day 11 –18
No of pupils: B257 G289 VIth141
Fees: FB £2080–£3465 WB £2080–£3465 DAY £105

County Down

Holywood

ROCKPORT PREPARATORY SCHOOL
Craigavad, Holywood, County Down BT18 0DD
Tel: 01232 428372
Head: Mrs H Pentland BEd
Type: Co-educational Day & Boarding 3 –13
No of pupils: B102 G94
Fees: FB £4710–£6705 DAY £1185–£5130

County Londonderry

Coleraine

COLERAINE ACADEMICAL INSTITUTION
Castlerock Road, Coleraine, County Londonderry BT51 3LA
Tel: 01265 44331
Head: Mr R S Forsythe BSc, DASE
Type: Boys Day & Boarding 11 –18
No of pupils: 870 B870 VIth198
Fees: DAY £300

County Tyrone

Dungannon

ROYAL SCHOOL DUNGANNON
Northland Row, Dungannon, County Tyrone BT71 6AP
Tel: 01868 722710
Head: Mr P D Hewitt MA, DipEd, FRSA, FInstMgt
Type: Co-educational Day & Boarding 8 –18
No of pupils: B340 G350 Vlth180
Fees: FB £6500 DAY £2990

Scotland

Angus

Montrose

LATHALLAN PREPARATORY SCHOOL
Brotherton Castle, Montrose, Angus DD10 0HN
Tel: 01561 362220
Head: Mr Peter Platts-Martin MA
Type: Co-educational Boarding & Day 3 –13
No of pupils: B90 G40
Fees: FB £9501–£9720 DAY £4284 –£6144

Argyll & Bute

Helensburgh

LOMOND SCHOOL
10 Stafford Street, Helensburgh, Argyll & Bute G84 9JX
Tel: 01436 672476
Head: Mr A D Macdonald MA(Hons)(Cantab), DipEd
Type: Co-educational Day & Boarding 3 –18
No of pupils: B210 G190 VIth40
Fees: FB £10,350–£11,190 DAY £1650 –£5220

Borders

Melrose

ST MARY'S PREP SCHOOL
Abbey Park, Melrose, Borders TD6 9LN
Tel: 01896 822517
Head: Mr J A Brett
Type: Co-educational Boarding & Day 4 –13
No of pupils: B40 G38
Fees: FB £8925WB £8745 DAY £3510 –£5625

City of Edinburgh

Edinburgh

CARGILFIELD
Barnton Avenue West, Edinburgh EH4 6HU
Tel: 0131 336 2207
Head: Andrew S Morrison MA, CertEd
Type: Co-educational Boarding & Day 3 –13
No of pupils: B126 G51
Fees: FB £9510 DAY £1575 –£6810

FETTES COLLEGE
Carrington Road, Edinburgh EH4 1QX
Tel: 0131 332 2281
Head: M C B Spens MA
Type: Co-educational Boarding & Day 10 –18
No of pupils: 484 B284 G200 VIth174
Fees: FB £9735–£14,205 DAY £6105 –£9585

GEORGE WATSON'S COLLEGE
Colinton Road, Edinburgh EH10 5EG
Tel: 0131 447 7931
Head: Mr Frank E Gerstenberg MA(Cantab), FRSA, FIMgt
Type: Co-educational Day & Boarding 3 –18
No of pupils: B1242 G1018 VIth423
Fees: FB £9798 DAY £1194 –£4800

MERCHISTON CASTLE SCHOOL
294 Colinton Road, Edinburgh EH13 0PU
Tel: 0131 312 2200
Head: Mr A R Hunter BA
Type: Boys Boarding & Day 10 –18
No of pupils: B375 VIth133
Fees: FB £10,395–£13,470 DAY £7425 –£9045

ST DENIS AND CRANLEY SCHOOL
Ettrick Road, Edinburgh EH10 5BJ
Tel: 0131 229 1500
Head: Mrs Sally M Duncanson MA
Type: Girls Day & Boarding B3–9 G3–18
No of pupils: B4 G162 VIth12
Fees: FB £8670–£10,470 WB £8670–£10,470
DAY £2595 –£5340

ST GEORGE'S SCHOOL FOR GIRLS
Garscube Terrace, Edinburgh EH12 6BG
Tel: 0131 332 4575
Head: Dr Judith McClure MA, DPhil(Oxon), FRSA, FSAScot
Type: Girls Day & Boarding B3–5 G3–18
No of pupils: 954 G954 VIth153
Fees: FB £8535–£10,005 DAY £2700 –£5040

ST MARGARET'S SCHOOL & ST DENIS AND CRANLEY
East Suffolk Road, Edinburgh EH16 5PJ
Tel: 0131 668 1986
Head: Miss A C Mitchell MA
Type: Girls Day & Boarding B3–8 G3–18
No of pupils: B20 G730 VIth110
Fees: FB £7290–£9390 DAY £2685 –£4785

ST MARY'S MUSIC SCHOOL
Coates Hall, 25 Grosvenor Crescent, Edinburgh EH12 5EL
Tel: 0131 538 7766
Head: Mrs J Jennifer Rimer BMus(Hons), LRAM, DipEd
Type: Co-educational Day & Boarding 9 –19
No of pupils: B31 G33 VIth19

STEWART'S MELVILLE COLLEGE
Queensferry Road, Edinburgh EH4 3EZ
Tel: 0131 332 7925
Head: P F J Tobin MA, FRSA
Type: Boys Day & Boarding 12 –18
No of pupils: 780 B780
Fees: FB £9810 DAY £5091

*THE EDINBURGH ACADEMY
42 Henderson Row, Edinburgh EH3 5BL
Tel: 0131 556 4603
Head: Rector J V Light MA
Type: Boys Day & Boarding B11–18 G16–18
No of pupils: 460 B460 VIth224
Fees: FB £11,469–£12,159 DAY £5013 –£5703

THE EDINBURGH ACADEMY PREPARATORY SCHOOL
10 Arboretum Road, Edinburgh EH3 5BL
Tel: 0131 552 3690
Head: Campbell R F Paterson MA, PGCE
Type: Boys Day & Boarding B3–11 G3–4
No of pupils: B361 G10
Fees: FB £8517–£8706 DAY £963 –£3849

THE MARY ERSKINE SCHOOL
Ravelston, Edinburgh EH4 3NT
Tel: 0131 337 2391
Head: Mr P F J Tobin MA, FRSA
Type: Girls Day & Boarding 11 –18
No of pupils: G700 VIth100
Fees: FB £9810 DAY £4800 –£5091

Clackmannanshire

Dollar

DOLLAR ACADEMY
Dollar, Clackmannanshire FK14 7DU
Tel: 01259 742511
Head: Mr J S Robertson MA
Type: Co-educational Day & Boarding 5 –18
No of pupils: 1132 B600 G532 VIth254
Fees: FB £9513–£10,701 DAY £3645 –£4833

Dumfries & Galloway

Thornhill

CADEMUIR INTERNATIONAL SCHOOL
Crawfordton House, Moniaive, Thornhill, Dumfries &
Galloway DG3 4HG
Tel: 01848 200212
Head: Robert Mulvey DIL
Type: Co-educational Boarding & Day 3 –19
No of pupils: B68 G32 VIth20
Fees: FB £11,100–£13,200 WB £10,050–£12,150
DAY £1950 –£6000

East Lothian

Dunbar

BELHAVEN HILL
Dunbar, East Lothian EH42 1NN
Tel: 01368 862785
Head: Mr I M Osborne MA(Cantab)
Type: Co-educational Boarding & Day 8 –13
No of pupils: 100 B70 G30
Fees: FB £9570 DAY £6810

Musselburgh

LORETTO JUNIOR SCHOOL
North Esk Lodge, North High Street, Musselburgh,
East Lothian EH21 6JA
Tel: 0131 665 2628
Head: David P Clark BA
Type: Co-educational Boarding & Day 8 –13
No of pupils: B60 G27
Fees: FB £8550–£9540 DAY £6015 –£6450

LORETTO SCHOOL
Musselburgh, East Lothian EH21 7RE
Tel: 0131 653 4444
Head: Keith J Budge MA
Type: Co-educational Boarding & Day 13 –18
No of pupils: 310 B250 G60 VIth155
Fees: FB £12,870 DAY £8580

Fife

St Andrews

ST KATHARINES PREP SCHOOL
The Pends, St Andrews, Fife KY16 9RB
Tel: 01334 472446
Head: Mrs Joan Brittain LTCL, CertEd, AdvDipEd(Bristol)
Type: Girls Boarding & Day B3–9 G3–12
No of pupils: B8 G78
Fees: FB £10,428 WB £10,128 DAY £1575 –£5607

ST LEONARDS AND ST KATHARINES SCHOOLS & ST LEONARDS SIXTH FORM COLLEGE
St Andrews, Fife KY16 9QU
Tel: 01334 476211
Head: Mrs M C James BA(Hons) York, St Anne's College Oxford
Type: Girls Boarding & Day 12 –18
No of pupils: 324 G324 VIth105
Fees: FB £13,752 DAY £7347

Moray

Aberlour

ABERLOUR HOUSE
Aberlour, Moray AB38 9LJ
Tel: 01340 871267
Head: J W Caithness MA
Type: Co-educational Boarding & Day G88 –13
No of pupils: B60 G40 VIth35
Fees: FB £8865 DAY £6069

Elgin

GORDONSTOUN SCHOOL
Elgin, Moray IV30 2RF
Tel: 01343 837837
Head: Mr Mark C Pyper BA London
Type: Co-educational Boarding & Day 13 –18
No of pupils: B250 G180 VIth215
Fees: FB £13,563 DAY £8754

Perth & Kinross

Blairgowrie

BUTTERSTONE SCHOOL
Meigle, Blairgowrie, Perth & Kinross PH12 8QY
Tel: 01828 640528
Head: Christopher Syers-Gibson MA(Cantab)
Type: Girls Boarding & Day B2–7 G2–13
No of pupils: B25 G90
Fees: FB £9390 DAY £3093 –£6153

By Pitlochry

RANNOCH SCHOOL
Rannoch, By Pitlochry, Perth & Kinross PH17 2QQ
Tel: 01882 632332
Head: Dr John D Halliday BA, PhD
Type: Co-educational Boarding & Day 10 –18
No of pupils: 210 B130 G80 VIth88
Fees: FB £9702–£11,655 DAY £6105

Crieff

★ARDVRECK SCHOOL
Gwydyr Road, Crieff, Perth & Kinross PH7 4EX
Tel: 01764 653112
Head: N W Gardner BA, CertEd(Dunelm)
Type: Co-educational Boarding & Day 3 –13
No of pupils: 166
Fees: FB £9045–£9465 DAY £2730 –£5865

MORRISON'S ACADEMY
Crieff, Perth & Kinross PH7 3AN
Tel: 01764 653885
Head: G H Edwards MA(Oxon)
Type: Co-educational Day & Boarding 5 –18
Fees: FB £9996–£11,121 DAY £2550 –£3828

MORRISON'S ACADEMY JUNIOR
Crieff, Perth & Kinross PH7 3AN
Tel: 01764 653885
Head: H A Ashmall MA, MLitt, FBIM
Type: Co-educational Day

Dunkeld

THE NEW SCHOOL
Butterstone, Dunkeld, Perth & Kinross PH8 0HJ
Tel: 01350 724216
Head: Dr William Marshall BSc, PhD
Type: Co-educational Boarding 12 –18
No of pupils: 40 B19 G21
Fees: WB £11,100 DAY £8400

Perth

★GLENALMOND COLLEGE, PERTH
Glenalmond, Perth PH1 3RY
Tel: 01738 880442
Head: I G Templeton MA, BA
Type: Co-educational Boarding & Day 12 –18
No of pupils: 367 B257 G110 VIth153
Fees: FB £10,335–£13,785 DAY £6900 –£9195

KILGRASTON (A SACRED HEART SCHOOL)
Bridge of Earn, Perth PH2 9BQ
Tel: 01738 812257
Head: Mrs Juliet L Austin BA(Hons)
Type: Girls Boarding & Day B5–8 G5–18
No of pupils: B4 G235 VIth60
Fees: FB £10,020–£11,730 DAY £4140 –£6750

STRATHALLAN SCHOOL
Forgandenny, Perth PH2 9EG
Tel: 01738 812546
Head: Mr Angus W McPhail MA(Oxon)
Type: Co-educational Boarding & Day 10 –18
No of pupils: 483 B323 G160 VIth184
Fees: FB £10,080–£13,500 DAY £6870 –£9300

Pitlochry

CROFTINLOAN SCHOOL
Pitlochry, Perth & Kinross PH16 5JR
Tel: 01796 472057
Head: Mr Robert Horton CertEd(London)
Type: Co-educational Boarding & Day 7 –14
No of pupils: 61 B34 G27
Fees: FB £9555 DAY £3750 –£5700

Stirling

Dunblane

QUEEN VICTORIA SCHOOL
Dunblane, Stirling FK15 0JY
Tel: 01786 822288
Head: B Raine BA(Hons), PGCE
Type: Co-educational Boarding 11 –18
No of pupils: B195 G40 VIth25

West Dunbartonshire

Dumbarton

KEIL SCHOOL
Helenslee Road, Dumbarton, West Dunbartonshire G82 4AL
Tel: 01389 763855
Head: J Cummings BA, MA
Type: Co-educational Boarding & Day 10 –18
No of pupils: B94 G72 VIth29
Fees: FB £9450–£10,509 DAY £4173 –£5892

Wales

Bridgend

Porthcawl

ST JOHN'S SCHOOL
Newton, Porthcawl, Bridgend CF36 5SJ
Tel: 01656 783404
Head: Mr R A Sockett BEd
Type: Co-educational Day & Boarding 3 –16
No of pupils: B166 G71
Fees: FB £6630–£8430 DAY £2850 –£5325

Cardiff

Cardiff

THE CATHEDRAL SCHOOL, LLANDAFF
Llandaff, Cardiff, Cardiff CF5 2YH
Tel: 01222 563179
Head: Mr P L Gray MA(Cantab), ARCO, PGCE
Type: Co-educational Day & Boarding 3 –13
No of pupils: B276 G105
Fees: FB £8505 DAY £3450

Carmarthenshire

Llandovery

LLANDOVERY COLLEGE
Llandovery, Carmarthenshire SA20 0EE
Tel: 01550 723000
Head: Dr C E Evans CChem, MRSC
Type: Co-educational Boarding & Day 11 –18
No of pupils: B138 G69 VIth77
Fees: FB £11,097 DAY £7368

Conwy

Colwyn Bay

RYDAL PENHROS SENIOR SCH CO-ED DIVISION
Pwllycrochan Avenue, Colwyn Bay, Conwy LL29 7BT
Tel: 01492 530155
Head: N W Thorne BEd, MSc
Type: Co-educational Boarding & Day 11 –18
No of pupils: B170 G90 VIth120
Fees: FB £8877–£10,383 DAY £6486 –£7515

Denbighshire

Denbigh

HOWELL'S SCHOOL
Denbigh, Denbighshire LL16 3EN
Tel: 01745 813631
Head: Mrs Sandra Gordon MEd, BA
Type: Girls Boarding & Day 11 –18
No of pupils: G200 VIth35
Fees: FB £8985–£10,785 DAY £6585 –£7485

Ruthin

RUTHIN SCHOOL
Ruthin, Denbighshire LL15 1EE
Tel: 01824 702543
Head: Mr J S Rowlands BSc
Type: Co-educational Day & Boarding 3 –18
No of pupils: B169 G77 VIth55
Fees: FB £9285–£11,235 WB £7725–£11,235
DAY £2775 –£7185

Gwynedd

Barmouth

TOWER HOUSE
Harlech Road, Barmouth, Gwynedd LL42 1RF
Tel: 01341 280127
Head: Mrs Joan Pugh BSc(Hons)
Type: Co-educational Day & Boarding 4 –16
No of pupils: B25 G50
Fees: FB £8850 DAY £2505 –£3510

Llandudno

ST DAVID'S COLLEGE
Gloddaeth Hall, Llandudno, Gwynedd LL30 1RD
Tel: 01492 875974
Head: Mr W G Seymour MA
Type: Boys Boarding & Day 11 –18
No of pupils: B200 VIth65
Fees: FB £10,740–£11,265 DAY £6987 –£7326

Monmouthshire

Chepstow

ST JOHN'S-ON-THE-HILL
Tutshill, Chepstow, Monmouthshire NP6 7LE
Tel: 01291 622045
Head: Mr I K Etchells BEd
Type: Co-educational Day & Boarding 2 –13
No of pupils: B178 G119
Fees: FB £7620 DAY £3375 –£5640

Monmouth

HABERDASHERS' MONMOUTH SCHOOL FOR GIRLS
Hereford Road, Monmouth NP5 3XT
Tel: 01600 711100
Head: Dr B Despontin MA, PGCE
Type: Girls Day & Boarding 7 –18
No of pupils: G675 VIth159
Fees: FB £9837–£10,215 DAY £4452 –£5601

★MONMOUTH SCHOOL
Monmouth NP5 3XP
Tel: 01600 713143
Head: Mr Timothy H P Haynes BA
Type: Boys Day & Boarding 11 –18
No of pupils: 735 VIth169
Fees: FB £9780 DAY £5871

Pembrokeshire

Saundersfoot

NETHERWOOD SCHOOL
Saundersfoot, Pembrokeshire SA69 9BE
Tel: 01834 813360
Head: D H Morris BA, CertEd, FRGS, FCollP
Type: Co-educational Boarding & Day 3 –16
No of pupils: B72 G83
Fees: FB £5550–£7500 DAY £2100 –£3450

Powys

Brecon

CHRIST COLLEGE
Brecon, Powys LD3 8AG
Tel: 01874 623359
Head: S W Hockey MA(Cantab)
Type: Boys Boarding & Day B11–18 G16–18
No of pupils: 351
Fees: FB £8913 DAY £6804

Section Three:
State Boarding Schools

Adams' Grammar School

(Founded 1656)

Newport, Shropshire TF10 7BD

Tel: 01952 810698 Fax: 01952 812696

e-mail: admin@agsn.demon.co.uk

Internet: http://www.rmplc.co.uk/eduweb/sites/adamsgs/index.html.

A Grant Maintained School, therefore, no tuition fees, parents pay only for boarding costs. Outstanding academic results and strong in sport and music. Wide range of extra-curricular activities. Adams' combines a traditional Grammar School ethos with a modern curriculum and facilities. Affiliated to the Technology Colleges Trust, Adams' has excellent provision for IT across the curriculum.

Head: J M Richardson

Date of appointment: January 1994

Member of: STABIS, Technology Colleges Trust

Grant Maintained Boys Day & Boarding

Religious affiliation: Non-denominational

Age range of pupils: 11 – 18

Boarders from 11

No. of students enrolled as at 1.9.98: 720

520 VIth Form: 160 Boys 40 Girls

Average size of class: 20 to 25

Teacher/Pupil ratio: 1:16 (excluding extra music and boarding staff)

Curriculum: Pupils are prepared for GCSE and A level examinations in all principal academic subjects and a variety of newer subjects such as Politics, Geology, IT, Business Studies, Design and PE. Our

excellent range of facilities support this and enable the use of IT across the curriculum. Adams' gained a new Technology Centre (1992), a Drama Studio (1993), a refurbished Library, Resources Centre and Careers Room (1994), a new Modern Languages Lab and Music Recording Studio (1996). In 1996 our new centre for IT, Mathematics and Business Studies opened and the School gained Technology College Status. The consequent funding provided for extensive networked computer facilities.

Entry requirements: Selection based on tests, school report and interview. For Sixth Form entry based on interview, school report and GCSE results.

Subject specialities and academic track record: The School has an outstanding academic track record.

Range of fees per annum as at 1.9.98:

Weekly Boarding: £4650

Boarding: £4860

Examinations offered including boards: GCSE and A level in a wide variety of subjects. MEG, SEG, NEAB, UCLES, Oxford and Cambridge.

Destination/careers prospects of leavers: Over 98% of leavers go on to university, including Oxford and Cambridge.

Academic & leisure facilities: Junior boarding is set in some of the finest playing fields in the country, incorporating five rugby pitches, three hockey pitches and two cricket squares. The extensive grounds and woodland are superb for athletics and cross-country and the School has a fishing lake and swimming pool.

The well-equipped gym is used for a variety of sports. Adams' has highly successful teams in a variety of sports and a number of pupils play at County, Regional and even National levels. Adams' is ideally placed for outdoor activities with the Shropshire countryside and the Welsh borders close-by. Adams' has a strong music tradition and holds an Annual Music Festival.

Religious activities: Non-denominational. However, a number of boarders attend local places of worship and confirmation classes can be arranged.

Adams' has a long tradition of academic excellence but aims to give an all-round education so that each pupil can discover and achieve their full potential. Sporting and cultural activities are important as are the School's strong international links. Trips and exchanges abroad take place annually and students can gain work experience abroad. The CCF and Duke of Edinburgh's Award develop independence and leadership skills. Pupils enter, and are successful in, a variety of national competitions in many curriculum areas from Maths to Design Technology. Our boarding houses offer a disciplined, caring, family environment with many organised activities and trips. A high staff to pupil ratio ensures strong pastoral care. We aim to produce confident, well-mannered, happy and successful young men who are ready to take on challenging and leading roles.

Adams' Grammar School is a registered charity which exists to provide high quality day and boarding education for children.

Burleigh Community College

(Founded 1691)

Thorpe Hill, Loughborough, Leicestershire LE11 0SQ

Tel: 01509 268996 Fax: 01509 233159

e-mail: BCCCMT@aol.com

Our model is the responsible family. Through high standards in a friendly yet structured environment we commit ourselves whole-heartedly to the education and welfare of your child.

Principal: Mr Philip Watson BSc, MA

Date of appointment: 1994

Member of: STABIS

Co-educational Boarding & Day

Age range of pupils: 14 – 19

Boarders from 10-19

No. of students enrolled as at 1.9.98: 1321

Boys: 645 Girls: 676 VIth Form: 471

Average size of class: Main School 22, Sixth Form 12

Teacher/Pupil ratio: 1:12

Curriculum: Burleigh College and its three feeder high schools provide a full range of artistic, sporting and cultural programmes and have an excellent academic reputation. Our size enables us to offer an above average range of subjects at GCSE and, especially at A level where results are always amongst the best in the county. Arts and Sciences are strong and the wide variety of sporting and expressive arts activities further enhances the College's reputation. Our community college status has significantly improved the facilities we have to offer and which are the envy of other schools.

Vocational courses have been successfully incorporated into the college curriculum at both Key Stage 4 and in the Sixth Form with many students now taking this route to university.

Entry requirements: Below 16 years, open entry - although all prospective boarders are interviewed. Post 16 years - a number of GCSE passes at certain grades as required, depending on course(s) applied for.

Range of fees per annum as at 1.9.98:

Boarding: £4725 – £5550

Tuition free.

Sports College: In September 1997 Burleigh was designated one of the first six specialist Sports Colleges in the UK, in recognition of high academic standards and excellent links with our community.

General: Loughborough is a pleasant market town in the heart of England. It is well served by major road and rail routes, and has East Midland airport very close by.

Boarding is at Field House which is a delightful Victorian building situated in superb grounds close to Burleigh, the University and the town centre. Up to 40 students, both boys and girls, are accommodated in comfortable, spacious bedrooms with excellent facilities. A warm family atmosphere prevails.

Cranbrook School

(Founded 1518)

Waterloo Road, Cranbrook, Kent TN17 3JD

Tel: 01580 712163 Fax: 01580 715365
e-mail: registrar@cranbrook.kent.sch.uk
Internet: http://www.cranbrook.kent.sch.uk

Cranbrook School (GM) existing to promote education in Cranbrook

Head: P A Close MA, FRSA

Member of: ISBA, STABIS

Co-educational Boarding & Day

Age range of pupils: 13 – 18

Boarders from 13

No. of students enrolled as at 1.9.98: 696

Boys: 392 Girls: 304

Average size of class: 26

Teacher/Pupil ratio: 1:15

Curriculum: 5 year course leading to 9 or more GCSEs, followed by 3 A levels.

Entry requirements: Day pupils enter by school reference/Entrance Test and local residence qualification; boarders by interview and assessment or Common Entrance.

Range of fees per annum as at 1.9.98:

Boarding: £5700

Tuition free.

Cranbrook is a selective, co-educational Upper School with 290 boarders and places for 290 Sixth Formers, situated in a pleasant country town within an hour of London. Our academic record is excellent with 99% pass rate at GCSE and 98% pass rate at A level (with 55% of grades being A or B).

Cranbrook's story is a remarkable one - established in 1518 as the free Grammar School of Queen Elizabeth I, it is now translated into a thriving Grant Maintained co-educational, academic day and boarding School. Cranbrook caters for the top 20% to 25% of the ability range, and candidates may be registered at any time prior to 31st October of the year preceding proposed entry.

At Cranbrook we expect and obtain high standards of personal behaviour and self discipline and we seek to realise the following educational aims:

To maintain and develop in pupils lively enquiring minds.

To foster attitudes which will instil self-confidence in pupils and create in them a sense of personal excellence.

To emphasise the importance of language, number, the aesthetic and physical areas of learning and to develop competence in them.

To help pupils to develop personal, spiritual and moral values, a tolerance of others and to be caring members of their community.

To help pupils to understand the world in which they live.

Boarding Houses are in the care of resident staff with small dormitories or single study bedrooms and generous common rooms and we ensure that the atmosphere in the Houses is both warm and friendly. Since boarding is on a termly basis, there are activities arranged for each weekend, including inter-house competitions, theatre and cinema trips and away-days.

We have a 400 seat fully equipped theatre which is used for musical as well as dramatic productions. Other facilities include a new Design Technology Centre, playing fields, a heated swimming pool, squash and tennis courts, a Sports Hall with dance studio, climbing wall and multi-gym and an Astroturf pitch. Boys' and girls' teams compete at the highest levels in all the major sports throughout the country and Cranbrook was awarded the prestigious Sportsmark Gold Award in 1998.

The most recent OFSTED inspection in 1997 listed Cranbrook as 'an outstanding school'.

Cranbrook School is a Grant Maintained Educational Charity.

Lady Manners School

(Founded 1636)

Bakewell, Derbyshire DE45 1JA

Tel: 01629 812671 Fax: 01629 814984

A caring Grant Maintained comprehensive School committed to academic excellence, personal and social development and traditional values in education and relationships. Expectations are high (OFSTED 1994 conclusion: School of 'excellence in both academic and pastoral spheres'). Success is reflected in the large, active Sixth Form and strong university entrance. Residential accommodation is in a comfortable mansion in extensive grounds and within the scenic national park.

Headmistress: Miss M P Sellers MA(Oxon), MA, FRSA

Date of appointment: 1996

Member of: BSA, STABIS

Co-educational Boarding & Day

Religious affiliation: None

Age range of pupils: 11 – 19

No. of students enrolled as at 1.9.98: 1531

VIth Form: 328

Average size of class: Lower School 29; Upper School 30; Sixth Form 12

Teacher/Pupil ratio: 1:18

Curriculum: Balanced curriculum leading to 28 GCSEs and 26 A level courses. Preparation for university including Oxbridge, S levels, STEP. Young Enterprise scheme. Careers programme.

Entry requirements: By informal interview and school report. Application direct to the Headteacher.

Range of fees per annum as at 1.9.98:

Weekly Boarding: £4737

Boarding: £5220

Lady Manners School is situated in the market town of Bakewell in the Peak District. Rural location. Outdoor education opportunities. Music, Sport, Drama, Duke of Edinburgh Award strong. Family style boarding. High staffing ratio.

Royal Grammar School

(Founded 1562)

Amersham Road, High Wycombe,
Buckinghamshire HP13 6QT

Tel: 01494 524955 Fax: 01494 510604

The School has a strong academic and sporting tradition with over 98 per cent going on to degree courses at universities of whom about 26 each year proceed to Oxford and Cambridge. There are currently national representatives in four sports at the school. Supportive, caring atmosphere.

Head: Mr David R Levin BEcon, MA, FRSA

Date of appointment: September 1993

Boys Day & Boarding

Religious affiliation: Inter-denominational Christian Foundation

Age range of pupils: 11 – 18

Boarders from 11+ (5 day only)

No. of students enrolled as at 1.9.98: 1350

Boys: 1350 VIth Form: 400

Average size of class: 20

Teacher/Pupil ratio: 1:16

Curriculum: Boys are prepared for GCSE, GCE A and S levels, and AS level, and entry to Oxford and Cambridge. Boys take at least nine GCSE subjects. At Sixth Form students choose three or four subjects from 23 A levels and 10 AS level subjects.

Entry requirements: At 11+ by Bucks CC selection procedure and by school assessment and interview at 12+ and upwards.

Range of fees per annum as at 1.9.98:

Fees on application

The 55 boarders are accommodated in two small, comfortable houses adjacent to the School each house having a resident Housemaster with family and resident Housetutor.

A new purpose built Boarding House for up to 70 boys will open in September 1999. It will have state of the art communication facilities and 36 single en suite rooms for the senior boys. There will be two resident Housemasters with families and five resident Housetutors.

There is a family environment where the individual is supported and cared for.

The Royal Grammar School is a registered charity (No. 310627) providing education in the community.

Sir Roger Manwood's School

(Founded 1563)

Manwood Road, Sandwich, Kent CT13 9JX

Tel: 01304 613286 Fax: 01304 615336

e-mail: headsrms@rmplc.co.uk

Head: Mr C R L Morgan MA(Cantab)

Date of appointment: 1996

Member of: BSA, STABIS

Co-educational Day & Boarding

Religious affiliation: Non-denominational

Age range of pupils: 11 – 18

Boarders from 11

No. of students enrolled as at 1.9.98: 750

VIth Form: 180

Teacher/Pupil ratio: 1:16

Curriculum: All pupils, boys and girls, do a wide common curriculum, including two foreign languages in years 8 to 9 leading to GCSE courses in years 10 and 11. GCE A levels, S levels and Oxbridge entry are taken at Sixth Form level.

Entry requirements: Entry is by interview and assessment. All pupils must be able to cope with a selective grammar school academic curriculum.

Range of fees per annum as at 1.9.98:

Boarding: £4734

Boarding fee only – no tuition fee

We have an excellent track record with over 95% of the Sixth Form entering Higher Education, including Oxbridge. GCSE and A level pass rates are extremely high; the school features prominently in the National League Tables.

Academic and leisure facilities offered are: 30 acres of playing fields, a swimming pool, shooting range, tennis courts, an astro-turf pitch, gymnasium and Sports Hall, a new Science Block and a new Technology Block and other specialist teaching accommodation.

Sir Roger Manwood's School stands in delightful grounds in the ancient town of Sandwich, near to Dover and the Continent and with regular train services to London.

The School is a charity which exists to provide education for children.

Steyning Grammar School

A Community Technology College

(Founded 1614)

Church Street, Steyning, West Sussex BN44 3LB

Tel: 01903 814786 Fax: 01903 879146

We are a learning community, living and working together. All who study through school, adult education, residence, the youth service or sports centre are encouraged to strive for excellence and personal achievement and to contribute to community life. Our successes range from Oxbridge entrance to basic literacy competence.

Head: P J Senior MA, BEd, FRSA, MIMgt

Date of appointment: September 1995

Member of: STABIS, BSA

Co-educational Day & Boarding

Age range of pupils: 11 – 18

No. of students enrolled as at 1.9.98: 1706

VIth Form: 393

Average size of class: 25

Teacher/Pupil ratio: Under 16, 1:18; Over 16, 1:12

Curriculum: Full national curriculum with many options available in KS4. Twenty-four A level subjects plus GNVQs – Post 16. Leisure activities enhanced by excellent community facilities in sport and performing arts.

Range of fees per annum as at 1.9.98:

Boarding: £4875

Sixth Form bursaries

The School still uses the original fifteenth century buildings with many modern additions, in a delightful South Downs village convenient to Gatwick, London and South Coast.

The Royal Alexandra & Albert School

(Founded May 1758)

Gatton Park, Reigate, Surrey RH2 0TW

Tel: 01737 643052 Fax: 01737 642294

Our lively, stimulating and caring environment and unique parkland setting combine to make the Royal Alexandra and Albert School an attractive option for many pupils and their parents. We are one of the fastest growing boarding schools in the country with quality boarding facilities which are second to none.

Head: R Bushin MA(Cantab), MA(Educ)London

Date of appointment: September 1993

Member of: BSA, STABIS

Co-educational Day & Boarding

Religious affiliation: Protestant

Age range of pupils: 7 – 19

Boarders from 7

No. of students enrolled as at 1.9.98: 540

Boys: 310 Girls: 230 VIth Form: 26

Average size of class: Junior School 25, Secondary School 20

Curriculum: Situated in the beautiful 18th century landscape of Gatton Park, Reigate, minutes from Junction 8 off the M25, and within 30 minutes of Gatwick Airport and an hour from Heathrow, the Royal Alexandra and Albert School offers high quality boarding education at a modest cost. Our junior and secondary schools offer all the subjects of the National Curriculum to a high standard. Our Sixth Form provision represents a unique partnership with Reigate Sixth Form and East Surrey Colleges. Sixth Form boarders, therefore, have access to the widest possible range of further education courses.

Subject specialities and academic track record: Recent results in Drama and Art and Design have been outstanding. Science has the 'most approved' accolade.

Entry requirements: Initial application is made through our Admissions Secretary. All potential

boarders are interviewed by the Headmaster. There are no formal academic requirements for admission.

Range of fees per annum as at 1.9.98:

Day: £750

Boarding: £5895 – £6285

Examinations offered including boards: Key Stage 2 and 3 tests, GCSE: NEAB, MEG and SEG.

Destination/career prospects of leavers: Majority of leavers go on to further and higher education. There are no particular career emphases.

Academic & leisure facilities: We offer a teaching and learning environment of the highest quality. Our computer facilities are second to none among maintained schools in Surrey and all pupils develop high levels of computer literacy. Our recreational facilities afford, in addition to the 'usual', a riding school, indoor heated swimming pool and a lake for keen anglers.

Religious activities: Whole school assemblies are held weekly in the School Chapel. All boarders attend Evensong each Sunday. Special 'occasions' include Harvest Festival, Remembrance Sunday, Christmas Carols and Founders' Day. Pupils are frequently involved in the preparation of services.

Scholarships: Bursaries are available in the event of 'social need'. These are assessed by our Bursary Committee after completion of a detailed questionnaire regarding individual circumstances.

Aims and objectives: We are different from many schools in that we welcome children irrespective of their abilities. In close partnership with parents we seek to ensure that all fulfil their potential.

The aims of the School are:

to create responsible citizens who will play a positive part in society

to encourage the virtues of self-discipline, thought and care for others

to enable all pupils to optimise their potential in whatever field it might be displayed.

We have created a lively, stimulating and caring environment out of which we seek to create lively, interested and caring pupils.

The Royal Alexandra and Albert Foundation, a registered charity, exists to provide boarding facilities, pastoral care and bursary support for pupils completing their education at the Royal Alexandra and Albert School.

Wymondham College

(Founded 1951)

Golf Links Road, Morley, Wymondham,
Norfolk NR18 9SZ

Tel: 01953 605566 Fax: 01953 603313

Principal: Mr John D Haden MA, BPhil

Date of appointment: 1992

Co-educational Boarding & Day

Religious affiliation: Non-denominational

Age range of pupils: 11 – 18

Boarders from 11

No. of students enrolled as at 1.9.98: 883

Boys: 480 Girls: 403 VIth Form: 299

Average size of class: 25

Teacher/Pupil ratio: 1:15

Curriculum: Broadly based, strong core, options do not close any career doors.

Entry requirements: School reports and interview with the Principal.

Range of fees per annum as at 1.9.98:

Boarding: £4923

The boarding houses cater for both boys and girls with clearly stated rules. There is a separate Year 7 house that provides a secure and supportive induction to College life and a separate pre-university House that offers an excellent preparation for university life. The 82 acre site is that of an ex US Air Force hospital. The College is well equipped and has a strong tradition of academic achievement. It is situated in the country, 15 miles south west of the city of Norwich on the road to London and Cambridge.

Wymondham College is a statutory charity and exists to provide high quality boarding education for boys and girls.

Directory of State Boarding Schools

Berkshire

Reading

READING SCHOOL
Erleigh Road, Reading, Berkshire RG1 5LW
Tel: 0118 9261406
Head: Dr P R Mason BSc, PhD, CChem, MRSC
Type: Boys Boarding & Day 11–18
No of pupils: B766 Vlth224
Fees: FB £4290

Buckinghamshire

High Wycombe

★ROYAL GRAMMAR SCHOOL
Amersham Road, High Wycombe,
Buckinghamshire HP13 6QT
Tel: 01494 524955
Head: Mr David R Levin BEcon, MA, FRSA
Type: Boys Day & Boarding 11–18
No of pupils: 1350 Vlth400
Fees: On application

Cornwall

Launceston

LAUNCESTON COLLEGE
Dunheved Road, Launceston, Cornwall PL15 9JN
Tel: 01566 772468
Head: A Wroath MA
Type: Co-educational Day & Boarding 11–18
No of pupils: 1100
Fees: FB £3200

Cumbria

Keswick

KESWICK SCHOOL
Main Street, Keswick, Cumbria CA12 5NF
Tel: 01768 772605
Head: H W Allen MA(Cantab), ACE(Oxon)
Type: Co-educational Day & Boarding 11–18
No of pupils: B604 G528
Fees: FB £3675–£4050

Milnthorpe

DALLAM SCHOOL
Haverflatts Lane, Milnthorpe, Cumbria LA7 7EH
Tel: 015395 63224
Head: A G Bancroft MA
Type: Co-educational Day & Boarding 11–18
No of pupils: 650
Fees: FB £3300–£3975

Derbyshire

Bakewell

★LADY MANNERS SCHOOL
Bakewell, Derbyshire DE45 1JA
Tel: 01629 812671
Head: Miss M P Sellers MA(Oxon), MA, FRSA
Type: Co-educational Boarding & Day 11–19
No of pupils: 1531 Vlth328
Fees: FB £5220 WB £4737

Devon

Crediton

QUEEN ELIZABETH'S COMMUNITY COLLEGE
Western Road, Crediton, Devon EX17 3LU
Tel: 01363 773401
Head: Mrs V Brasington MEd
Type: 11–18
No of pupils: 1384 B683 G701 Vlth178
Fees: FB £4200 WB £3600

Dorset

Lyme Regis

THE WOODROFFE SCHOOL
Uplyme Road, Lyme Regis, Dorset DT7 3LS
Tel: 01297 442232
Head: Mr Redman
Type: Co-educational Day & Boarding 11 –18
No of pupils: 850
Fees: FB £4050

Shaftesbury

SHAFTESBURY SCHOOL
Salisbury Road, Shaftesbury, Dorset SP7 8ER
Tel: 01747 854498
Head: A D Jeavons BA, MPhil, FRSA
Type: Co-educational Day & Boarding 13 –18
No of pupils: 671 B334 G337 VIth180
Fees: FB £4050

Essex

Colchester

COLCHESTER ROYAL GRAMMAR SCHOOL
Lexden Road, Colchester, Essex CO3 3ND
Tel: 01206 577971/2
Head: Stewart Francis MA
Type: Boys Day & Boarding B11–18 G16–18
No of pupils: 662 VIth181
Fees: FB £4710 WB £3090

Hampshire

Winchester

KINGS' SCHOOL, WINCHESTER
Romsey Road, Winchester, Hampshire SO22 5PN
Tel: 01962 861161
Head: R W Bradbury MA
Type: Co-educational Day & Boarding 11 –16
No of pupils: 990
Fees: FB £5079

THE WESTGATE SCHOOL
Cheriton Road, Winchester, Hampshire SO22 5AZ
Tel: 01962 854757
Head: P D Jenner BA, ACP
Type: Co-educational Day & Boarding 11 –16
No of pupils: 950
Fees: FB £5079

Hertfordshire

Harpenden

ST GEORGE'S SCHOOL
Sun Lane, Harpenden, Hertfordshire AL5 4TD
Tel: 01582 765477
Head: N F Hoare MA, FRSA
Type: Co-educational Boarding & Day 11 –18
No of pupils: 931 B498 G433 VIth205
Fees: FB £5175

Kent

Cranbrook

*CRANBROOK SCHOOL
Waterloo Road, Cranbrook, Kent TN17 3JD
Tel: 01580 712163
Head: P A Close MA, FRSA
Type: Co-educational Boarding & Day 13 –18
No of pupils: 696 B392 G304
Fees: FB £5700

Sandwich

*SIR ROGER MANWOOD'S SCHOOL
Manwood Road, Sandwich, Kent CT13 9JX
Tel: 01304 613286
Head: Mr C R L Morgan MA(Cantab)
Type: Co-educational Day & Boarding 11 –18
No of pupils: 750 VIth180
Fees: FB £4734

Lancashire

Lancaster

LANCASTER ROYAL GRAMMAR SCHOOL
East Road, Lancaster LA1 3EF
Tel: 01524 32109
Head: P J Mawby MA(Cantab)
Type: Boys Day & Boarding 11 –18
No of pupils: B915 Vlth270
Fees: FB £3840

Leicestershire

Ashby-de-la-Zouch

ASHBY GRAMMAR SCHOOL
Leicester Road, Ashby-de-la-Zouch,
Leicestershire LE6 5DH
Tel: 01530 413759
Head: Mrs V Keller-Garnett
Type: Co-educational Boarding & Day 14 –19
No of pupils: 1320
Fees: FB £4590–£4950

Loughborough

★BURLEIGH COMMUNITY COLLEGE
Thorpe Hill, Loughborough, Leicestershire LE11 0SQ
Tel: 01509 268996
Head: Mr Philip Watson BSc, MA
Type: Co-educational Boarding & Day 14 –19
No of pupils: 1321 B645 G676 Vlth471
Fees: FB £4725–£5550

Lincolnshire

Grantham

KING'S SCHOOL
Brook Street, Grantham, Lincolnshire NG31 6RP
Tel: 01476 563180
Head: S B Howarth MA(oxon)
Type: Boys Day & Boarding 11 –18
No of pupils: B825
Fees: FB £3975WB £3825

Market Rasen

DE ASTON SCHOOL
Willingham Road, Market Rasen, Lincolnshire LN8 3RF
Tel: 01673 843415
Head: A H Neal MA(Cantab)
Type: Co-educational Day & Boarding 11 –18
No of pupils: 1110
Fees: FB £2940

Skegness

SKEGNESS GRAMMAR SCHOOL
Skegness, Lincolnshire PE25 2QS
Tel: 01754 610000
Head: A Rigby
Type: Co-educational Boarding & Day 11 –18
No of pupils: 660
Fees: FB £3147

Norfolk

Wymondham

*WYMONDHAM COLLEGE
Golf Links Road, Morley, Wymondham, Norfolk NR18 9SZ
Tel: 01953 605566
Principal: Mr John D Haden MA, BPhil
Type: Co-educational Boarding & Day 11 –18
No of pupils: 883 B480 G403 VIth299
Fees: FB £4923

Oxfordshire

Oxford

BURFORD SCHOOL
Cheltenham Road, Burford, Oxford, Oxfordshire OX18 4PL
Tel: 01993 823283/823303
Head: R J D Back BA
Type: Co-educational Day & Boarding 11 –18
No of pupils: 1200
Fees: FB £4530 WB £4380

Rutland

Oakham

RUTLAND SIXTH FORM COLLEGE
Barleythorpe Road, Oakham, Leicestershire LE15 6QH
Tel: 01572 722863
Head: L A Kidd BSc, MEd
Type: Co-educational Day & Boarding 16 –19
Fees: FB £5700

Shropshire

Newport

*ADAMS' GRAMMAR SCHOOL
Newport, Shropshire TF10 7BD
Tel: 01952 810698
Head: J M Richardson
Type: Grant Maintained Boys Day & Boarding 11 –18
No of pupils: 720 VIth B160 G40
Fees: FB £4860 WB £4650

Shrewsbury

ADAMS' SCHOOL WEM & ADAMS' COLLEGE
Lowe Hill, Wem, Shrewsbury, Shropshire SY4 5UB
Tel: 01939 232328
Head: P G Arnold BA
Type: Co-educational Day & Boarding 11 –18
No of pupils: 955
Fees: FB £4485 WB £3345

Somerset

Bridgwater

BRYMORE SECONDARY TECHNICAL COLLEGE
Cannington, Bridgwater, Somerset TA5 2NB
Tel: 01278 652369
Head: T J Pierce BSc
Type: Boys Day & Boarding 13 –17
No of pupils: B210
Fees: FB £3465

Bruton

SEXEY'S SCHOOL
Cole Road, Bruton, Somerset BA10 ODF
Tel: 01749 813393
Head: Stephen Burgoyne BA
Type: Co-educational Boarding & Day 11 –18
No of pupils: B223 G183 VIth195
Fees: FB £4140

Surrey

Reigate

*THE ROYAL ALEXANDRA & ALBERT SCHOOL
Gatton Park, Reigate, Surrey RH2 0TW
Tel: 01737 643052
Head: R Bushin MA(Cantab), MA(Educ)London
Type: Co-educational Day & Boarding 7 –19
No of pupils: 540 B310 G230 VIth26
Fees: FB £5895–£6285 DAY £750

Woking

GORDON'S SCHOOL
West End, Woking, Surrey GU24 9PT
Tel: 01276 858084
Head: D A Mulkerrin MA
Type: Co-educational Boarding & Day 11 –18
No of pupils: 310
Fees: FB £5196 WB £4680 DAY £2856

West Midlands

Stourbridge

OLD SWINFORD HOSPITAL
Stourbridge, West Midlands DY8 1QX
Tel: 01384 370025
Head: C F R Potter MA(Cantab)
Type: Boys Boarding 11 –18
No of pupils: B565 VIth180
Fees: FB £4200

West Sussex

Steyning

*STEYNING GRAMMAR SCHOOL
Church Street, Steyning, West Sussex BN44 3LB
Tel: 01903 814786
Head: P J Senior MA, BEd, FRSA, MIMgt
Type: Co-educational Day & Boarding 11 –18
No of pupils: 1706 VIth393
Fees: FB £4875

North Yorkshire

Ripon

RIPON GRAMMAR SCHOOL
Clotherholme Road, Ripon, North Yorkshire HG4 2DG
Tel: 01765 602647/8
Head: Mr A M Jones BA
Type: Co-educational Day & Boarding 11 –18
No of pupils: 620
Fees: FB £3150–£4395 WB £2250–£3150

Wales

Wales Denbighshire

Denbigh

ST BRIGID'S SCHOOL
Denbigh, Denbighshire LL16 4BH
Tel: 01745 815228
Head: Sister Elizabeth Kelly CSB
Type: 3 –18
No of pupils: 250 VIth50
Fees: FB £3900

Section Four:
Boarding at 16+

Peter Symonds' College

(Founded 1897)

Owens Road, Winchester, Hampshire SO22 6RX

Tel: 01962 852764 Fax: 01962 849372

One of only two Sixth Form colleges to offer boarding. By valuing individuals, achieves remakable academic success.

Head: Mr N A Hopkins BSc, MEd

Date of appointment: 1993

Member of: FEFC, STABIS

Co-educational Day & Boarding

Age range of pupils: 16 – 19

No. of students enrolled as at 1.9.98: 1874

Boys: 940 Girls: 934

Average size of class: 20

Teacher/Pupil ratio: 1:12

Curriculum: 35 A level subjects, 5 GNVQ, GCSE, Business Skills courses plus 56 sports and activities on offer each year.

Range of fees per annum as at 1.9.98:

Boarding: £5802 – £6200

Large Sixth Form College half a mile from centre of Winchester.

Peter Symonds' College is an educational establishment with charitable status providing education for 16-19 year olds.

Information about day schools can be found in
Which School ?
also published by John Catt Educational Ltd

St Clare's, Oxford

(Founded 1953)

139 Banbury Road, Oxford, Oxfordshire OX2 7AL

Tel: 01865 552031 Fax: 01865 310002
e-mail: admission@stclares.ac.uk
Internet: www.stclares.ac.uk

Head: Mr Boyd Roberts MA(Oxon) CertEd, CBiol, MIBiol

Date of appointment: 1998

Member of: ARELS, ECIS. Accredited by BAC.

Co-educational Boarding & Day

Age range of pupils: 16 – 20

Boarders from 16 years

No. of students enrolled as at 1.9.98: 310

Boys: 123 Girls: 187

Average size of class: 8

Teacher/Pupil ratio: 1:7

Curriculum: Courses offered: International Baccalaureate, (two year, broadly based A level equivalent requiring study of six subjects. Accepted by all universities in the UK, US and in most other countries). 1 year pre-IB course. 1 year university foundation course. English Language courses, academic year 16+ and summer courses 10-16 and 16+. Liberal Arts/Study Abroad course for US undergraduates.

Range of fees per annum as at 1.9.98:

Day: £9415

Boarding: £15,050

St Clare's is a co-educational international college in North Oxford with a high standard of academic achievement and a friendly, mature atmosphere. The minimum age is 16. Over 40 nationalities are represented, the major nationality being British.

The International Baccalaureate is an exciting and demanding course, which provides a strong, broad base for higher study. Three subjects are studied at 'Higher Level' and three at 'Standard' level. In addition, students submit an extended essay of 4,000 words, take part in our Creativity, Action and Service Programme, and also follow a course of 'Theory of Knowledge' which develops their capacity for critical thinking. Almost all students go on to higher education assisted by our careers advisers, one full time.

St Clare's offers a wealth of subjects for study, supported by the Academic Resources Centre and social/cultural activities organised by the Student Activities Office including environmental action, community service, horseriding, taekwan-do, music and drama.

St Clare's, Oxford is a charitable foundation which aims to promote and advance education generally, and in particular to promote international education and understanding.

The Norland College

(Founded 1892)

Denford Park, Hungerford, Berkshire RG17 OPQ

Tel: 01488 682252 Fax: 01488 685212

The requests for Norland Nurses exceed demand and students who successfully complete the course can be assured of a choice of employment.

Headmistress: Mrs L E Davis MPhil, RGN, FRSH

Date of appointment: 1980

Specialist Training for Professional Qualifications in the Early Years Care and Education

Religious affiliation: None

Age range of pupils: 17 and over

Boarders from 17 years

No. of students enrolled as at 1.9.98: 80

Average size of class: 25

Teacher/Pupil ratio: 1:18

Curriculum: Two year course leading to the award of:

a) Diploma in Nursery Nursing (entry - Three GCSEs at Grade C or above) *OR*

b) Diploma in Higher Education (Early Childhood Studies) (entry - two A level passes)

Plus the coveted Norland Diploma.

Range of fees per annum as at 1.9.98:

Day: £6306

Boarding: £10,881

The College is situated in parkland together with Day Care and Nursery School facilities providing onsite opportunities for practical training.

Directory of Schools
offering Boarding at 16+

Berkshire

Hungerford

*THE NORLAND COLLEGE
Denford Park, Hungerford, Berkshire RG17 OPQ
Tel: 01488 682252
Head: Mrs L E Davis MPhil, RGN, FRSH
Type: Co-educational Day & Boarding from 17
No of pupils: 80
Fees: FB £10,881 DAY £6306

Reading

PADWORTH COLLEGE
Padworth, Reading, Berkshire RG7 4NR
Tel: 0118 983 2644/5
Head: Eric Reynolds BA, PGCE
Type: Girls Boarding & Day 14 –19
No of pupils: G125
Fees: FB £12,495 DAY £6248

Cambridgeshire

Cambridge

CAMBRIDGE ARTS & SCIENCES
13-14 Round Church Street, Cambridge CB5 8AD
Tel: 01223 314431
Head: Mr Peter McLaughlin CertEd, BEd(Cantab)
Type: Co-educational Boarding & Day 14 –19
No of pupils: B94 G98 VIth135
Fees: FB £10,800–£14,000   DAY £7000 –£10,800

CAMBRIDGE CENTRE FOR SIXTH FORM STUDIES
1 Salisbury Villas, Station Road, Cambridge CB1 2JF
Tel: 01223 716890
Head: Mr P C Redhead MA, PGCE
Type: Co-educational Day & Boarding 14 –19
No of pupils: 180 B95 G85 VIth155
Fees: FB £11,790–£15,354   DAY £6162 –£9846

Devon

Plymouth

PLYMOUTH TUTORIAL COLLEGE (EGAS)
The Pines, 131 Pomphlett Road, Plymstock, Plymouth,
Devon PL9 7BU
Tel: 01752 401942
Heads: Mr B A E Stoyel FCollP, CertEd &
Mrs M M Stoyel BSc
Type: Co-educational Day 6 –80

Hampshire

Winchester

*PETER SYMONDS' COLLEGE
Owens Road, Winchester, Hampshire SO22 6RX
Tel: 01962 852764
Head: Mr N A Hopkins BSc, MEd
Type: Co-educational Day & Boarding 16 –19
No of pupils: 1874 B940 G934
Fees: FB £5802–£6200

Kent

Rochester

ROCHESTER TUTORS INDEPENDENT COLLEGE
New Road House, 3 New Road, Rochester, Kent ME1 1BD
Tel: 01634 828115
Heads: B Pain BSc(Hons) & Simon de Balder BA(Hons)
Type: Co-educational Day & Boarding 14 –50
No of pupils: 150 B75 G75
Fees: FB £10,550 DAY £7250

Tonbridge

THE OLD VICARAGE
Marden, Tonbridge, Kent TN12 9AG
Tel: 01622 832200
Head: Mrs P G Stevens LRAM(S&D)
Type: Girls Day & Boarding 9 –50
No of pupils: G6
Fees: FB £7830

Leicestershire

Leicester

IRWIN COLLEGE
164 London Road, Leicester LE2 1ND
Tel: 0116 2552648
Head: Mr A J Elliott BA(Oxon), MPhil(Cantab), TEFL
Type: Co-educational Day & Boarding 14 –22
No of pupils: B50 G50 Vlth60
Fees: FB £11,550–£12,600 DAY £6200

Market Harborough

BROOKE HOUSE COLLEGE
Leicester Road, Market Harborough, Leicestershire
LE16 7AU
Tel: 01858 462452
Head: Mr F Colombo BSc, CertEd, MIBiol
Type: Co-educational Boarding & Day 13 –20
No of pupils: B60 G28 Vlth73
Fees: FB £12,060 DAY £6975

London

London

LUCIE CLAYTON SECRETARIAL COLLEGE
4 Cornwall Gardens, Kensington, London SW7 4AJ
Tel: 0171 581 0024
Head: Mrs Denise Perry
Type: Girls Boarding & Day 16 –21
No of pupils: G100
Fees: FB £6300 DAY £3000

Northamptonshire

Northampton

BOSWORTH TUTORIAL COLLEGE
Nazareth House, Old University Blding, Barrack Road,
Northampton, Northamptonshire NN2 6AF
Tel: 01604 239995
Head: Mark A V Broadway BSc, PGCE
Type: Co-educational Day & Boarding 4 –20
No of pupils: 127 B71 G56
Fees: FB £11,795–£12,085 DAY £6440 –£6590

Oxfordshire

Oxford

CHERWELL TUTORS
Greyfriars, Paradise Street, Oxford OX1 1LD
Tel: 01865 242670
Head: P J Gordon BA, CertEd
Type: Co-educational Boarding & Day

EDWARD GREENE'S TUTORIAL ESTABLISHMENT
45 Pembroke Street, Oxford OX1 1BP
Tel: 01865 248308
Head: E P C Greene MA
Type: Co-educational Boarding & Day

OXFORD TUTORIAL COLLEGE
12 King Edward Street, Oxford OX1 4HT
Tel: 01865 793333
Head: Ralph Dennison BA, PGCE
Type: Co-educational Day 16 –25
No of pupils: 108 B57 G51
Fees: FB £3500 DAY £3306

★ST CLARE'S, OXFORD
139 Banbury Road, Oxford OX2 7AL
Tel: 01865 552031
Head: Mr Boyd Roberts MA(Oxon) CertEd, CBiol, MIBiol
Type: Co-educational Boarding & Day 16 –20
No of pupils: 310 B123 G187
Fees: FB £15,050 DAY £9415

Section Five:
International Schools in the UK
and Overseas

American Community Schools

(Founded 1967)

Heywood, Portsmouth Road, Cobham, Surrey KT11 1BL

Tel: 01932 867251 Fax: 01932 869798
e-mail: trovillard@acs-england.co.uk
Internet: http://www.acs-england.co.uk

Headmaster: Mr T Lehman

Member of: NEAS & C (New England Association of Schools & Colleges); IB; ISC, ECIS, SATS and AP

Co-educational Boarding & Day

Religious affiliation: Non-sectarian

Age range of pupils: 3 – 19

No. of students enrolled as at 1.9.98: 1265

Boys: 629 Girls: 636

Average size of class: 16

Teacher/Pupil ratio: 1:10

Curriculum: Courses offered: English, Maths, French, German, Spanish, Biology, Chemistry, Physics, History, Economics, Art, Computer Studies, Psychology, Music, Drama. 10 Advanced Placement courses and 15 International Baccalaureate courses.

Range of fees per annum as at 1.9.98:

Tuition and accommodation fees upon application. Financial aid is available.

The modern, purpose-built boarding division provides study-bedrooms with bathroom accommodation for 120 students in grades 7-13 with a choice of 5 or 7 day programs.

ACS offers college-preparatory programs leading to the American High School Diploma and International Baccalaureate Diploma (for university entrance worldwide). Students regularly achieve a 95-100% pass rate on the full Baccalaureate Diploma.

Hockerill Anglo-European School

(Founded 1980)

Dunmow Road, Bishops Stortford, Hertfordshire CM23 5HX

Tel: 01279 658451 Fax: 01279 755918

Hockerill is a caring boarding community sited within a leafy and spacious campus, very easily accessible by road, train or air. It has a strong international dimension, a curriculum which includes an internationally acclaimed bilingual (French/English) option and excellent IT facilities. It is recognised by the UK Government as one of the UK's small number of specialist Language Colleges.

Headmaster: Dr Robert Guthrie BSc, PhD, MBA

Date of appointment: 1996

Member of: BSA, STABIS, JBO

Co-educational Boarding

Age range of pupils: 11 – 18

Boarders from 11 years

No. of students enrolled as at 1.9.98: 500

Boys: 265 Girls: 235

Average size of class: 22

Teacher/Pupil ratio: 1:14

Curriculum: This is based on the National Curriculum. The international dimension includes an extensive and growing network of links and exchanges with schools in Poland, China, Hungary, Morocco, Italy, Germany, France, Holland, Romania and the USA. Many students opt for the award-winning bilingual section which includes studying History and some Geography using the French language and resources. It also involves some study in Lyon, Aix-en-Provence, and at the School's base in the Loire Valley.

Work experience is available overseas. Science includes a Rural Science option. Support is provided for the able (links with the GIFT Partnership) as well as those with learning difficulties (trained full time staff).

Entry requirements: Admission is usually based on interview and school reports.

Range of fees per annum as at 1.9.98:

Boarding: £4030

Examinations offered including boards: GCSE; International Baccalaureate.

Distinctive facilities include a network of over 180 computers with Internet access, a floodlit all weather sports pitch and a small farm. The School occupies buildings listed for their architectural importance within a beautiful site situated midway between London and Cambridge. It is 35 minutes from London by regular express rail link, one mile from the M11 and three miles from London Stansted Airport.

Hockerill Anglo-European School is a Grant Maintained exempt charity

Marymount International School

(Founded 1955)

George Road, Kingston upon Thames, Surrey KT2 7PE

Tel: 0181 949 0571 Fax: 0181 336 2485

Marymount offers superb teaching by experienced and highly qualified staff. Each student's schedule is individually tailored to the subjects she wishes to follow. Marymount offers excellent facilities including a state-of-the-art Computer Centre and Sports Hall. Academic success leads to a university entrance rate of over 95% each year.

Principal: Sr Rosaleen Sheridan RSHM, MSc Psychology and Social Sciences (University College, Dublin)

Date of appointment: 1990

Member of: MSA, ECIS, IBO, GSA

Girls Day & Boarding

Religious affiliation: Roman Catholic Multi-faith

Caring environment fostered by Sisters of the Sacred Heart of Mary

Age range of pupils: Girls 11 – 18

No. of students enrolled as at 1.9.98: 235

Girls: 235 VIth Form: 100

Average size of class: 15

Teacher/Pupil ratio: 1:10

Curriculum: Marymount offers a full International Baccalaureate Curriculum, integrated with the American College Preparatory programme. The IB Middle Years programme is followed by all students aged 11-16, who then may elect to take the two-year IB Diploma syllabus, leading to UK university admission and US college credit. Over 98% of our graduates go on to third-level education in the UK and abroad.

Entry requirements: Previous reports, teacher's recommendations and interview.

Range of fees per annum as at 1.9.98:

Day: £8100 – £9050

Weekly Boarding: £14,400 – £15,350

Boarding: £14,600 – £15,550

The beautiful seven acre campus is situated just 12 miles southwest of London. Facilities include modern science centre, full size sports complex, classroom block with library and computer centre, and music centre and Design Technology room.

Marymount International School (Institution of the Religious Sisters of the Sacred Heart of Mary the Immaculate Virgin), a registered charity, strives to provide high quality education for its students.

Sherborne School International College

(Founded: Sherborne School - 1550, International College - 1977)

Newell Grange, Newell, Sherborne, Dorset DT9 4EZ

Tel: 01935 814743 Fax: 01935 816863

Principal: Dr Christopher Greenfield MA, MEd

Date of appointment: 1997

Co-educational Boarding

Religious affiliation: Multi-denominational

Age range of pupils: 10 – 16

No. of students enrolled as at 1.9.98: 120

Average size of class: 7

Teacher/Pupil ratio: 1:4

Curriculum: The International College of Sherborne School provides a 'bridge' which enables pupils educated in other countries to prepare themselves thoroughly and carefully for success in top UK schools. Our aim is to ensure that when our pupils go on to other schools they have a good command of spoken and written English, and a sound foundation in other subjects. With this preparation they are able to thrive, rather than merely survive, when they join in the larger classes of native English speaking children.

Subject specialities and academic track record: We specialise in preparing boys and girls from overseas for entrance to good independent boarding schools. Some pupils are native English speakers, but most are learning English. Excellent success rate at Common Entrance and GCSE examinations.

Entry requirements: Previous school report requested. No entry examination.

Range of fees per annum as at 1.9.98:

Boarding: £17,250

Lab fees, textbooks and essential materials are included.

Examinations offered including boards: Common Entrance examination at 13+, GCSE (All Boards), University of Cambridge Examinations in English.

Destination/career prospects of leavers: Our pupils gain admission to the best of UK Schools, *eg* Winchester, Sherborne, Westminster, Harrow, and achieve high levels of success there as a result of the sound foundation acquired in the College.

Academic & leisure facilities: Classes are small - average seven pupils. Every pupil receives careful personal attention, in and out of lessons, and lives and studies in the happy family atmosphere of a small school which believes in helping every pupil to make the most of his or her potential. Standards of good manners and discipline are high. In 1991 we moved into new buildings with first-class living accommodation and excellent classroom and laboratory facilities. A new classroom block is being completed this year.

Our aim in the International College is to provide a happy and hard-working atmosphere in which children from overseas can prepare themselves, academically and socially for the more robust conditions which they will find.

Sherborne School is a Registered Charity which exists to provide a complete and well-balanced education for children.

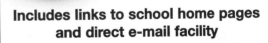

St George's School in Switzerland

(Founded 1927)

1815 Clarens, Montreux,

Tel: ++41 21 964 34 11 Fax: ++41 21 964 49 32

Principal: Mrs L G Zünd-Cooper BA, HDE, NUI

Member of: BSA, ECIS, COBISEC, AVDEP, SHA, ADISR, FSEP

Religious affiliation: Non-denominational

Age range of pupils: 5 – 19

Co-educational day school

No. of students enrolled as at 1.9.98: 150

Curriculum: Pupils are prepared for the full range of IGCSE and A levels (Cambridge and London Boards), the Alliance Française (University of Paris), the Royal Schools of Music exams and the Pitman examinations in Typing and Word Processing. The US College Board exams, PSAT, SAT, TOEFL and ACH tests can also be taken. Full details of all courses are available upon request.

The Junior department follows the National Curriculum from Pre-reception to year 6 for day boys and day girls. Day boys are accepted in the senior school.

Entry requirements: Pupils are admitted on the basis of interview where possible, or on the basis of recent reports from their previous school as well as a confidential report from its principal.

Range of fees per annum as at 1.9.98:

Secondary Day: SFr 20,620-22,050 Boarding: SFr 43,690-45,430. Junior dept. rates on request. Fees are reviewed yearly by the governing body.

With small classes and a highly qualified staff, pupils are assured of the best individual attention.

There is a high level of success in public examinations. The academic programme is supplemented by a wide range of extra-curricular activities including photography, choir, computer art club, aerobics. Music and drama occupy an important place both in and out of the curriculum. The school has excellent sports facilities including a fully equipped sports hall with indoor tennis court, seven outdoor tennis courts and a swimming pool. Off-campus sports include skiing, horse-riding, windsurfing, and squash. The school has a well-stocked computerised library with over 10,000 books, videos and audiotapes; two modern science laboratories and a school hall.

Cultural visits are organised to a number of European destinations. Excursions are arranged every weekend.

Accommodation: Purpose-built in 1927, the school stands in a park of 45,000m² with magnificent uninterrupted views of the mountains and lake. It is within easy reach of Geneva airport, 50 minutes away. Boarders live in the main building in single or double rooms.

Summer courses in July: Intensive English or French courses for boys and girls aged 10-16 years.

TASIS England American School

(Founded 1976)

Coldharbour Lane, Thorpe, Surrey TW20 8TE

Tel: +44 (0) 1932 565252 Fax: +44 (0) 1932 564644
e-mail: ukadmissions@tasis.com; uksummer@tasis.com
Internet: http://www.tasis.com

'The American School in a Class by Itself'

Headmaster: Mr Dennis G Manning BA, MA

Date of appointment: 01/09/84

Co-educational Boarding & Day

Age range of pupils: 4 – 18

Boarders from 14

No. of students enrolled as at 1.9.98: 725

Boys: 369 Girls: 356

Range of fees per annum as at 1.9.98:

Day: £4365 – £9950

Boarding: £15,990

TASIS England, frequently cited as the premier American school in the United Kingdom, is now into its third decade of offering an American college-preparatory curriculum to day students from grades

Pre-K through to 12 and to boarding students from grades 9-12. Mrs M Crist Fleming, who established The American School in Switzerland in 1955, founded TASIS England in 1976. Located on a stunningly beautiful historic estate of Georgian mansions and 17th century cottages some miles southwest of London, TASIS combines an excellent academic program with exceptional facilities for art, drama, music, computers, and sports. Small classes and a dedicated, experienced faculty numbering in excess of 100 provide highly individualised attention and an outstanding environment for learning.

TASIS England embraces three divisions: Lower (grades PK-5; ages 4-10), Middle (grades 6-8; ages 11-13), and Upper (grades 9-12; ages 14-18). Students in each division regularly benefit from the opportunity to work closely with visiting artists, actors, musicians, and sports professionals. The comprehensive athletics program includes intramurals in the Lower School and interschool games for Middle School, JV, and Varsity teams. Throughout the year, students enjoy numerous field trips, weekend activities, and in-program travel to London, elsewhere within the UK, and abroad.

TASIS' ongoing effort to provide its students with the very best educational experience was recently underscored with the opening of the Early Childhood Center. Linked to the Lower School's Thorpe House, a Grade II listed building, the Center adds five classrooms and a multi-purpose room for dining, assemblies, and physical education. The three-storey Georgian-style building represents the latest stage in the School's on-going development plan, which has also included the inauguration of the 400-seat Fleming Theatre, the scene of student and professional productions throughout the year.

Virtually all TASIS graduates gain admission to the universities of their choice in the United Kingdom, the United States, Canada, and elsewhere. Recent placements have included Oxford, London, the LSE, Exeter, Plymouth, Edinburgh, Aberdeen and a variety of other UK universities. In the United States, graduates are currently enrolled at Harvard, Yale, Stanford, Dartmouth, Johns Hopkins, the University of Virginia, Washington and Lee, Texas, and many others.

Admissions decisions for the academic school year are made on a rolling basis upon receipt of a completed application form together with the application fee, three teachers' recommendations, and three years of transcripts. Standardised test scores and a student questionnaire are requested, but are not required. An interview is recommended unless distance is a prohibiting factor.

For additional information please contact Dr Duncan Rollo, Director of Admissions.

The TASIS England Summer Program, open to students ages 12-18 from the UK and around the world, is both rigorous and exciting. Intensive summer programs include high school credit and enrichment courses, theatre workshops, ESL, TOEFL, and SATReview. Students also enjoy a range of sports, activities, and travel, both international and within the UK. For admission to the summer program, a completed application, deposit, and teacher recommendation form are required.

TASIS England is accredited by the European Council of International Schools (ECIS), and the New England Association of Schools and Colleges (NEASC), and is a member of the National Association of Independent Schools (NAIS).

Directory of International Schools in the UK and Overseas

Bristol

Bristol

BADMINTON SCHOOL
Westbury-on-Trym, Bristol, BS9 3BA
Tel: 0117 905 5200
Head: Mrs Jan Scarrow BA, PGCE
Type: Girls Boarding & Day 4 –18
No of pupils: G389
Fees: FB £9375–£13,425 DAY £3525 –£7425

Hertfordshire

Bishops Stortford

*HOCKERILL ANGLO-EUROPEAN SCHOOL
Dunmow Road, Bishops Stortford, Hertfordshire CM23 5HX
Tel: 01279 658451
Head: Dr Robert Guthrie BSc, PhD, MBA
Type: Co-educational Boarding 11 –18
No of pupils: 500 B265 G235
Fees: FB £4030

Kent

Sevenoaks

SEVENOAKS SCHOOL
Sevenoaks, Kent TN13 1HU
Tel: 01732 455133
Head: T Cookson MA
Type: Co-educational Day & Boarding 11 –18
No of pupils: 940 B525 G415
Fees: FB £11,178–£11,961 DAY £6804 –£7587

Lancashire

Fleetwood

ROSSALL SCHOOL
Fleetwood, Lancashire FY7 8JW
Tel: 01253 774247/774201
Head: R D W Rhodes JP, BA
Type: Co-educational Boarding & Day 11 –18
No of pupils: B165 G96 VIth135
Fees: FB £7710–£11,400 WB £7710–£11,400 DAY £4200

London

London

SCHILLER INTERNATIONAL UNIVERSITY
Royal Waterloo House, 51-55 Waterloo Road,
London SE1 8TX
Tel: 0171 928 1372
Head: Dr Richard Taylor PhD
Type: Co-educational Day

Somerset

Street

MILLFIELD
Street, Somerset BA16 0YD
Tel: 01458 442291
Head: Mr P M Johnson MA
Type: Co-educational Boarding & Day 13 –18
No of pupils: B726 G496 VIth570
Fees: FB £15,105 DAY £9870

Suffolk

Felixstowe

FELIXSTOWE INTERNATIONAL COLLEGE
Cranmer House, Maybush Lane, Felixstowe,
Suffolk IP11 7LX
Tel: 01394 282388
Head: Mrs M Longhurst
Type: Girls Boarding 11 –17
No of pupils: G35
Fees: FB £14,400

Surrey

Cobham

*AMERICAN COMMUNITY SCHOOLS
Heywood, Portsmouth Road, Cobham, Surrey KT11 1BL
Tel: 01932 867251
Head: Mr T Lehman
Type: Co-educational Boarding & Day 3 –19
No of pupils: 1265 B629 G636
Fees: On application

Dorking

HURTWOOD HOUSE
Holmbury St Mary, Dorking, Surrey RH5 6NU
Tel: 01483 277416
Head: K R B Jackson MA, FRSA
Type: Co-educational Boarding 16 –18
No of pupils: B130 G150
Fees: FB £4750

Kingston upon Thames

*MARYMOUNT INTERNATIONAL SCHOOL
George Road, Kingston upon Thames, Surrey KT2 7PE
Tel: 0181 949 0571
Head: Sr Rosaleen Sheridan RSHM, MSc Psychology and
Social Sciences (University College, Dublin)
Type: Girls Day & Boarding 11 –18
No of pupils: 235 G235 Vlth100
Fees: FB £14,600–£15,550 WB £14,400–£15,350
DAY £8100 –£9050

Thorpe

*TASIS ENGLAND AMERICAN SCHOOL
Coldharbour Lane, Thorpe, Surrey TW20 8TE
Tel: +44 (0) 1932 565252
Head: Mr Dennis G Manning BA, MA
Type: Co-educational Boarding & Day 4 –18
No of pupils: 725 B369 G356
Fees: FB £15,990 DAY £4365 –£9950

East Sussex

Uckfield

BUCKSWOOD GRANGE
Uckfield, East Sussex TN22 3PU
Tel: 01825 747000
Head: Mr M B Reiser BSc(Econ)
Type: Co-educational Day & Boarding 4 –18
No of pupils: B72 G65 Vlth14
Fees: FB £11,880 DAY £6000

West Midlands

Birmingham

THE BLUE COAT SCHOOL
Somerset Road, Edgbaston, Birmingham,
West Midlands B17 0HR
Tel: 0121 454 1425
Head: Mr A D J Browning MA(Cantab)
Type: Co-educational Day & Boarding 3 –13
No of pupils: 420 B240 G180
Fees: FB £8100 DAY £3480 –£5250

Wales

Vale of Glamorgan

Barry

ATLANTIC COLLEGE
St Donat's Castle, Llantwit Major, Barry,
Vale of Glamorgan CF6 9WF
Tel: 01446 792530
Head: C Jenkins
Type: Co-educational Day

Switzerland

Montreux

*ST GEORGE'S SCHOOL IN SWITZERLAND
1815 Clarens, Montreux, Switzerland
Tel: ++41 21 964 34 11
Head: Mrs L G Zünd-Cooper BA, HDE, NUI
Type: 5 –19
No of pupils: 150

Glossary of Abbreviations

AEB	Associated Examining Board for the General Certificate of Education
ALBC	Associate of The London Bible College
ARELS	Association of Recognised English Language Schools/Federation of English Language Course Organisers
ATI	The Association of Tutors Incorporated
BA	Bachelor of Arts
BD	Bachelor of Divinity
BEd	Bachelor of Education
BLitt	Bachelor of Letters
BSA	Boarding Schools Association
BSc	Bachelor of Science
BTEC	Business and Technician Education Council
Cantab	Cambridge University
CE	Common Entrance Examination
C & G	City & Guilds Examination
CertEd	Certificate of Education
CIFE	Conference for Independent Further Education
CSE	Certificate of Secondary Education. Now replaced by GCSE
DipEd	Diploma of Education
ECIS	European Council of International Schools
EFL	English as a Foreign Language
ESL	English as a Second Language
FCollP	Fellow of the College of Preceptors
FEFC	Further Education Funding Council
GBA	Association of Governing Bodies of Public Schools
GBGSA	Association of Governing Bodies of Girls' Public Schools
GCE	General Certificate of Education. GCE 'O' level was replaced in 1988 by GCSE. GCE A level remains
GCSE	New single system of examinations replacing GCE O level & CSE
GDST	Girls' Day School Trust
GNVQ	General National Vocational Qualifications
GSA	Girls' Schools Association
HMC	Headmasters' and Headmistresses' Conference Schools
IAPS	Incorporated Association of Preparatory Schools
ISA	Independent Schools' Association

Western Isles

Moray

Aberdeenshire

Highland

Aberdeen
City

Angus

Perthshire & Kinross

Dundee
City

Argyle
and Bute

Stirling

Fife

Clackmananshire

Falkirk

East
Dumbarton-
shire

North
Lanarkshire

City of
Edinburgh

E. Lothian

Dumbarto
& Clydebank

City of
Glasgow

W. Lothian

Moray

Renfrewshire

Inverclyde

Renfrewshire

North
Ayrshire

S. Lanarkshire

Borders

North
Ayrshire

East
Ayrshire

South
Ayrshire

Dumfries and Galloway

Londonderry

Antrim

Tyrone

Fermanagh

Armagh

Down

© RH Publications (1999)

Index

A

Abberley Hall, Worcester D186
Abbot's Hill Junior School St Nicholas House,
      Hemel Hempstead 51, D155
Abbot's Hill School, Hemel Hempstead 51, D155
Abbots Bromley, Nr Lichfield....................................D173
Abbotsholme School, Uttoxeter D174
Aberlour House, Aberlour D195
Abingdon School, Abingdon............................53, D168
Ackworth School, Pontefract....................................D190
Acorn School, Nailsworth D151
Adams' Grammar School, Newport................201, D216
Adams' School Wem & Adams' College,
      Shrewsbury...D216
Adcote School for Girls, Shrewsbury......................D170
Aldenham School, Elstree D155
Aldro School, Godalming..D177
Aldwickbury School, Harpenden D155
Alexanders International School, Woodbridge D175
All Hallows College, Lyme Regis D148
All Hallows School, Shepton Mallet.........................D172
American Community Schools, Cobham.........231, D241
Amesbury School, Hindhead D177
Ampleforth College, York...............................131, D188
Ampleforth College Junior School, York............47, D188
Ardingly College, Haywards Heath D181
Ardingly College Junior School, Haywards Heath ...D181
Ardvreck School, Crieff.....................................27, D195
Arnold Lodge School, Leamington Spa...................D183
Ashby Grammar School,
      Ashby-de-la-Zouch...D215
Ashdown House School, Forest Row D179
Ashfold School, Aylesbury D139
Ashford School, Ashford....................................54, D158
Ashville College, Harrogate.....................................D187
Atlantic College, Barry D242
Austin Friars School, Carlisle D143
Aysgarth School, Bedale D187

B

Badminton Junior School, Bristol D138
Badminton School, Bristol..D241
Ballard College, New Milton D153
Ballard Lake Preparatory School, New Milton........D153
Barlborough Hall School, Chesterfield D144
Barnard Castle School, Barnard Castle..................D149
Barnardiston Hall Prep School, Haverhill.................D174

Baston School, Bromley D158
Battle Abbey School, Battle.....................................D178
Beachborough School, Brackley D166
Bearwood College, Wokingham D137
Beaudesert Park, Stroud D152
Bedales Junior School (Dunhurst), Petersfield D153
Bedales School, Petersfield......................................D153
Bedford High School, Bedford D135
Bedford Modern School, Bedford D135
Bedford Preparatory School, Bedford D135
Bedford School, Bedford..D135
Bedgebury School, Cranbrook 56, D158
Bedstone College, Bucknell.....................................D170
Beechwood Park, St Albans D156
Beechwood Sacred Heart, Tunbridge Wells............D160
Beeston Hall School, Cromer D165
Belhaven Hill, Dunbar D194
Bellerbys College Mayfield and Wadhurst,
      Wadhurst..D180
Belmont Preparatory School, Dorking D176
Benenden School, Cranbrook D159
Bentham Grammar School, Lancaster D161
Berkhamsted Collegiate School, Berkhamsted D155
Bethany School, Cranbrook......................................D159
Bilton Grange, Rugby D183
Birchfield School, Wolverhampton D183
Bishop's Stortford College, Bishops Stortford D155
Bishop's Stortford College Junior School,
      Bishops Stortford...D155
Bloxham School, Banbury D168
Blundell's School, Tiverton D146
Bootham School, York.....................................131, D188
Bosworth Tutorial College, Northampton D228
Boundary Oak School, Fareham..............................D152
Bow School, Durham D149
Box Hill School, Dorking D176
Bradfield College, Reading D136
Brambletye, East Grinstead D181
Bramcote Lorne School, Retford D167
Bramcote School, Scarborough D187
Bramdean Grammar School, Exeter........................D145
Bramdean Prep & Grammar School, Exeter D145
Bredon School, Tewkesbury.............................57, D152
Bredon School - Junior School, Tewkesbury D152
Brentwood School, Brentwood................................D150
Brighton College, Brighton D178
Brockwood Park School, Bramdean D152
Bromsgrove Lower School, Bromsgrove..................D185
Bromsgrove School, Bromsgrove............................D185
Bronte House School, Bradford D189

Brooke House College, Market Harborough D228
Broomham School, Hastings D179
Bruton School for Girls, Bruton D171
Bryanston School, Blandford Forum D147
Brymore Secondary Technical College,
   Bridgwater D216
Burford School, Oxford...D216
Burgess Hill School, Burgess Hill D180
Burleigh Community College,
   Loughborough 203, D215
Butterstone School, Blairgowrie D195

C

Cabin Hill School, Belfast D191
Cademuir International School, Thornhill................D194
Caldicott, Farnham Royal D139
Cambridge Arts & Sciences, Cambridge...............D227
Cambridge Centre for Sixth Form Studies,
   Cambridge D227
Campbell College, Belfast D191
Canford School, Wimborne D149
Cargilfield, Edinburgh D193
Casterton School, Carnforth.................................D161
Caterham School, Caterham D176
Catteral Hall, Settle D187
Cawston College, Norwich D166
Chafyn Grove School, Salisbury D184
Chapter House Preparatory School, York D188
Charterhouse, Godalming.....................................D177
Chase Academy, Cannock D173
Cheam Hawtreys, Newbury D136
Cheltenham College, Cheltenham D151
Cheltenham College Junior School, Cheltenham....D151
Cherwell Tutors, Oxford..D228
Chetham's School of Music, Manchester...............D164
Chigwell School, Chigwell D150
Chilton Cantelo School, Yeovil D173
Christ Church Cathedral School, Oxford.................D168
Christ College, Brecon..D198
Christ's Hospital, Horsham....................................D181
City of London Freemen's School, Ashtead............D176
Claremont Fan Court Middle School, Esher D177
Clayesmore Preparatory School,
   Blandford Forum...D147
Clayesmore School, Blandford Forum....................D147
Clevedon House, Ilkley D189
Clifton College, Bristol D138
Clifton College Preparatory School, Bristol D138
Clifton High School, Bristol...................................D138
Cobham Hall School, Gravesend D159
Cokethorpe School, Witney D169
Colchester Royal Grammar School, Colchester......D214
Coleraine Academical Institution, Coleraine...........D191
Colston's Collegiate School, Bristol D138

Concord College, Shrewsbury................................D170
Convent of the Sacred Heart School, Swaffham.....D166
Copthorne School Trust, Crawley...........................D181
Cothill House, Abingdon D168
Cottesmore School, Pease Pottage 28, D182
Cranbrook School, Cranbrook.......................204, D214
Cranleigh Preparatory School, Cranleigh D176
Cranleigh School, Cranleigh D176
Croftdown School, Malvern D185
Croftinloan School, Pitlochry D196
Culford School, Bury St Edmunds.........................D174
Cumnor House School, Haywards Heath...............D181
Cundall Manor School, York.............................47, D188

D

d'Overbroeck's College, Oxford 58, D168
Dallam School, Milnthorpe....................................D213
Dauntsey's School, Devizes D184
De Aston School, Market Rasen............................D215
Dean Close Junior School, Cheltenham............29, D151
Dean Close School, Cheltenham......................60, D151
Denstone College, Uttoxeter D174
Dollar Academy, Dollar D194
Dorset House School, Pulborough D182
Douai School, Reading...D136
Dover College, Dover..D159
Downe House School, Thatcham 61, D137
Downside School, Bath D171
Dragon School, Oxford.....................................30, D169
Duke of Kent School, Cranleigh............................D176
Duke of York's Royal Military School, Dover.....62, D159
Dulwich College, London................................63, D163
Dulwich College Preparatory School,
   London...D163
Dulwich Preparatory School, Cranbrook 30, D159
Dumpton School, Wimborne D149
Durham School, Durham D149
Durlston Court, New Milton D153

E

Eagle House, Sandhurst D137
Eastbourne College, Eastbourne D179
Eccles Hall School, Norwich..................................D166
Edge Grove School, Aldenham Village D155
Edgeborough, Farnham...D177
Edgehill College, Bideford D145
Edward Greene's Tutorial Establishment,
   Oxford D228
Elizabeth College, Guernsey.................................D141
Ellesmere College, Ellesmere...............................D170
Elmfield Rudolf Steiner School, Stourbridge D183
Elmhurst Ballet School, Camberley D176
Elstree School, Reading..D136

Eltham College, London 64, D163
Embley Park School, Romsey D153
Epsom College, Epsom D177
Eton College, Windsor D137
Exeter Cathedral School, Exeter...........................D145
Exeter School, Exeter D145

F

Falcon Manor School, Towcester............................D166
Farleigh School, Andover.....................................D152
Farlington School, Horsham 65, D181
Farringtons & Stratford House, Chislehurst.......66, D158
Farringtons & Stratford House Junior School,
    Chislehurst 31, D158
Felixstowe International College, Felixstowe...........D241
Felsted Preparatory School, Great Dunmow D150
Felsted School, Great Dunmow.............................D150
Feltonfleet School, Cobham D176
Fettes College, Edinburgh D193
Finborough School, Stowmarket D175
Forest Boys School, London D163
Forest Prep School, London.................................D163
Forres Sandle Manor, Fordingbridge......................D153
Framlingham College, Woodbridge 67, D175
Framlingham College Junior School,
    Woodbridge 67, D175
Frensham Heights School, Farnham 68, D177
Friars School, Ashford D158
Friends' School, Saffron Walden D150
Friends' School, Lisburn D191
Fulneck School, Leeds D189
Fyling Hall School, Whitby D188

G

George Watson's College, Edinburgh D193
Giggleswick School, Settle 69, D187
Glebe House School, Hunstanton D165
Glenalmond College, Perth.............................70, D196
Godstowe Preparatory School, High Wycombe......D139
Gordon's School, Woking.....................................D217
Gordonstoun School, Elgin..................................D195
Gosfield School, Halstead D150
Grace Dieu Manor School, Coalville D162
Great Ballard School, Chichester D180
Great Walstead School, Haywards Heath D181
Green Hill School, Evesham D185
Greenfields School, Forest Row D179
Grenville College, Bideford D145
Grenville College Junior (Stella Maris), Bideford D145
Grenville College Junior School, Bideford..............D145
Gresham's Preparatory School, Holt......................D165
Gresham's School, Holt.......................................D165

Grosvenor House School, Harrogate.....................D187
Gyosei International School UK, Milton Keynes D139

H

Haberdashers' Monmouth School for Girls,
    Monmouth D198
Haileybury, Hertford...D156
Hammond School, Chester D141
Handcross Park School, Haywards Heath D181
Hanford School, Blandford Forum.........................D147
Harecroft Hall School, Seascale D143
Harrogate Ladies' College, Harrogate D187
Harrow School, Harrow 71, D165
Hatherop Castle Preparatory School, Cirencester ..D151
Hawkhurst Court School, Brighton D178
Hazelwood School, Oxted D178
Hazlegrove, Yeovil D173
Headington School, Oxford D169
Heath Mount School, Hertford.............................D156
Heathfield School, Ascot 72, D135
Hereford Cathedral Junior School, Hereford D154
Hethersett Old Hall School, Norwich D166
Highfield School, Liphook....................................D153
Hillstone Malvern College, Malvern D185
Hockerill Anglo-European School,
    Bishops Stortford.....................................232, D241
Hoe Bridge and The Trees School, Woking............D178
Holme Park Preparatory School, Kendal D143
Holmewood House, Tunbridge Wells D160
Holmwood House, Colchester..............................D150
Homefield School (Prep & Senior Depts),
    Christchurch D148
Hordle Walhampton School, Lymington.................D153
Horris Hill, Newbury D136
Howell's School, Denbigh....................................D197
Howsham Hall, York 47, D188
Hunterhouse College, Belfast D191
Hurst Lodge, Ascot..D135
Hurstpierpoint College, Hassocks D181
Hurstpierpoint Junior School, Hassocks D181
Hurtwood House, Dorking D242

I

Ipswich School, Ipswich D174
Irwin College, Leicester......................................D228

K

Keil School, Dumbarton......................................D196
Kelly College, Tavistock......................................D146
Kent College, Canterbury D158
Kent College Junior School, Tunbridge Wells D160

Kent College, Pembury, Tunbridge Wells D160
Keswick School, Keswick D213
Kilgraston (A Sacred Heart School), Perth..............D196
Kimbolton School, Huntingdon...............................D140
King Edward's School Witley, Godalming 73, D177
King William's College, Castletown D157
King's Bruton, Bruton D172
King's College, Taunton...D172
King's College School, Cambridge..........................D140
King's Hall School, Taunton D172
King's Junior School, Canterbury D158
King's Junior School, Worcester D186
King's Preparatory School, Rochester D160
King's School, Rochester, Rochester D160
Kingham Hill School, Chipping Norton D168
King's School, Grantham..D215
Kingsland Grange, Shrewsbury D170
Kingsmead School, Wirral D164
Kings' School, Winchester......................................D214
Kingswood School, Bath D171
Kirkham Grammar School, Preston 74, D161
Kitebrook House, Moreton-in-Marsh.....................D151
Knighton House, Blandford Forum D147

L

Lady Manners School, Bakewell......................205, D213
Lambrook Haileybury School, Bracknell..................D136
Lancaster Royal Grammar School,
    Lancaster D215
Lancing College, Lancing D182
Langley School, Norwich..................................76, D166
Lathallan Preparatory School, Montrose D193
Launceston College, Launceston D213
Lavant House Rosemead, Chichester D180
Leaden Hall School, Salisbury 33, D184
Leighton Park School, Reading D136
Licensed Victuallers' School, Ascot........................D135
Lichfield Cathedral School, Lichfield D173
Lime House School, Carlisle.............................78, D143
Lincoln Minster Preparatory School, Lincoln..........D162
Lincoln Minster School, Lincoln.............................D162
Littlemead Grammar School, Chichester.................D180
Llandovery College, Llandovery.............................D197
Lockers Park School, Hemel Hempstead................D156
Lomond School, Helensburgh D193
Longridge Towers School, Berwick-upon-Tweed ...D167
Lord Wandsworth College, Hook............................D153
Loretto Junior School, Musselburgh.......................D194
Loretto School, Musselburgh D194
Loughborough Grammar School,
    Loughborough 79, D162
Lucie Clayton Secretarial College, London D228
Luckley-Oakfield School, Wokingham.....................D137
Ludgrove, Wokingham...D137

M

Maidwell Hall, Northampton D166
Malsis School, Skipton D188
Malvern College, Malvern D186
Malvern Girls' College, Malvern D186
Manor House School, Honiton D146
Marlborough College, Marlborough........................D184
Marlborough House School, Hawkhurst..................D159
Marlston House Preparatory School, Newbury D136
Marymount International School,
    Kingston upon Thames.................................233, D242
Merchant Taylors' School, Northwood D165
Merchiston Castle School, Edinburgh D193
Methodist College, Belfast....................................D191
Michael Hall School, Forest Row............................D179
Mill Hill School, London D163
Millbrook House School, Abingdon D168
    Millfield, Street D241
Millfield Preparatory School, Glastonbury D172
Milton Abbey School, Blandford Forum D147
Moffats School, Bewdley.......................................D185
Moira House Junior School, Eastbourne D179
Moira House School, Eastbourne D179
Monkton Combe Junior School, Bath D171
Monkton Combe Senior School, Bath....................D171
Monmouth School, Monmouth..........................82, D198
Moor Park School, Ludlow.....................................D170
Moorland School, Clitheroe...................................D161
Moreton Hall, Bury St Edmunds............................D174
Moreton Hall, Oswestry.....................................83, D170
Morrison's Academy, Crieff...................................D195
Morrison's Academy Junior, Crieff.........................D195
Moulsford Preparatory School, Wallingford D169
Mount House Preparatory School, Tavistock D146
Mount St Mary's College, Near Sheffield 84, D144
Mowden Hall School, Stocksfield D167
Mowden School, Hove D179
Moyles Court School, Ringwood..........................D153

N

Netherwood School, Saundersfoot.....................D198
Nevill Holt School, Market Harborough...............D162
New Hall Preparatory School, Chelmsford D150
New Hall School, Chelmsford 86, D150
Newlands School, Seaford....................35, 87, D180
Norman Court Preparatory School,
    Salisbury...D184
North Foreland Lodge, Nr Basingstoke..............D152
Northbourne Park School, Deal D159

O

Oakham School, Oakham D169
Oakwood School, Chichester D180
Ockbrook School, Derby....................................D144
Old Buckenham Hall School, Ipswich 37, D174
Old Swinford Hospital, Stourbridge D217
Orwell Park School, Ipswich.........................38, D174
Osho Ko Hsuan School, Chulmleigh..................D145
Oswestry School, Oswestry D170
Oundle School, Peterborough...........................D140
Oxford Tutorial College, Oxford D228

P

Packwood Haugh, Shrewsbury....................40, D170
Padworth College, Reading................................D227
Pangbourne College, Reading 89, D136
Papplewick, Ascot.......................................41, D135
Parkside School, Cobham.................................D176
Perrott Hill School, Crewkerne D172
Peter Symonds' College, Winchester.........221, D227
Peterborough High School, Peterborough..........D140
Pinewood School, Swindon D184
Pipers Corner School, High Wycombe 90, D139
Plymouth College, Plymouth 91, D146
Plymouth Tutorial College (EGAS), Plymouth.....D227
Pocklington School, York......................92,131, D188
Polam Hall, Darlington......................................D149
Polam Hall Junior School, Darlington.................D149
Polwhele House School, Truro D142
Port Regis, Shaftesbury D148
Pownall Hall School, Wilmslow D141
Prestfelde Preparatory School, Shrewsbury D170
Princethorpe College, Rugby D183
Prior Park College, Bath D171
Prior Park Preparatory School, Swindon.............D185
Prior's Field School, Godalming...................93, D177

Q

Queen Anne's School, Reading D136
Queen Elizabeth's Hospital, Bristol D138
Queen Elizabeth's Community College,
    Crediton...D213
Queen Ethelburga's College, York D188
Queen Margaret's School, York 131, D188
Queen Mary's School, Thirsk 131, D188
Queen Victoria School, Dunblane D196
Queen's College, Taunton.................................D172
Queen's College Junior School, Taunton............D172
Queenswood School, Hatfield............................D155

R

Radley College, Abingdon D168
Ramillies Hall School, Cheadle D141
Ranby House, Retford D167
Rannoch School, By Pitlochry 94, D195
Ratcliffe College, Leicester 95, D162
Rathdown School, Co Dublin 96
Read School, Selby...................................131, D187
Reading Blue Coat School,
    Sonning-on-Thames D137
Reading School, Reading D213
Red House Prep School, York...........................D188
Reed's School, Cobham....................................D176
Rendcomb College, Cirencester........................D151
Repton Preparatory School, Derby....................D144
Repton School, Repton.....................................D144
Riddlesworth Hall, Diss.....................................D165
Ripon Cathedral Choir School, Ripon.................D187
Ripon Grammar School, Ripon D217
Rishworth School, Halifax...........................97, D189
Rochester Tutors Independent College,
    Rochester...D227
Rockport Preparatory School, Holywood D191
Rodney School, Newark D167
Roedean School, Brighton.................................D178
Rookesbury Park School, Wickham 42, D154
Rookwood School, Andover D152
Rose Hill School, Wotton-under-Edge D152
Rossall Preparatory School, Fleetwood D161
Rossall School, Fleetwood D241
Rossholme School, Highbridge D172
Royal Grammar School,
    High Wycombe 206, D213
Royal Hospital School, Ipswich D175
Royal Russell Prep School, Croydon..................D176
Royal School Dungannon D192
Rugby School, Rugby D183
Ruthin School, Ruthin D197
Rutland Sixth Form College, Oakham D216
Rydal Penhros Senior School Co-Ed Division,
    Colwyn Bay...D197
Ryde School with Upper Chine, Ryde D157
Rye St Antony School, Oxford............................D169

S

S Anselm's School, Bakewell D144
Saint George's School, Southwold.....................D175
Saint Michael's College, Tenbury Wells..............D186
Salisbury Cathedral School, Salisbury................D184
Sandroyd School, Salisbury D184
Scarborough College, Scarborough D187
Scarborough College Junior School,
    Scarborough D187
Schiller International University, London D241

Seaford College, Petworth............................D182
Sedbergh School, Sedbergh D143
Sevenoaks School, Sevenoaks.....................D241
Sexey's School, Bruton 216, D216
Shaftesbury School, Shaftesbury 214, D214
Shebbear College, Beaworthy D145
Sherborne Preparatory School, Sherborne D148
Sherborne School, Sherborne D148
Sherborne School for Girls, Sherborne..............D148
Sherborne School International College,
    Sherborne 98, 234, D148
Sherrardswood School, Welwyn...................D157
Shiplake College, Henley-on-Thames D168
Shrewsbury School, Shrewsbury.............99, D170
Sibford Junior School, Banbury.....................D168
Sibford School, Banbury.............................D168
Sidcot School, Winscombe 100, D173
Sir Roger Manwood's School,
    Sandwich, ...207, D214
Skegness Grammar School, Skegness D215
Slindon College, Arundel D180
Smallwood Manor Prep School, Uttoxeter.......D174
Sompting Abbotts Preparatory School, Lancing.....D182
St Andrew's School, Eastbourne...................D179
St Andrew's School, Reading........................D136
St Anne's, Windermere D143
St Anne's School (Junior Dept), Windermere D143
St Antony's-Leweston Preparatory School,
    Sherborne D148
St Antony's-Leweston School, Sherborne D148
St Aubyn's School, Tiverton D146
St Aubyns, Brighton D178
St Bede's Preparatory School, Eastbourne.............D179
St Bede's School, Hailsham 101, D179
St Bede's School, Stafford D173
St Bees School, St Bees 102, D143
St Benedict's Convent School, Andover D152
St Brigid's School, Denbigh.........................D217
St Catherine's School, Guildford 103, D177
St Christopher School, Letchworth 105, D156
St Clare's, Oxford 222, D228
St David's School for Girls, Ashford D165
St David's College, Llandudno D198
St Denis and Cranley School, Edinburgh D193
St Dunstan's Abbey School, Plymouth...............D146
St Edmund's College, Near Ware 107, D156
St Edmund's Junior School, Canterbury D158
St Edmund's School, Canterbury D158
St Edmund's School, Hindhead.....................D177
St Edward's, Oxford 108, D169
St Elphin's School, Matlock.........................D144
St Felix School, Southwold..........................D175
St Francis' College, Letchworth.....................D156
St George's School, Ascot D135
St George's School, Windsor D137
St George's School for Girls, Edinburgh D193

St George's School, Harpenden............................D214
St George's School in Switzerland,
    Montreux.......................................236, D242
St Helen's School For Girls, Northwood.................D165
St Hugh's School, Faringdon.........................D168
St Hugh's School, Woodhall Spa D163
St James' School, Grimsby D163
St James's and The Abbey, Malvern D186
St John's Beaumont, Windsor.......................D137
St John's College, Southsea D154
St John's College School, Cambridge................D140
St John's School, Hindhead D178
St John's School, Sidmouth D146
St John's School, Porthcawl.........................D197
St John's-on-the-Hill, Chepstow D198
St Joseph's School, Launceston D142
St Katharines Prep School, St Andrews D195
St Lawrence College in Thanet, Ramsgate.............D159
St Leonards and
    St Katharines Schools, St Andrews, ...D195
St Leonards-Mayfield School, Mayfield.................D179
St Margaret's School, Bushey 109, D155
St Margaret's School & St Denis and Cranley,
    Edinburgh..D193
St Martin's School, York.........................47, D189
St Mary's Hall, Brighton......................110, D178
St Mary's Hall, Stonyhurst D161
St Mary's Music School, Edinburgh D194
St Mary's Prep School, Melrose D193
St Mary's School, Ascot 111, D135
St Mary's School, Calne 112, D184
St Mary's School, Cambridge.......................D140
St Mary's School, Shaftesbury D148
St Mary's School, Wantage D169
St Mary's Westbrook, Folkestone............112, D159
St Michael's School, Barnstaple.....................D145
St Olaves School (Junior of St Peter's), York 47, D189
St Paul's Cathedral School, London.............44, D163
St Paul's Preparatory School, London D164
St Peter's School, Exmouth.........................D146
St Peter's School, York.......................131, D189
St Petroc's School, Bude D142
St Richard's School, Bromyard 44, D154
St Ronan's, Hawkhurst D159
St Swithun's School, Winchester............113, D154
St Teresa's School, Dorking D176
Stamford High School, Stamford............113, D162
Stamford High School Junior School, Stamford D162
Stamford School, Stamford.................114, D162
Stamford School Junior School, Stamford.............D163
Stanborough School, Watford D157
Stanbridge Earls School, Romsey 115, D154
Stancliffe Hall, Matlock.............................D144
Stewart's Melville College, Edinburgh 81, D194
Steyning Grammar School, Steyning............207, D217
Stoke College, Sudbury............................D175

Stonar School, Melksham.....................................D184
Stonyhurst College, Clitheroe D161
Stoodley Knowle School, Torquay D147
Stover School for Girls, Newton Abbot D146
Stowe School, Buckingham..................................D139
Strathallan School, Perth D196
Summer Fields, Oxford..D169
Summerhill School, Leiston D175
Sunningdale School, Ascot.................................D135
Sutton Valence School, Maidstone.......................D159
Swanbourne House School, Milton Keynes D139

T

TASIS England American School, Thorpe 237, D242
Taunton Preparatory School, Taunton....................D172
Taunton School, Taunton D172
Taverham Hall School, Norwich D166
Temple Grove School, Uckfield D180
Terra Nova School, Crewe...................................D141
Terrington Hall, York 47, D189
Tettenhall College, Wolverhampton........................D183
The Arts Educational School, Tring D156
The Blue Coat School, Birmingham........................D242
The Bolitho School, Penzance..............................D142
The Buchan School, Castletown D157
The Cathedral School, Llandaff, Cardiff D197
The Cheltenham Ladies' College, Cheltenham D151
The Chorister School, Durham D149
The Downs School, Bristol D138
The Downs School, Malvern D186
The Duchy Grammar School, Truro D142
The Edinburgh Academy, Edinburgh..............116, D194
The Edinburgh Academy Preparatory School,
   Edinburgh..D194
The Elms, Malvern D186
The Godolphin School, Salisbury D184
The Hereford Cathedral School, Hereford..............D154
The International School of Choueifat,
   Marshfield 117, D184
The Junior School, St Lawrence College,
   Ramsgate..D160
The King's School, Canterbury.......................118, D158
The King's School, Gloucester D151
The King's School Ely 120, D140
The Leys School, Cambridge D140
The Mary Erskine School, Edinburgh 81, D194
The Mount School, York 131, D189
The New Beacon, Sevenoaks..............................D160
The New School, Dunkeld D195
The Norland College, Hungerford.................223, D227
The Old Hall School, Telford...............................D170
The Old Malthouse, Swanage...............................D148
The Old Vicarage, Tonbridge D227
The Oratory Preparatory School, Reading...............D136

The Oratory School, Reading D136
The Park School, Yeovil......................................D173
The Pilgrims' School, Winchester.........................D154
The Prebendal School, Chichester D181
The Princess Helena College, Hitchin...................D156
The Purcell School, London, Bushey.....................D155
The Red Maids' School, Bristol 121, D138
The Royal Alexandra & Albert School,
   Reigate...208, D217
The Royal Masonic School for Girls,
   Rickmansworth 122, D156
The Royal School, Armagh D191
The Royal School, Haslemere..............................D177
The Royal School, Hampstead, London,.........123, D164
The Royal Wolverhampton Junior School,
   Wolverhampton......................................124, D183
The Royal Wolverhampton School,
   Wolverhampton,.....................................124, D183
The Ryleys School, Alderley Edge D141
The Towers, Steyning D182
The Westgate School, Winchester........................D214
The Woodroffe School, Lyme Regis D214
The Yarlet Schools, Stafford...............................D173
Thornlow Junior School, Weymouth......................D148
Thornlow School, Weymouth...............................D149
Thornton College, Milton Keynes.........................D139
Tockington Manor School, Bristol D138
Tonbridge School, Tonbridge D160
Tower House, Barmouth.....................................D198
Town Close House Preparatory School, Norwich ...D166
Treliske School, Truro..D142
Trent College, Nottingham..................................D167
Trinity School, Teignmouth D146
Truro High School for Girls, Truro...................125, D142
Truro School, Truro...D142
Tudor Hall School, Banbury................................D168
Twyford School, Winchester................................D154

U

Uppingham School, Uppingham D169
Ursuline College, Westgate-on-Sea D160

V

Vernon Holme, Canterbury D158
Victoria College Belfast, Belfast...........................D191
Vinehall School, Robertsbridge D179

W

Walthamstow Hall, Sevenoaks D160
Warminster Preparatory School, Warminster D185
Warminster School, Warminster D185
Warwick School, Warwick 126, D183
Wellesley House, Broadstairs D158
Wellingborough School, Wellingborough D166
Wellington College, Crowthorne D136
Wellington School, Wellington D172
Wellow House School, Newark................................D167
Wells Cathedral Junior School, Wells D172
Wells Cathedral School, Wells D173
Wentworth College, Bournemouth D148
West Buckland Preparatory School, Barnstaple D145
West Buckland School, Barnstaple D145
West Hill Park Preparatory School, Fareham D153
Westbourne House School, Chichester...................D181
Westbrook Hay School, Hemel Hempstead.............D156
Westminster Abbey Choir School, London D164
Westminster Cathedral Choir School, London D164
Westminster School, London D164
Westonbirt School, Tetbury D152
Winchester College, Winchester............................D154
Winchester House, Brackley...................................D166
Windlesham House, Pulborough 46, D182
Wispers School, Haslemere............................128, D177
Witham Hall, Bourne D162
Wolborough Hill School, Newton Abbot D146
Woldingham School, Woldingham D178
Woodcote House School, Windlesham D178
Woodhouse Grove School, Apperley Bridge...........D189
Woodleigh School Langton, Malton D187
Worksop College, Worksop D167
Worth School, Crawley D181
Wrekin College, Telford D171
Wychwood School, Oxford..............................130, D169
Wycliffe College, Stonehouse.................................D151
Wycombe Abbey School, High Wycombe...............D139
Wymondham College, Wymondham 210, D216
Wynstones School, Gloucester D151

THE 2000 GUIDE

Ensure your institution's inclusion in the Thirteenth Edition of the *Guide to Boarding Schools and Colleges 2000.*

Reserve your space now by ticking one of the following boxes. Advance details will be sent to you before the general mailing campaign begins in Autumn 1999.

☐ 1) I wish to have my institution re-listed as in this edition of the Guide

☐ 2) I wish to take a larger listing than included in this edition of the Guide

☐ 3) I wish to include my institution in the 2000 edition of the Guide for the first time

☐ 4) I wish to repeat my advertisement as in this edition of the Guide

☐ 5) I wish to increase the size of my advertisement in this edition of the Guide

☐ 6) I wish to advertise in the 2000 edition of the Guide for the first time

No contractual obligation is entered into by ticking any of the above boxes. *A booking form containing fees and details of listings will be sent later.*

Name and Address of Institution or Organisation:. . . . .

. . . .

. . . .

Post Code:. . . . . Tel:. . . . .

Signed:. . . . . Name:. . . . .

Position:. . . . . Date: . . . .

Return to:

John Catt Educational Limited

Great Glemham, Saxmundham, Suffolk IP17 2DH, UK

Telephone: +44 (0)1728 663666 • *Facsimile:* +44 (0)1728 663415
Website: http://www.johncatt.co.uk • *E-mail:* enquiries@johncatt.co.uk

Please use this form if you would welcome the support of our advisory service and telephone us if you have any questions on how best to proceed.

THIS FORM MAY BE PHOTOCOPIED TO BE FAXED OR MAILED

Please complete in CAPITALS

To: **John Catt Educational Ltd**   *From:*
Great Glemham
Saxmundham
Suffolk IP17 2DH UK

Fax No: **+44 (0)1728 663 415**   *Fax No:*
Tel No: **+44 (0)1728 663 666**   *Tel No:*

In response to the information provided below please suggest the names of three schools which could fulfil my requirements and request them to send me their prospectuses and any other specific information relevant to my needs.

I understand that this form, when completed, may be faxed to the schools concerned.

Details of pupil

1. Family Name: ....
2. First Name(s): ....
3. Male / Female: ....
4. Date of Birth: ....
5. Nationality: ....
6. Religion: ....
7. First Language: ....
8. Competence in English (if not first language): ....
9. Current School & Dates: ....

    Previous Schools & Dates ....

10. Examinations & Certificates: ....
11. Special Achievements: ....
12. Special Needs: ....
13. Reason for seeking new school: ....

School required

14. Type (Full / Weekly Boarding, Day, Co-ed, Single Sex): ....
15. Proposed Starting Date: ....
16. Area of UK preferred (relatives, friends and travel considerations): ....
17. Examinations sought: GCSE / 'A' Level, I.B., Vocational: ....
18. Is Guardianship required: ....

Disclaimer: John Catt Educational Limited shall not be liable nor accept responsibility for the accuracy of the information given to the applicant and the applicant is advised that should he rely on the information he would do so at his own risk and the applicant is therefore advised to make his own independent enquiries.

Signature: ....   Relationship to pupil: ....

Date: ....

International Reader Enquiry Card

For more information about schools and colleges listed in **Boarding Schools and Colleges 1999**, write the name of the school(s) or college(s) that interest(s) you below:

_____   _____

_____   _____

_____   _____

If you live outside the UK, simply post this card to John Catt Educational Limited. No stamp is necessary. Brochures and information concerning the institution(s) you have requested will be sent to you as soon as possible.

Your Name: _____

Address: _____

_____

_____ Postcode: _____

Tel No: _____ Fax No: _____

Age of prospective pupil: _____ Sex: **M** OR **F** (CIRCLE AS APPROPRIATE)

International Reader Enquiry Card

For more information about schools and colleges listed in **Boarding Schools and Colleges 1999**, write the name of the school(s) or college(s) that interest(s) you below:

_____   _____

_____   _____

_____   _____

If you live outside the UK, simply post this card to John Catt Educational Limited. No stamp is necessary. Brochures and information concerning the institution(s) you have requested will be sent to you as soon as possible.

Your Name: _____

Address: _____

_____

_____ Postcode: _____

Tel No: _____ Fax No: _____

Age of prospective pupil: _____ Sex: **M** OR **F** (CIRCLE AS APPROPRIATE)

By air mail
Par avion

PHQ-D/956/IP

NE PAS AFFRANCHIR

NO STAMP REQUIRED

REPONSE PAYEE
GRANDE-BRETAGNE

John Catt Educational Ltd
Great Glemham
SAXMUNDHAM
Suffolk
GREAT BRITAIN
IP17 2BR

By air mail
Par avion

PHQ-D/956/IP

NE PAS AFFRANCHIR

NO STAMP REQUIRED

REPONSE PAYEE
GRANDE-BRETAGNE

John Catt Educational Ltd
Great Glemham
SAXMUNDHAM
Suffolk
GREAT BRITAIN
IP17 2BR

BUSINESS REPLY SERVICE
Licence No. JSL. 26

John Catt Educational Limited
Great Glemham
SAXMUNDHAM
Suffolk
IP17 2BR

BUSINESS REPLY SERVICE
Licence No. JSL. 26

John Catt Educational Limited
Great Glemham
SAXMUNDHAM
Suffolk
IP17 2BR

BUSINESS REPLY SERVICE
Licence No. JSL. 26

John Catt Educational Limited
Great Glemham
SAXMUNDHAM
Suffolk
IP17 2BR

BUSINESS REPLY SERVICE
Licence No. JSL. 26

John Catt Educational Limited
Great Glemham
SAXMUNDHAM
Suffolk
IP17 2BR

READER ENQUIRY CARD

For more information about schools and colleges listed in **Boarding Schools and Colleges 1999**, write the name of the school(s) or college(s) that interest(s) you below:

_____

_____

_____

Post this card if you live within the UK. No stamp is necessary. If you do not, please use the International Reader Enquiry Card. Brochures and information concerning the institution(s) you have requested will be sent to you as soon as possible.

Your Name Mr, Mrs, Ms: _____

Address: _____

_____

Postcode: _____

Tel No: _____ Fax No: _____

Age of prospective pupil: _____ Sex: M or F (CIRCLE AS APPROPRIATE)

READER ENQUIRY CARD

For more information about schools and colleges listed in **Boarding Schools and Colleges 1999**, write the name of the school(s) or college(s) that interest(s) you below:

_____

_____

_____

Post this card if you live within the UK. No stamp is necessary. If you do not, please use the International Reader Enquiry Card. Brochures and information concerning the institution(s) you have requested will be sent to you as soon as possible.

Your Name Mr, Mrs, Ms: _____

Address: _____

_____

Postcode: _____

Tel No: _____ Fax No: _____

Age of prospective pupil: _____ Sex: M or F (CIRCLE AS APPROPRIATE)

READER ENQUIRY CARD

For more information about schools and colleges listed in **Boarding Schools and Colleges 1999**, write the name of the school(s) or college(s) that interest(s) you below:

_____

_____

_____

Post this card if you live within the UK. No stamp is necessary. If you do not, please use the International Reader Enquiry Card. Brochures and information concerning the institution(s) you have requested will be sent to you as soon as possible.

Your Name Mr, Mrs, Ms: _____

Address: _____

_____

Postcode: _____

Tel No: _____ Fax No: _____

Age of prospective pupil: _____ Sex: M or F (CIRCLE AS APPROPRIATE)

READER ENQUIRY CARD

For more information about schools and colleges listed in **Boarding Schools and Colleges 1999**, write the name of the school(s) or college(s) that interest(s) you below:

_____

_____

_____

Post this card if you live within the UK. No stamp is necessary. If you do not, please use the International Reader Enquiry Card. Brochures and information concerning the institution(s) you have requested will be sent to you as soon as possible.

Your Name Mr, Mrs, Ms: _____

Address: _____

_____

Postcode: _____

Tel No: _____ Fax No: _____

Age of prospective pupil: _____ Sex: M or F (CIRCLE AS APPROPRIATE)